THE MAKING OF INDIA

THE MAKING OF INDIA:

A BRIEF HISTORY OF THE DIFFERENT ELEMENTS, GEOGRAPHICAL, ETHNICAL, MATERIAL, MORAL AND POLITICAL, THAT WENT TO THE BUILDING UP OF THE INDIAN PEOPLE,

WITH AN ACCOUNT OF

THE FOUNDATION, CONSOLIDATION, AND PROGRESS OF BRITISH RULE IN INDIA

A. YUSUF ALI

GYAN

Published by

GYAN

Gyan Publishing House
5, Ansari Road
Daryaganj, New Delhi-110002
Phone: 011-47034999, 9811692060
E-mail: books@gyanbooks.com

Distribution Network
gyanbooks.com
India, USA, Canada, UK, Australia

ISBN: 978-93-7014-321-0 (HB)

First Published, 1925

2nd Impression 2025

Printed at: Gyan Press, Delhi.

THE MAKING OF INDIA
Author: A. YUSUF ALI

THE MAKING OF INDIA

THE MAKING OF INDIA

A BRIEF HISTORY OF THE DIFFERENT ELEMENTS, GEOGRAPHICAL, ETHNICAL, MATERIAL, MORAL AND POLITICAL, THAT WENT TO THE BUILDING UP OF THE INDIAN PEOPLE

WITH AN ACCOUNT OF

THE FOUNDATION, CONSOLIDATION, AND PROGRESS OF BRITISH RULE IN INDIA

BY

A. YUSUF ALI

C.B.E., M.A., LL.M. (CANTAB.), F.R.S.L., ETC.

BARRISTER-AT-LAW; LATE OF THE INDIAN CIVIL SERVICE
AUTHOR OF "LIFE AND LABOUR OF THE PEOPLE OF INDIA," "MESTROVIC AND SERBIAN SCULPTURE," ETC.; EDITOR OF SIR ROLAND WILSON'S "DIGEST OF ANGLO-MOHAMMEDAN LAW"

1925

PREFACE

The new spirit that has recently affected the writing, teaching, and study of history has been applied very little yet to Indian history. It is not my purpose in this Preface to expound that spirit, but a few words are necessary to enable the reader to appreciate the writer's point of view. I look upon history as a whole, and not in water-tight compartments. I have tried, within the brief compass available to me, to relate Indian facts to connected events whose primary interest lay outside India. In the study of causes and tendencies, this method may be found helpful, especially if pursued on a larger scale. Military and political history has not been ignored, for both these are factors in the "Making of India," but in our age-long history they are really very subordinate factors, and have been treated as such. Social, economic, and religious movements—some of which are obscure to the general reader—have been given what I consider their due prominence. Atrocities and unedifying "facts"—even if they *are* facts—are merely referred to, in order to save the space for the things that matter, the abiding factors that have made and are making India. I want my countrymen to understand, not only the particular sections to which they may severally belong, but India as a whole—a living and growing reality that must command our devotion. I want them further to understand their historic relations to the outside world; for their position in the world will depend on what they make it. In this spirit I want the Dominions and Colonies, as well as the Mother country of the Empire, to understand India. And in these days of world solidarity I want the world to realize India; to think of it not as a vague and remote abstraction, but as a living reality whose history touches the world's history at so many points. This may appear an impossible ambition for so small a book, but it is merely a sketch for what I hope may emerge as a larger scheme in the future.

I have consulted original authorities wherever possible, but I have not considered it necessary or desirable to burden this sketch with numerous footnotes and references. The needs of schools and colleges and the general reader have been held in view. The list of seventy-four books for further study aims at naming only easily accessible books which may help to supplement my very rapid story at any given point. I should have mentioned Lord Curzon's *British Government in India*, published in June, if it had appeared before my List was printed, although the interest of Lord Curzon's study is mainly psychological. It reveals not only his individual psychology, but that of his nation as read by him.

It will be noticed that I have discarded the word "Mahomedan" or "Mohammedan," and used the more correct, as well as more usual, form "Muslim" according to the best modern practice in India. In the spelling of Indian names I have usually adopted the official Hunterian system, except in well-established forms like "Cawnpore" and "Lucknow," which are also retained in official use. The forms "Kahnpur" and "Lakhnau," apart from their apparent uncouthness, would not enable those names to be pronounced by English lips as other than "Cawnpore" and "Lucknow." "Punjab" is still sometimes used officially, and entraps the unwary student of Hunterianism to pronounce it "*Poonjab*"; there is absolutely no reason why it should not always be written "Panjab," and I have consistently done so. On the same principle "Burma" ought to be "Barma"; but Hunterianism has not been consistently applied to Burmese names, and I have followed the universal practice of writing "Burma." In the case of the name "Haidarabad" I have introduced a distinction. There are two places of that name: one is the Nizam's capital in the Deccan, and the other is a town in Sindh. I have spelt the Nizam's capital as the Nizam's Government spells it, "Hyderabad"; the town in Sindh I write as *Haidarabad*, as it should be written. I have tried to be reasonably consistent, but not slavishly.

Among friends who have helped I may mention Sir William Foster, historiographer at the India Office, who has always, with ready courtesy, answered any points referred to him on the British period; Mr. H. C. Barnard, who is responsible for the Chronological Summary and the Index; and my publishers, Messrs. A. and C. Black, whose indulgence has enabled me to improve the maps and bring them up to date. For instance, I have shown the Khaibar railway, which is to be opened by the Viceroy in November, 1925.

A. YUSUF ALI.

"Marash,"
12, Grange Park, Ealing,
July 8, 1925.

CONTENTS

CHAPTER I

GEOGRAPHICAL INFLUENCES

CHAPTER II

THE PEOPLE, LANGUAGES, AND POLITICAL DIVISIONS

CHAPTER III

THE ROOTS OF HINDUISM

CHAPTER IV

THE MESSAGE OF BUDDHA

CHAPTER V

FOREIGN INVASIONS AND INFLUENCES

CHAPTER VI

THE IMPERIAL IDEA IN HINDU INDIA

CHAPTER VII

MUSLIM INVASIONS, 1000–1206

CHAPTER VIII

ESTABLISHMENT OF THE MUSLIM EMPIRE IN INDIA, 1206–1526

CHAPTER IX

THE MUGHAL EMPIRE IN THE MAKING

CHAPTER X

THE MUGHAL EMPIRE AT ITS ZENITH

CHAPTER XI

HOW ENGLAND WON AGAINST PORTUGAL AND HOLLAND

CHAPTER XII

THE GROWTH OF ENGLISH COMMERCE AND OF THE EAST INDIA COMPANY

CHAPTER XIII

THE THREE PRESIDENCIES: THE COMPANY'S ORGANIZATION IN INDIA IN THE COMMERCIAL PERIOD

CHAPTER XIV

THE MUGHAL EMPIRE IN ITS DECLINE

CHAPTER XVII

THE COMPANY'S POSITION AT HOME: PARLIAMENTARY REGULATION (1765–1781)

CHAPTER XVIII

CONSOLIDATION IN BENGAL: EXPANSION IN MADRAS AND BOMBAY

CHAPTER XIX

FIGHT FOR SUPREMACY, 1789-1819

CHAPTER XX

REFORM AND PHILANTHROPY: MOVEMENTS, MORAL, SOCIAL, AND RELIGIOUS, 1819–1836

CHAPTER XXI

PUSH TO THE NORTH-WEST: PANJAB, SINDH, AND AFGHANISTAN, 1836–1856

CHAPTER XXII

THE GREAT MUTINY AND THE EXTINCTION OF THE COMPANY, 1857–1858

CHAPTER XXIII

BRITISH SPIRIT SUPREME: MILITARY, ADMINISTRATIVE, AND ECONOMIC REFORMS; SAFEGUARDING THE FRONTIERS, 1860–1888

CHAPTER XXIV

GROWTH OF NATIONALISM, AND THE SPIRIT OF DISCONTENT, 1888–1910

CHAPTER XXV

THE GREAT WAR AND THE NEW CONSTITUTION, 1910–1925

APPENDICES

LIST OF MAPS

THE MAKING OF INDIA

CHAPTER I

GEOGRAPHICAL INFLUENCES

India's Central Position.—In the map of Asia India occupies a central position. If we take a map of the Eastern Hemisphere, including the continents of Europe, Asia, Africa, and Australia, India again occupies a central position. Ancient Indian civilization was in touch with the other civilizations of Asia and Egypt. Greek influences can be traced in Indian art and science after a certain period. Buddhism linked India to Central and Eastern Asia. Islam gave her a fresh Western orientation. Her membership of the British Empire gives her a place in world politics. It is probable that in the new unity of the world India may occupy a yet more important place, commensurate with her geographical position.

Prehistoric Geology.—Geologically, the southern Peninsula of India has a different history from the northern portion. The two alluvial tracts which form the Gangetic and the Indus systems respectively formed a shallow sea, drained from the Himalayas. The Himalayas themselves are a comparatively new system of mountains compared with the ancient rocks of the south. The separation of the north from the south by water continued in the Secondary Epoch and a good deal of the Tertiary—perhaps even after the advent of man. On the other hand, Peninsular India was joined on with Ceylon in the south, with Burma, the Malay Peninsula, and the Islands, on to Australia in the east, and with Madagascar and East Africa on the west. Geologists also tell us that West Africa was united with Brazil in South America. This great, ancient, equatorial continent, called Gondwana, accounts for many physical affinities to be found in India, in rocks, in fauna and flora, and also possibly in the remotely ancient strata of ethnic and linguistic stocks.

Boundaries.—Broadly speaking, India's boundaries on the north, north-east, and north-west are made up of high mountain chains. Her eastern and western coasts are washed by the sea, and as they converge to a point in the south, there is no southern boundary.

Isolation in the North.—The northern chain of hills is the main Himalayas, whose peak, Mount Everest, is the highest in the world, with an altitude roughly of 29,000 feet above sea-level. Behind this enormous chain is the high plateau of Tibet, which is sparsely populated, and isolated from China in the east and Mongolia in the north. The northern barrier of India, therefore, shuts her off almost completely from other parts of Asia.

Importance of the North-West Frontier.—The north-west mountain barriers are scarcely separated by the Indus from the main Himalayan Range, and are connected with the mountain chain that runs right across Asia from Baluchistan to Lake Baikal and beyond. This mountainous region has passes which have been accessible to troops and large bodies of men from prehistoric times to the present day. This region is therefore of great importance from an ethnical, historical, and strategic point of view.

North-East.—On the north-east the river Brahmaputra separates the main Himalayas from their eastern extensions—a series of mountain chains which, in the first instance, cut off India from Burma except by sea, and ultimately divide Burma from Siam by mountains that continue northwards, and constitute roughly the boundary between China and Tibet. Burma is not thus absolutely cut off from India, and her civilization, like that of Siam and Indo-China, looks both towards India and China. Burma now forms one of the major provinces of British India. The 1,000 miles of her Chinese frontier, a good deal of which is undemarcated, may possibly possess some strategic value in the event of a military awakening in China. At present this frontier is of no importance.

East.—On the east of India proper (not including Burma) is the Bay of Bengal, which receives at its northern apex the waters of the Brahmaputra river, the sources of which are north of the Himalayas, and which forms the main fertilizing agent of the provinces of Assam and Eastern Bengal. This Bay, with numerous islands near the coast of Burma, forms really a great sea, with a width of more than 1,200 miles between Madras and the Malay Peninsula. In historic times there has been a stream of Indian emigration eastwards through the straits of Malacca into the Pacific Islands, in which Java has a civilization based on that of the Hindus. No great irruptions have come from the opposite direction, because the Pacific islands were uncivilized and thinly peopled, and the Chinese, with a settled civilization, were content to remain within their own borders. In this they were unlike the nomadic and restless peoples of Central Asia, whose migrations shook the old world of Asia and Europe.

West.—The western boundary of India is the Arabian Sea, which, like the Bay of Bengal, is an inlet of the Indian Ocean. Across this sea India maintained communications with Arabia, Egypt, and the Roman Empire. The latest invasions of India by various European nations also came from the west and south-west, round the Cape of Good Hope. India's main channel of communication at the present day is in this direction, through the Red Sea and by the Suez Canal. Her frontier post of Aden (whose foreign relations are now under the Middle East department of the Colonial Office) is about 1,700 miles away from Bombay, across the Arabian Sea.

Ceylon.—The island of Ceylon is separated from India by a narrow channel, and belongs physically, though not politically, to India. Politically Ceylon is governed as a Crown Colony within the British Empire.

Length of Frontier.—The huge extent of this sub-continent will be gathered from the fact that its land frontier, measured merely along straight lines from the south-east corner of Baluchistan to the southern-most point of Tenasserim, is more than 4,000 miles, and its coastline similarly measured between the same points without taking account of indentations, measures more than 4,500 miles. The real coastline of India may be taken to be over 6,000 miles.

Harbours—(*a*) *Modern.*—The principal harbours within British territory on the western coast are Karachi and Bombay.

The Portuguese hold Goa, which was a well-used harbour before their advent, and there are some minor harbours situated in Indian States. The Bay of Bengal is not furnished with so many good harbours, which is not surprising on this inhospitable, surf-beaten coast. Madras is the only harbour of first-class importance. The harbour of Calcutta in the north is situated eighty-five miles up the Hugli river. Rangoon on the Irawadi is the principal harbour of Burma, twenty miles from the sea. All the harbours just mentioned have been developed within the last four and a half centuries—that is, since the advent of European maritime nations to India.

(*b*) *Older Harbours and their Trade.*—From very ancient times, however, there were numerous harbours, both on the western and the eastern coasts of Southern India, which carried on a flourishing trade with Arabia, Egypt, and Europe in the West, and China in the East. Those early harbours have now fallen into a position of minor importance, or been silted up, or have disappeared altogether owing to changes in the eastern coastline. On the west coast old river harbours, like Broach and Surat, have become useless for modern maritime trade. When Julius Cæsar became master of Alexandria, 47 B.C., the Romans developed the Red Sea trade with India. The discovery of the south-west monsoons by western navigators in A.D. 47 gave a further stimulus to Arab and Eastern trade, mainly with Southern India. The pepper of Malabar, the pearls of Ceylon, and the beryl of Coimbatore District in the Madras Presidency, and later on the diamond mines near the Krishna river, formed the main attractions of the early trade. There is reason to suppose also that gold was mined in Southern India, although Pliny (*d.* A.D. 79) laments the drain of gold to India, possibly referring to gold coins. The Periplus, which describes the navigation of the Arabian Sea (A.D. 80), mentions as Indian exports ivory, perfumes, and cotton fabrics. Large hoards of Roman coins, mostly of the reigns of Augustus and Tiberius, but also some of Claudius and Caligula, are found in the Madras Presidency. Few Roman coins have been found in Northern India.

River Basins of Northern India.—The rivers of Northern India have from the earliest times acted as the chief lines of communication. The Indus and its tributaries serve the Panjab and Sindh, and communicate from the gates of India near Peshawar to the Indian Ocean. The Ganges and the Jamna were navigable from very near their upper reaches in the plains to their junction at Allahabad, and the combined river between Allahabad and the Bay of Bengal formed a very broad highway of communication between Upper India and Lower Bengal. The distance between Delhi on the Jamna and the delta of the Ganges in Bengal, measured along the river, without taking account of minor bends, is over a thousand miles. There were thus from the earliest times easy means of communication all over Northern India, which may be taken to be the country covered by the river systems of the Ganges and the Indus. There were, moreover, a few trunk roads in this tract, mainly with the two communicating gates of India: one leading through Kabul to Central Asia, and the other through Kandahar towards Persia. Besides this land route, the coasting sea route to Persia and Arabia was also used, until Western knowledge of the monsoons enabled ships to sail right across the Arabian Sea.

Three Central Tracts.—The central country immediately south of the Indo-Gangetic plains has three tracts of varying physical features, which may, however, be treated as one from historical considerations. One is the large, sandy desert of Rajputana. To the south-west of this desert is the peninsula of Kathiawar and the rich, alluvial plains of Gujarat. East of Gujarat is the hill tract of Central India, and the greater part of the modern Central Provinces. The desert of Rajputana was an isolating factor as between the north and the south, but it did not form as complete a barrier as the one we shall presently mention. Gujarat and Kathiawar were accessible from the Panjab either by way of Sindh or by way of the valleys of those rivers of Central India which feed the Jamna, notably the Chambal basin. The central portion of India was covered until recent times with dense forests, inhabited by wild tribes, which also acted as a barrier between the north and the south.

Barriers between North and South.—The three barriers which practically cut off Northern from Southern India were (1) the Vindhya Mountains, north of the Narbada river; (2) the Narbada river, which rises from hills in the Central Provinces, and after passing through picturesque gorges and descending through rapids, falls into the Arabian Sea; although its total length is nearly 800 miles, very little of it is navigable; (3) the Satpura Range, south of the Narbada, which is the home of some of the oldest aborigines of India. This triple barrier acted as an obstacle to the invasions based on the north-west frontier of India. They did not, however, affect communications between Bengal and the south by the east coast of India, via Orissa and the Telugu country. No river communications acted as a link between Northern and Southern India.

South India : the Deccan Plateau.—Southern India, which for all practical purposes we may consider the peninsular tract south of the Narbada, has no great navigable rivers. The Narbada and the Tapti, which rise in Central India and fall into the Arabian Sea, are useless as channels of communication. Further south, on account of the great mountain chain, the Western Ghats, there are no important rivers flowing from the peninsula to the west. These Ghats have rendered sea communication with the West difficult, except in the extreme south, through the Coimbatore Gap and beyond the termination of the Ghats. The east coast of India has also its Eastern Ghats. A little triangular tract in the extreme south, and facing the island of Ceylon, has been at all times a prosperous country. This little triangular tract in the extreme south may be called the Tamil country, from the prevailing language and people. Just north of it is a strip of fertile territory on the East Coast called the Telugu, or Andhra, country. It includes the deltas of the Godavari and the Krishna. Between the Eastern and the Western Ghats is the famous Deccan Plateau, of which the Eastern and Western Ghats, converging to the south, may be considered the flanks.

East Coast Rivers.—The chief rivers of the east coast, the Mahanadi, the Godavari, the Krishna, and the Kaveri, are not navigable to any great extent, and usually lie in deep, rocky channels. Their deltas, however, have an elaborate system of irrigation. The agricultural staple, as in Bengal, is rice. The climate is enervating, and the population is not physically hardy.

Ancient Towns : Taxila and Delhi.—The situation of important towns in India has naturally varied with the political conditions of the country. Probably one of the most ancient inhabited sites was near modern Peshawar, in a buried town called Taxila, where excavations have revealed a large number of Buddhist remains. Under another name it was probably a pre-Buddhist town. The site owed its importance to its being at the gateway of India from the north-western passes, on the road by which the earliest invasions of the Aryans took place. Later, as the Aryans penetrated further into the country, the sacred tract became that round the upper reaches of the river Jamna, indicated by the neighbourhood of modern Delhi. This tract is of great strategic and historical importance, as is evident from the fact that more than five battles have been fought at or in the neighbourhood of Panipat within recorded times. It may be mentioned that this is a sort of bottle-neck entrance from the Panjab into the spacious plains of Northern India on the one side, or the fertile lands of Central India on the other. West and south-west lies the sandy desert. North is the range of the Himalayas, and east and south-east is the Jamna, which is a sufficiently wide river to act as a barrier for early invasions. The importance of the position of Delhi will thus be understood, but its importance was greater when India looked towards the north-west and was a land-power, than now, when, under British rule, it looks more to the sea by way of either Calcutta or Bombay, and its government rests ultimately on British sea-power.

Benares, Patna, Ujjain, etc.—Benares (also called Kashi), the sacred city of the Hindus, is also an ancient city, but obviously its importance can only date from the time when the Hindus had spread over the Jamna and Ganges valleys, and could look upon the position of Benares as central. Benares also plays an important part in Buddha's teaching. Ajodhya (modern town Fyzabad) and Muttra (Mathura) in the east and west respectively of the United Provinces, are ancient, sacred cities, and centres of different cults. Ajodhya is the city of Rama, the hero of the Hindu epic Ramayana, and the mother city of many Rajput families. Thousands of the devotees of Rama flock there for pilgrimage. On the other hand, the centre of

Krishna worship is at Muttra, known to the Alexandrian geographer, Ptolemy, as "Modoura of the gods," and a focus of Buddhist learning and art in the early centuries of the Christian era. Perhaps the most important city during Buddhist times was on the various sites represented by the modern Patna. Ujjain, in Central India, was reputed to be the centre of Sanskrit learning in classical times, and was also the capital of various Indian kingdoms. Hindu astronomy counts its longitudes from Ujjain Observatory as zero. In Buddhist literature it figures prominently as the capital of the Avanti kingdom. Its geographical importance is due to its central position in India. It is also at the confluence of the ancient routes from the west coast and from the Deccan to Northern India. On the west coast the town of Broach dates back to before the Christian era. It was an important port for communications westwards across the sea, as Surat was in the fourteenth to the seventeenth centuries. In Southern India, besides the ports already mentioned, the town of Madura was an important centre some centuries before the Christian era. Kanchi (modern Conjeeveram, near Madras) was an important centre of Northern culture in Southern India, and was the capital of the Pallava dynasty from about A.D. 200 to about A.D. 800.

The "Presidency Towns" : Other Towns.—The biggest cities of modern India—Calcutta, Bombay, and Madras—are creations of British rule. They are called Presidency Towns because they were the seats of a President and Council in the days of the East India Company. They owe their importance to the fact that they were the chief outlets for the East India Company's trade before the Company became a territorial power. Karachi, on the Indus delta, is a harbour of still more modern creation. Lahore and Agra rose into importance in Mughal times, and still retain their interest, the one as the capital of the Panjab, and the other as the centre of the finest Mughal architecture in India. Rangoon is the chief port of Burma, and the third seaport of British India. It is the outlet for the chief staples of Burma—namely, rice, rubies, petroleum, teak, and other timbers. The size of the biggest towns may be judged by the fact that the population of Calcutta with suburbs approaches a million and a quarter, while that of Bombay is well over a million. There are twenty-eight towns with a population of over 100,000, and many other towns of historical importance or of moderate size scattered all over India, many of them in ruins. About a tenth of the total population lives in municipal areas.

Variations of Climate: Principal Crops.—It will be readily understood that in a sub-continent extending from Latitude 37° N. to 8° N. and Longitude 61° E. to 101° E. the climate, flora and fauna, must vary enormously. This variation is rendered still wider by varying altitudes above the sea-level, and by differences of soil and rainfall. The snowline on the Northern Himalayas is 19,500 feet above the sea-level, and yet a long line of perpetual snow can be seen from the lower Himalayas. The dry, sandy deserts of Rajputana offer a striking contrast to the wet, submontane districts of Northern Bengal, where there are places with an annual rainfall of over 400 inches. The average rainfall all over India is between 40 and 45 inches. The rich, alluvial soils of the Indus and the Jamna-Ganges basins yield two main harvests in the year, with a third extra harvest in many places. Wheat, barley, rice, pulses, oil-seeds, sugar-cane, and, in suitable local areas, indigo, jute, and cotton, are grown in abundance. In moist areas with abundant rainfall two crops of rice are raised. The tableland of the Deccan has the characteristic black cotton soil which grows cotton, and has grown it from very ancient times. Not much wheat is grown in this area, but maize and the millets form the staple food. Rice is grown further south and in the coastal areas where abundance of water is available for irrigation. There is a system of water tanks by which the rain-water is collected and stored and utilized for the various rice crops as required.

Irrigation.—Tank irrigation is a very ancient system in India. Other systems, such as that of utilizing the waters of the snow-fed rivers from the higher reaches, by means of long and scientifically aligned canals and distributaries, have been extensively developed within British times. A network of canals extends over the United Provinces and the Panjab, and a big project in hand will supply Sindh with abundant river water for irrigation. In the alluvial tracts also the water level is not at any great distance from the surface of the soil, and numerous wells are dug, from which water is drawn by bullock and other power for irrigation purposes. Fourteen million acres are under well irrigation, 21 millions are irrigated from canals, and 7 millions from storage tanks.

Seasons.—The seasons in the Indian area are somewhat different from those in other countries. Instead of the four seasons of Europe—spring, summer, autumn, and winter—the well-marked periods are: (1) the cold weather, roughly from September-October to March-April, according to latitude and altitude; (2) the hot weather, from March-April to June-July; and (3) the monsoons, or the periods of the rains, from June-July to September-October. The classical Sanskrit writers further subdivided each of these periods into two, making six theoretical seasons for India. But there are great local variations, especially as we get to the extreme north, or the Himalayan country, or near the seacoast, or towards the Equator. The tract of the perpetual snows of the Himalayas is uninhabitable. When we get to the region of the glaciers we find an alpine flora, and flowers like the edelweiss can be picked up. As we descend in altitude, the climate and the flora and fauna become more and more like that of the temperate climates, until we come to the bananas, the coco-nut palms, and the pepper and spices of the tropics. There is an abundant variety of trees, yielding shade, fruit, and timber. The State forests cover an area of nearly one-fourth of British India. In Northern India most English flowers and vegetables will grow in the cold weather, and there is a delightful and bracing climate for man and beast. Further south, as we get within the tropics, there are two factors which temper the climate—namely, the equability of the sea coast and the altitude of the Deccan Plateau. On the whole, it must be confessed that the climate is very hot and trying in the hot weather, and has undoubtedly affected adversely the physical qualities of the successive races that have inhabited India.

Famines.—The capricious variations in rainfall frequently cause local famines. With the development of roads, and the 37,000 miles of open railways, foodstuffs can easily be moved about, but the distress is chiefly caused by the shortage of water and fodder for cattle. The whole of India is never simultaneously affected by famine, but whenever the affected area is large, organized measures for famine relief on a large scale become necessary, and are undertaken by Government. The development of manufactures and mineral resources will tend to minimize the distress caused by agricultural depressions.

Minerals.—The mineral wealth of the country is both varied and abundant. Coal, mineral oil, iron, copper, silver and lead (Burma), mica, gold, manganese, salt, and precious stones may be mentioned among the chief mineral products.

CHAPTER II

THE PEOPLE, LANGUAGES, AND POLITICAL DIVISIONS

Ethnical Stocks: Pre-Dravidian and Dravidian.—The ethnical variations amongst the people of India are as wide as the variations in the flora and fauna. There is no doubt that the substratum of original stock, which is represented by certain very primitive tribes, now numerically insignificant, is of a negroid or Australian character, possibly dating from the early geological times when India was not separated east and west, as she is now. Tribes like the Bhils and Gonds, who live in the hilly and forest country of Central India, are either connected with that stock or represent a superimposed layer. The earliest historical stock that we can trace in the population of India is the Dravidian, which forms the main factor in the population of the Madras Presidency, the eastern half of Hyderabad State and Mysore and other States of Southern India. The Dravidians developed a high civilization of their own. There are no historical landmarks by which we can trace their advent into India. The Dravidian languages are extinct in Northern India, although fragments of them are found in Baluchistan. It is inferred that the Dravidians once peopled Northern India, and were pushed back by the subsequent invasions of the Aryans. This, however, is purely a matter of conjecture. Some of the prehistoric finds in the Dravidian country seem to have their counterpart in other prehistoric civilizations.

Indo-Aryans.—With the advent of the Aryans we come to a definite event which has stamped its mark upon the Indian population, Indian languages, and Indian civilization. They also form a connecting-link with the main population of Europe. Competent opinion has not yet been able to fix the definite centre from which the original Aryan stock radiated in all directions, or the roads which different waves of that stock followed. The Steppes of Central Asia, the region round the Baltic, and the plains of Hungary have been mentioned as the original centre and home of the Aryan race before its dispersion. To the separation of its various tribes, and their migrations in various directions, we cannot assign dates. The Hindu tradition would suggest an impossibly early date, but it is valueless for chronological purposes. As the result of the most recent researches, we may possibly conclude that the first wave of Aryan invasion into India, corresponding with the composition of the oldest hymns of the Rig-Veda, may be assigned to somewhere about 1200-1500 B.C.

Aryo-Dravidians.—But the Aryans did not come into an empty land. All their earliest literature in India indicates constant and unceasing warfare with the inhabitants whom they found in the country, and also amongst the Aryan tribes themselves. What was the stock which first felt their impact we cannot definitely decide. It was a dark race, which may correspond either to the civilized Dravidians, who are supposed to have been driven southwards, or some of the more primitive tribes, whose remnants live in the forests of Central India even now. Ethnologists trace the Aryo-Dravidian stock in the United Provinces and Bihar, while the Aryan stock seems to predominate in Kashmir and the Panjab.

Tibeto-Mongolians.—As the Aryans advanced eastwards in the Jamna-Ganges valley, they also encountered another ethnic stock, the Tibeto-Mongolian. The Mongolian stock, distinguished by its broad cheek-bones, narrow oblique eyes, scanty hair, and yellow skin, is one of the main stocks of Asia. The Chinese represent that stock in its highest and purest form. The Japanese are, according to modern standards, the most advanced representatives of that stock, but have other admixtures. The Tibetans, Burmans, Siamese, and the people of Indo-China represent mixed stocks in which the Mongolian blood predominates. The people of the countries north of China may possibly represent a more primitive branch of that stock. How that stock came into India, whether through the mountain passes of the Central Himalayas or through Burma on the north-east, or through Kashmir or the north-west frontier, remains doubtful. If they came through the north-west frontier passes, they must have been pushed forward eastwards by the Aryan invasions. In the population of Bengal, Assam, and Orissa, and to a less extent in Bihar and the United Provinces, and possibly even further south, the Tibeto-Mongolian stock can be traced. In the hill population of the Himalayas, including the Gurkhas of Nepal, Mongolian features appear prominently.

Turki, Persian, and other Stocks.—The Aryans themselves came in successive waves, each pushing forward the other until the force of the migrations was spent. While, however, they were dispersing eastwards and southwards in India, and establishing their institutions and civilization, other races, which were restlessly seeking new homes from Central Asia or Persia, also followed the same route, and mingled themselves in the population of India. Among these we can definitely trace the Turki races, the Bactrians and Scythians (who may possibly be of Turki affinities), the Persians, the Parthians, the Huns, and a vast mass of miscellaneous races.

Greeks, Arabs, and Modern Europeans.—When Alexander the Great overthrew the Persian Empire, his Macedonians also entered the Panjab, which had already been a province of the Persian Empire. The Greek stock left traces in the population of the Panjab and surrounding regions. After the rise of Buddhism there was much intercourse between Central Asia and China on the one hand and India on the other, and that must have further increased the race intermixture between India, Central Asia, and beyond. Quite early in the Christian era the Asiatic Christians established a colony in Southern India, and the remnants of the Jews who are found in Southern and Western India have also been established in the country for many centuries. With the rise of Islam in the seventh century and the expansion of the Muslim Empire in the following century, Arab influence was felt in India, thus renewing the Semitic influences of Assyria and Babylonia in remoter ages. After the invasion of the Portuguese at the end of the fifteenth century, the Dutch, the French, the English, and some of the minor European nations, came for trade in organized bands, while isolated Italians, Germans, and Russians are known to have visited India. From the eleventh century onwards, Arabs,

Persians, Afghans, and Turks (both from the West and from Central Asia) are known to have come in fair numbers and contributed to the Muslim population in India.

Modern Features : Hindus and Muslims.—It will thus be seen that ethnically the Indian population is a vast admixture. So far as modern India is concerned, the chief factors that count are the Dravidians in Southern India and the mixed Aryan races of Northern India. The vast majority of the people of India conform to Aryan civilization as developed in India, and modified by Muslim (also called "Muhammadan") and British civilizations, as we shall see in the course of this history. The Muslims, though in the mass they are not racially different from the Hindus, are sharply divided from the rest of the inhabitants of India on account of their religion, and as they number 69 millions out of a total population of 319 millions (by the census of 1921), they may be reckoned as one of the main subdivisions among the people of India. The Hindu castes will be referred to in the next chapter.

Vernacular Languages. — The numerous historical and geographical factors that have made up the population of India are also responsible for the large variety of languages to be found in India. Many of these languages are mere dialects, and many people are polyglot. A full survey of the Indian languages has revealed their true affinities, and rendered possible a scientific classification. The principal vernacular languages, with growing literatures, are:

1. Hindustani, which is the common term for the common language spoken in the United Provinces, Bihar, and in considerable areas around them, and understood more or less all over India. Its literary forms are Hindi and Urdu.

2. Bengali, spoken in the province of Bengal. It has a very fine recent literature, thanks to men of genius like Dr. Rabindranath Tagore, who writes both in the vernacular and the English language.

3. Marathi, the language of the Marathas, who inhabit the southern part of the Bombay Presidency, the western part of the Hyderabad State, and a considerable part of Berar and the Central Provinces.

4. Gujarati, the language of Gujarat, including Kathiawar, and some portions of Rajputana and Central India.

5. Panjabi, spoken in the Panjab.

6. Sindhi, confined to Sindh.

7. Tamil, which has an ancient and very fine literature, and is spoken in the tract of the Madras Presidency south of the Krishna river, and east of a rough line drawn through Raichur and Bangalore and so on to Cape Comorin.

8. Telugu, which is the language spoken in the northern parts of the Madras Presidency and the eastern half of the Hyderabad State.

9. Kanarese, the prevailing language in Kanara, Mysore, and generally the west coast of Southern India, west of the line mentioned under (7) above. There are sister Dravidian languages like Malayalam, which need not detain us.

10. Burmese, which is spoken in Burma.

The first six languages mentioned above are all based on Aryan dialects; Tamil, Telugu, and Kanarese are Dravidian; and Burmese is Tibeto-Mongolian, largely influenced by Sanskrit.

Indian Classical Languages.—Besides these living languages there is the old classical language, Sanskrit, and its derivative, Pali, which have both a considerable body of literature. Sanskrit is the sacred language of the Hindu scriptures, and Pali of a great portion of the Buddhist scriptures. The Muslims also introduced Arabic and Persian, which are not now spoken languages in India, but which have largely influenced Urdu and those forms of other vernaculars which are spoken by Muslims in India.

Historical Growth of the Provinces.—The division of India into provinces is not entirely based either on linguistic or racial or geographical considerations. But good historical reasons can be given for the present constitution of these provinces.

Nine Major Provinces : (1) Madras and (2) Bombay.—The acquisition of Madras on the east coast by the East India Company gave them a point of support from which, when the Company stood out to acquire territory, it spread north and south, and formed the Madras Presidency, mainly on the east coast of India, but also extending a little way on the west coast of South India. Similarly, the acquisition of the island of

Bombay and the subsequent wars with the Marathas gave the East India Company a hold on the west coast of India, and eventually made them masters of a good part of the Maratha country, and practically the whole of Gujarat; when the province of Sindh was conquered, the Punjab was not yet British territory, and the sea route from Bombay to Sindh being the only means of communication, the province of Sindh was attached to Bombay, and still remains part of the Bombay Presidency or Province.

(3) **Bengal,** (4) **Bihar,** (5) **United Provinces of Agra and Oudh,** (6) **Panjab,** (7) **Central Provinces,** (8) **Assam : formed out of the old Bengal Presidency:** (9) **Burma.**—The acquisition of Calcutta at the mouth of the Hugli gave the East India Company a jumping-ground for the rich basin of the Ganges. At first they acquired from the Mughal a share in the administration of Bengal and Bihar, which they constituted the Bengal Presidency. Later the tracts now forming the United Provinces were acquired on the break-up of the Mughal Empire and the annexation of Oudh. These tracts were also attached to the Bengal Presidency. The conquest of the Panjab from the Sikhs and its annexation added further to the enormous area of the old Bengal Presidency. When shortly before the Mutiny the East India Company also acquired the Central Provinces, they, too, were lumped in the Bengal Presidency. The old Bengal Presidency, therefore, practically included the whole of British India which was not included in the Bombay and Madras Presidencies. Since then the Bengal Presidency has been gradually broken up into provinces of manageable size. The word "Presidency," whether applied to Bengal, Bombay, or Madras, has no significance now, and we must speak of provinces as the true administrative divisions of India. The provinces into which Bengal broke up are the Panjab, the United Provinces of Agra and Oudh, Bihar including Orissa, Bengal properly so-called, Assam, and the Central Provinces. These six, with the provinces of Bombay and Madras, and the province of Burma, constitute the nine major provinces of India.

System of Government.—Each of the major provinces is administered by a Governor with an Executive Council of not more than four members, and a ministry of two or more members. The members of the Executive Council, English and Indian, are appointed by the Crown, and hold charge of special "reserved" departments, for which they are responsible to the Governor. The ministers are appointed by the Governor from among the elected members of the Legislative Council, and hold charge of other departments called "transferred," for which their responsibility is theoretically to the electorate. Each of these provinces has also a Legislative Council, consisting of at least 70 per cent. of elected members. These provincial councils will probably approach more and more as time goes on to the standard of local parliaments. Over all these provinces is the Government of India, whose head is the Viceroy and Governor-General, with an Executive Council of seven members (besides himself) appointed by the Crown. There are no popular members in the Government of India. The legislature of the Government of India consists of two houses. The Lower House is called the Legislative Assembly, and consists of 144 members, of whom 104 are elected. The Upper House, or Revising Chamber, or Senate, is called the Council of State, consisting of 34 elected and 26 nominated members, but the election is on a narrower franchise. The final responsibility for the policy of India rests with the Secretary of State for India, who is a member of the British Cabinet in England, and who has a council of twelve members to assist him. It is understood, however, in the new Constitution, that this ultimate responsibility to the Parliament of Great Britain does not imply ordinary interference with the details of administration in India, and it is an accepted principle of the Imperial Government that India should approach by gradual and successive stages to the status of a fully responsible Dominion.

Indian States.—Thus far we have described the administrative system of British India, but it must not be forgotten that within the total area of 1·8 million square miles and the total population of 319 millions of people in India as a whole, 709,000 square miles is not directly under British rule. Roughly two-fifths of India is governed by Indian princes or rulers, who have, under definite treaties with the British Government, various degrees of autonomous power. Some of these rulers have a very small extent of territory, and distinctly limited powers. But the greater number of the more important Princes of India have complete autonomous powers within their own limits, and are only precluded from having dealings with foreign countries or from having unlimited armed forces. The rulers of some of these States are Muslims, of others Rajputs, and of a few others Hindus of other tribes or castes. The most important Indian State is that of His Exalted Highness the Nizam of Hyderabad, who holds sway over the greater part of the Deccan Plateau, with an area of 82,700 square miles, and a population of 12 millions. Next in importance are the Maharajas of Mysore in Southern India, Baroda in Gujarat, Gwalior in Central India, and Kashmir in the extreme north. Mention may also be made of the interesting State of Bhopal, which has been ruled for three generations by a Muslim princess. Many of the smaller States are grouped together, and appear in the map as one big area, such as Rajputana or the peninsula of Kathiawar. The position of the Indian States collectively is not carefully defined, apart from the definition contained in the historic treaties with each of them separately. But the tendency of recent policy has been to leave their internal administration more and more without interference; to draw them together to an appreciation of common action in the Chamber of Princes; to consult them as friends and allies with regard to the administration of the British Indian Empire and the British Empire generally, and to make the British Crown a more and more real bond of union for the common advancement of mutual interests as between British territory and territory administered by Indian princes.

CHAPTER III

THE ROOTS OF HINDUISM

The Terms "Hindu" and "India."—The term "Hindu" is not found in the Vedas or in the ancient Sanskrit records. It is derived from the name of the river Indus. The Greeks and Persians, who came to know India from the Indus, called the contiguous country and its people from the name of the river. The Sanskrit name of the river was Sindhu. The Greeks characteristically omitted the sibilant, and called the people "Indoi." This name was adopted by the Romans for the people (Indi), and they called the whole country India.

Religious Divisions: Hindu and Muslim.—We have seen in the last chapter that the modern Hindus themselves are a mixed race. In the south the Dravidian stock predominates, but has an infusion of Aryan and other stocks. In the north the Aryan race contributes a considerable factor, but it has received an admixture of many other races. There are also some wild primitive tribes in the country. Putting aside the Europeans and other newly received foreigners, as well as the Jews and Parsis, who form an insignificant element in the vast permanent population, the main division of the people is by religion rather than by race. For the present purposes we may also exclude the 11 million Buddhists of Burma, which, although politically in British India, historically and geographically forms a separate country. In this way the main population of India would be divided between Muslims (69 millions) and Hindus (217 millions), and there are about 3 million Sikhs in the Panjab.

Who is a Hindu?—The Muslims have a definite religion, although many of them are ethnically related to various sections of their Hindu countrymen. The Sikhs also have a definite religion and scriptures, sprung from the contact of Hinduism with Islam. They became an organized, militant body in the Panjab about 250 years ago, and retain their martial ardour to the present day. The Parsis are descended from a small band of Persians who brought the Zoroastrian religion into Western India in the seventh century A.D. The Jews are a similar remnant of an older faith. The Christians, the bulk of whom belong to the Indian races or are of mixed descent, are gradually acquiring the consciousness of a separate community, in spite of their division into many denominations. They now number nearly 5 million souls in the Indian population. If we exclude these well-defined religions and the Buddhists, can we call the residue of the Indian population Hindus? This negative definition is sometimes adopted, but there are difficulties in the way of its acceptance, which we shall now consider.

Difficulties of Definition.—In the first place, there are the Animists, nearly 10 million in number, as recorded in the last Census. They consist mainly of members of the primitive forest tribes, whose religion is most rudimentary, and consists in the practice of magic and the propitiation of spirits, good and evil, but mostly evil, that reside in trees, rocks, streams, tigers, etc., or that haunt places or the bodies of human beings. Many of the elements of this magical religion have been absorbed into *popular* Hinduism, and some even into scriptural Hinduism outside the philosophies, especially in rites and ceremonials. The upper fringe of Animists tends to be absorbed into the Hinduism of castes, and the process has gone on for many centuries. In the second place, the Jains, who profess a religion older than Buddhists, and number over a million souls, are, from a religious point of view, sharply contrasted from Hindus of the *Sanatan Dharma* (orthodox religion), although in popular parlance they are spoken of as Hindus. Thirdly, the same may be said of modern reforming sects, like the Arya Samaj or the Brahmo Samaj, or mediæval reforming sects like the Kabir-Panthis (followers of Kabir), whose religious notions involve wide departure from the orthodox religion, however loosely we may define it. There is no reason why, if the Sikhs are excluded from the pale of Hinduism, these sects should be included in it, as they usually are. Finally, there is the more comprehensive definition attempted by the Hindu Maha Sabha (Central Association), with a view to political and religious solidarity. In their meeting at Benares in August 1923, they adopted the definition that a "Hindu" means "any person . . . professing to be a Hindu or following any religion of Indian origin, and includes *Sanatanists* [Orthodox], Arya Samajists, Jains, Sikhs, Buddhists, Brahmos, etc." This definition is not logically exact, and will be practically repudiated by Sanatanists, Sikhs, and Buddhists. If it aims at social or political solidarity it fails of its purpose, because it excludes Hindus converted or descended from converts to the Christian or Muslim faith. If its aim is purely religious it fails, because there is no common ground of faith, worship, or rites or ceremonies.

Historical Growth of Hinduism.—This confusion is historically intelligible. When the Aryans first came to India, about 2000 to 1000 B.C., they viewed the world as consisting of themselves (Aryans) and non-Aryans. The word "Hindu" had not then been invented, but the idea of exclusiveness, both religious and ethnic, soon gathered round the term "Aryan." To the present day many Hindu minds conceive of the terms "Aryan" and "Hindu" as synonymous. The Aryans had to contend with Dravidian civilization, and with the amorphous mass of Animism, which may have contained elements both Dravidian and Aboriginal. The Aryans gradually absorbed all these heterogeneous elements, but suffered much in the process. They changed their gods or cults or altered their characters; they developed new forms of social polity; and they built up a peculiar social organization, of which caste was the cornerstone and sacerdotalism (Brahmanism) the apex. This process was still in the early stages in the time of Buddha (fifth century B.C.) and at the invasion of Alexander the Great (326-325 B.C.). When the Greeks gave the name "Indoi" to the tribes round the Indus, there was not yet either an organized Hindu people or Hindu religion, and the name "Hindu" was not in use for centuries afterwards.

Fight between Narrow Sacerdotalism and more Catholic Movements.—Asoka's empire (third century B.C.) tried to give Buddhism an organization on non-sectarian lines. Its universality conquered Asia, but lost its hold on India. The Indian mind continued to develop its philosophies, cults, and floating ideas into numerous systems, but with a general trend towards exclusiveness and sacerdotalism. But the contact of Buddhism with the outer world and with the thought of Alexandria was not without its influence on the other schools of Indian thought. These latter have, besides the predominant Brahman tradition, a less exclusive warrior (Kshatriya) tradition, which has only begun to be studied quite recently. This warrior tradition was much strengthened by the foreign invasions and influences of the first six centuries of the Christian era (see Chapter V.).

Rise of Modern Hinduism.—Modern Hinduism aims at being a social and religious fabric with diverse compartments, and yet possessing a catholic ideal. Its foundations were laid in the dim past, but its chief modern features were developed during the four centuries (the seventh to the tenth of the Christian era) when Buddhism was extinguished, the foreign elements absorbed, the Sanskrit language became diffused throughout the peninsula as a classical language, and the clans and septs of the Rajput warriors were adopted as castes into the Hindu system, to do battle against the many races who came to fight under the united banner of Islam. Shankar Acharya, born in Southern India in A.D. 788, travelled all over the country, and established monasteries for the dissemination of the Brahmanical religion (and for the extinction of Buddhism) at the four strategic corners—viz., Dwarka on the west coast; Sringeri in the modern Mysore State; Jagannath or Puri on the east coast, south of Calcutta; and Badrinath in the extreme north, among the Himalayas. For a man who died at the age of thirty-two his work shows wonderful grasp and thoroughness. These centuries are sometimes called the period of the "revival" of Hinduism. In truth they witnessed the synthesis of a new religion.

Transformation of Deities.—Rudra, the Vedic god of roaring tempests, becomes in later periods Shiva "the Auspicious," and has gathered round him many accretions from Dravidian sources, especially those connected with sex worship. The goddess Kali, who delights in blood, and wears a garland of human skulls, is a relic of barbarous ages. She is identified with diseases, revenge, and slaughter in various forms. The nature gods Indra (thunder and rain), Agni (fire), Varuna (the sky), who are so prominent in the scheme of the Vedic hymns, have now become comparatively unimportant. There is scarcely a living temple to the Sun in modern India. The growth of the concepts that gather round the god Vishnu has been remarkable in its various stages. Originally a solar deity of very subordinate importance, he developed a character for personal beneficence. Then he became a rival to Shiva, or perhaps he was a protest against Shiva. Where Shiva was austere, Vishnu cared for men. Where Shiva was the Destroyer, Vishnu was the Preserver. The Vishnu cult came nearest to the idea of a personal god—a god whose love for humanity has induced him to assume various incarnations (Avatars), in which he has dwelt amongst men. Two of his incarnations were as Rama and Krishna, and round these names have grown up whole cycles of legends, literature, philosophy, and song. Rama is the self-denying god, the perfect model of a son, husband, and brother in private life, of a king and warrior in public life, and of a friend and helper in the godhead. Krishna is the sportive god, the god of mirth, dance, and dalliance in popular poetry, and the god of philosophy in the remarkable poem the *Bhagavad Gita*. Vaishnava poetry (that devoted to the god Vishnu) has made notable contributions to the world's devotional poetry. Between the eleventh and fifteenth centuries A.D., while Muslim saints poured their Sufi doctrines into India, Vaishnava Hindu bards evolved their doctrine of a personal god who wants love rather than service. This period was fruitful in minor Hindu sects which aimed at discarding caste, and some of which survive to the present day. This school of thought found its culmination in Tulsi Das (A.D. 1532-1623), the greatest poet of mediæval Hinduism, as it has found its international expression in Rabindranath Tagore, the finest flower of modern Vaishnavism.

Common Concepts of Hinduism.—This evolutionary glance at Hinduism shows the inherent difficulty of defining a system in which many historical strands are interwoven. Exclude the Muslims and Christians, whether of Hindu descent or not, as well as Parsis and Jews, and we may roughly speak of the rest of the permanent inhabitants of India as Hindus. The Animists are doubtful. But the Sikhs for certain purposes claim to be distinct from the Hindus, and so do the followers of the Brahmo Samaj, the Arya Samaj, and some of the minor sects, although the Arya Samajists claim that they are the true exponents of Hinduism, and the impetus which they have given to the reform of the Hindu social system, and the proselytizing zeal they have shown in enlarging their fold, have brought about a new conception of Hinduism. There are a few common features which are in the Hindu "atmosphere" which we proceed to examine, such as: (1) a belief in the Vedas as scriptures; (2) conformity to the practices of caste and burning of the dead; (3) the use of the services of Brahmans as priests; (4) the acceptance of certain theologico-philosophical concepts, including a vaguely comprehensive Pantheon, the doctrine of the transmigration of souls, and the doctrine of Karma. Let us consider each of these points in detail.

Belief in the Vedas.—Perhaps the most characteristically religious mark of Hinduism is a belief in the inspiration of certain ancient Sanskrit books called the Vedas. It can only be a vague belief, because none but Brahmans are allowed to study and expound these sacred books, and the lower classes are not even allowed to hear the Vedas. There are generally reckoned four Vedas, but even a learned and orthodox Brahman does not necessarily follow the four Vedas. There are some who follow two Vedas, and some three, and others all the four. To the Hindu every word and sound of the Vedas is inspired, and the books have existed from all time. Historically, as far as indications of language and internal evidence enable us to judge, the most ancient, and from a literary point of view the most interesting, is the Rig-Veda, which is mainly metrical. Latest research puts the age of the Rig-Veda at somewhere between 1000 and 1200 B.C. It consists of hymns to the forces of nature, which are personified as gods and goddesses. The Pantheon is simple, but implies a close priestly organization. The picture of life we get from the Vedas shows plain living in touch with Nature, but a not inconsiderable advance in the arts of civilization. In abstract concepts and the elaboration of priestly functions the later Vedas and their commentaries show all the subtleties of the Hindu intellect. The language of the earliest hymns is the oldest form of the Aryan tongue of which we have any literary record. The other Vedas consist of chants (mainly derived from the Rig-Veda), or prayers and formulæ for sacrifices, or spells and incantations for all kinds of religious rites.

Vedic Literature and the Puranas.—Along with the texts of the Vedas we have a large body of Sanskrit literature that grew up round the Vedas. These books are of various ages, and may be looked upon as commentaries, but in fact they show the germination of the religious ideas whose seeds we find in the Vedas. They follow up earlier suggestions in a series of logical aphorisms, probing into the very limits of abstract knowledge. The Upanishads are specially noteworthy as containing some very sublime doctrine and daring speculations as to the relations of man with the Godhead, the nature of the soul and matter, and the problems of life and eternity. Life in ancient India seems to have differentiated very early the special functions and privileges of the priests. As in other countries and ages, the priests were also the thinkers, writers, and teachers of the nation. These sages lived scattered in retreats in the forests, and studied and composed a great body of literature. As Brahmans they were the special repositories of the knowledge of God (Brahma) and the soul. Ancient Hindu polity assigns them a very lofty place, in public and private life. Even kings have to be guided by Brahmans. But political and social power must primarily have rested in the kingly or warrior class, who were called the Kshatriyas. The Kshatriyas as a class were probably illiterate, but in those early days it was not impossible for a Kshatriya to become learned in the Vedas and attain the status of a Brahman. There is a series of books called the Puranas, which are supposed to embody legendary lore and history without dates. They also give extensive genealogies of kings. Some of the latest writers of authority trace in some of these Puranas a Kshatriya tradition of history as distinct from the Brahman tradition. The Kshatriya tradition is less narrow socially, though the literature embodying it is not quite so exalted in philosophy and speculation as the literature specially identified with the Brahmans.

The Two Epics.—The two famous epics of India, the Mahabharat and the Ramayan, in their present form, are of comparatively recent date, but they comprise material of very different periods orally handed down, and finally edited into a complete whole. The Mahabharat has as the skeleton of its plot the story of the "Great War" of ancient India. But round that story are woven many episodes of Hindu tradition, and many stories meant to enlighten and edify the ordinary man or woman. One compact little body of philosophical argument, known as the Bhagavad Gita, may be specially mentioned. It enshrines all the characteristics of later Hindu theology in a poetic, philosophical, and semi-dramatic form, in language of singular beauty and moral elevation. The Ramayan tells a simpler story, and has more unity. Its hero is Rama, painted (as we saw) as the pattern of all that a Hindu son, husband, or brother ought to be in private life, and all that a Hindu king, warrior and saint ought to be in public life. To the Hindu, Rama is a perfect type of manhood, just as his wife, Sita, is a pattern of wifely devotion and womanly purity. It is possible that the story of Rama's exile into the forest, the devotion of his wife and brother who follow him to brave all hardships, the abduction of Sita by the demon king of Ceylon, the invasion of that island by Rama and his monkey allies, the destruction of the demon's city, the recovery of Sita in spotless purity, and the final restoration of Rama to his ancestral kingdom in Ajodhya (modern Oudh) embodied national historical memories. Possibly they refer to the advance of the Aryans into Southern India and Ceylon, the friendly non-Aryan tribes being typified by the monkeys and the hostile ones by the demons. The Ramayan and its dramatic story has made a deep impression on the Hindu mind, and although the original is in Sanskrit, vernacular versions in Hindi, Bengali, and other modern languages are acted and recited, and are thoroughly familiar to the minds of the people, both literate and illiterate.

The Shastras.—Besides the Vedas, the Upanishads, the body of Commentaries that are grouped round the Vedas, and the epics, there are a number of books relating to law and the sciences (as understood in ancient times) which are considered part of the body of Hindu sacred literature. These are collectively called the Shastras. The most important authoritative book on Hindu law is that of Manu. It is difficult to define its date precisely, and there are wide differences of opinion among those competent to judge. Like other ancient books, it has parts that belong to different ages, but from internal evidence it is probable that the system of law which it teaches was worked out about the time of the Christian era, and that the book in its present form was compiled a few centuries later. The Hindu law concepts are ultimately derived from the commentaries of the various Vedic schools, and no doubt embrace a certain body of customary law. The textbooks of Manu and of another old writer of a slightly later school are still used and applied by the British courts of law in India to the Hindus with regard to their domestic relations, such as marriage, inheritance, and other questions of personal law.

The Four Classical Castes.—The body of sacred scriptures mentioned above affects the majority of Hindus only theoretically and as a matter of belief, except as regards the law-books. The enforceable part of Hindu law again is confined to the domestic sphere, and may be over-ridden, as in the case of the lower castes, by local customs. The usages of caste are almost a universal symbol of the Hindu social system. In its origin, caste was probably an indefinite division into different orders of society. The original ideal castes are four in number: the Brahman, the Kshatriya, the Vaishya, and the Shudra. As we have already seen, the Brahman and the Kshatriya represent respectively the priestly and the warrior orders, and are co-extensive with the earliest organization of Aryan society. The Vaishya represented the agricultural and trading classes, the classes represented by those who were responsible for the skilled productive activities of society. The Shudras were the lowest caste, and were practically servile. Manu figuratively derives these castes from four members of the divine body—the Brahmans from the head, the Kshatriyas from the arms, the Vaishyas from the stomach, and the Shudras from the feet, of Brahma, the supreme and abstract deity of Hinduism. The Shudras were possibly non-Aryans, who accepted the Hindu social system, and had a place found for them at the bottom of the scale. Apart from these four classical castes, which had an accepted place in Hinduism, the people outside the system were grouped as Mlenchhas, which might mean the primitive forest savages, whom Hinduism did not recognize, or even foreigners of high culture like the Greeks or the Muslims when they first came to India.

Modern Castes.—The Rig-Veda in reality knows nothing of the caste system. The later literature speaks vaguely of the four classical castes. By the time we come to the lawbook of Manu, we find a large number of mixed castes, and conditions approaching more or less those at the present day, although the number of castes had not multiplied so enormously as they have done at the present day. In modern India there are hundreds of castes, each divided into many sub-castes. Members of a particular caste whose home is in one territorial area in India, but who migrate into another, sometimes lose touch with the home territory, and form a separate caste of their own. A caste may also be subdivided on the basis of trade or occupation. In this way race, occupation, and territorial habitat have each had something to do with the development of caste. At the present day a caste is simply a group of people who cannot eat cooked food with any persons outside their group, and who cannot inter-marry outside that group. Many of the castes are numerically not very strong, especially as those groups tend to split up. On the other hand, Hindus of modern education relax many of the rules of caste.

Hindu Social System dominated by Caste.—Caste remains the dominating factor in the Hindu social system. Even where individual members are willing to relax some of the rules, the question of caste comes up in the ceremonies connected with birth, marriage, and death, and in matters of inheritance. Each caste has its own ceremonies, and those ceremonies must be performed by Brahmans as regards most castes. The Brahmans themselves do not form one caste. There are numerous Brahman castes (or sub-castes), and the employment of any particular caste of Brahmans for any particular caste of clients and for any particular sets of ceremonies depends upon custom and hereditary practice. The idea of caste is so firmly rooted on Indian soil that groups not belonging to Hinduism are unconsciously affected by it, and tend to form castes of their own, although their rules may not be quite so rigid.

Burial Customs.—The Hindus burn their dead, unlike other communities of India. But it is not every Brahman who can officiate at the cremation ceremony. There are specialized Brahmans for funeral ceremonies, just as there are specialized Brahmans for performing the ceremonies connected with bathing at the various sacred places in India. The cremation is not usually complete. Charred remains are often floated down streams or sacred rivers. In the case of distinguished personages, mausolea are erected over the ashes of the deceased, or by way of cenotaphs, but this practice may be due to Muslim influences. The spirits of deceased ancestors are worshipped every year with solemn ceremonies.

Comprehensive Pantheon.—From the peculiar social organization which we have described arise some corollaries which are crystallized in certain beliefs and ideas which are ingrained in the very texture of Hinduism. One such idea is the comprehensive nature of the Pantheon. There are said to be 330 millions of Hindu gods and goddesses, but their cult is undefined. There are the old nature gods from the Vedic Hymns; there are gods and goddesses derived and absorbed from various cults that came into contact with Hinduism; there are national heroes like Rama and saints like Buddha, who have been absorbed into the Pantheon as reincarnations of the god Vishnu; and there are various local gods, goddesses, and godlings worshipped in villages, and considered as guardian deities, different in different localities. Snake worship, tree worship, river worship, sex worship, and similar cults belong to a wholly different circle of primitive ideas, but are nevertheless part of popular Hinduism.

Good and Malevolent Deities.—We have already glanced at the historical growth of the ideas grouped round Vishnu and Shiva. They form two persons in a Trinity: Brahma the creator, Vishnu the preserver, and Shiva the destroyer. Brahma is an embodiment of the abstract idea of God, and generally has no idols and no exclusive cult. Vishnu (in his many forms and incarnations) and Shiva have temples dotted over India, and have exclusive sects and devotees innumerable. Shiva is a contemplative god, and lives in the Himalayas. He and his consort Parvati, identified with the terrible goddess Kali, are associated with destruction, sacrifices, and vengeance. Philosophers explain these terrible deeds as connected with the destruction of evil as preparatory to the restoration of good, but village superstition believes in a malevolent goddess of smallpox or cholera who has to be appeased, or deities of all degrees, whose wrath at the sins, follies, and failings of mankind has to be pacified with formal and prolonged ceremonies.

Transmigration of Souls.—From the theory of the incarnation of the gods to the theory of the transmigration of souls is an easy step. Most of the schools of Hindu philosophy either believe that matter is an illusion, and the only reality is the Supreme Soul, of which all living souls are a part, as the drops of water are a part of the great ocean; or else that matter is eternal and indestructible, and that its various energies and activities explain what we call life and soul. For the popular mind it is enough to believe that each individual has a soul (or is part of a universal Soul), which takes a certain shape in this life, and which prepares itself for a rise or fall in the chain of evolution, leading to final absorption in the one primordial matter of Soul. There is thus a nice balance of ethical motives. The apparent inequalities of this life are connected with something that we did in our last, and the good or evil that we do in this life leads up to its corresponding results, a rise or a fall in the scale of evolution in the next life.

Doctrine of Karma.—The doctrine that every deed must have its inevitable consequence, not necessarily in one life, but possibly in thousands of lives, is the doctrine of Karma, and appears to be diametrically opposed to the doctrine of repentance and forgiveness of sins, although the Vishnu school of devotion attempts to hold both the doctrine of Karma and that of salvation by faith and devotion. The idea that each caste has its own place in the social system and should be content with that place, the present lower or higher caste being determined by previous Karma, leads to the logical deduction that the ethical duties of each caste may be different. For example, the duty of the warrior may be to fight, although it causes destruction of life, while the duty of a Brahman is to save life, and to preach extreme tenderness to all forms of life, high and low. The Bhagavad Gita elaborates this theme at great length, and tries to reconcile the apparent conflicts of duty which face everyone in practical life. One of the fundamental political ideas in Manu's lawbook is that a State exists in order to preserve the various castes or divisions of men, and not to allow them to be confounded.

Maya, or Illusion.—A very popular belief in the Hindu mind is indicated by the word *Maya,* or Illusion. According to this, all the material forms that we see and the events that seem to happen are only a subjective reflection of our own minds or our own Karma, and have no real existence. The problem of life is to get rid of these illusions. The only Reality is one and indivisible. There is no real meaning in the division between spirit and matter, between God and man, between life and inanimate nature, or between any of these. Individual existence is also an illusion, and the goal of life in philosophy is to destroy this illusion, and to reach final absorption into the Infinite, which is the only Existence. This doctrine has been very subtly elaborated by the Vedanta school of philosophy, but it vaguely affects all Hindu thought, and forms the background both of religious poetry and of the dreamy philosophy of the masses. It is more comprehensive than Western Pantheism.

Tenderness for Animal Life.—Among the root ideas of Hinduism must be mentioned extreme tenderness for animal life in all its forms. This feature is specially prominent among the sect of Jains, who number more than a million in the Indian population, and whose religion is older than that of the Buddha. Extreme votaries of the Jain faith cover their mouths and noses with fine cloth, in order to protect small insects from being destroyed by entering the human body. If this idea were given practical shape, it would lead to a more intelligent kindness for domestic animals, but theory and practice are often at variance in India, and the one does not necessarily affect the other. The sentiment, however, of tenderness to all life, and, indeed, of a sort of community of existence with lifeless matter itself, is of great value in moulding that type of universal goodwill which we find in the past thought of India in all ages. The worship of the cow is a characteristic feature of Hinduism.

Magic and Witchcraft.—The most primitive strata of population have still, in their floating beliefs, a haunting fear of magic and witchcraft. This has affected various phases of popular life and worship in India. All sorts of spirits are imagined to dwell in animals, trees, and even places, which are accordingly worshipped with peculiar rites varying with the localities. A belief of this kind, if undiluted with any other element of religion, is called Animism. The Indian census of 1921 enumerated 9¾ millions of Animists. These belong mainly to the primitive forest tribes. But vague ideas of that kind underlie a good deal of the rites and ceremonies of the masses. The worship of the energies of nature, as symbolized in sex, is also a factor in certain phases of religion, especially in Bengal. The popular superstitions of the country-side are numerous, but in that respect India is not peculiar.

Factors in Actual Hinduism.—Many of the ideas that we have last mentioned are probably foreign to the Aryan heritage of the Hindus. But they form large factors in the actual life of the country. If, as is the ordinary practice, we include amongst the Hindus the Dravidian as well as the Aryan races, and all the ethnic mixtures that form the Hindu population, these factors must be taken into account. In point of religion, although the Jains class themselves separately from the orthodox Hindus, the Jain religion can be, and is, rightly classed as a phase of the Hindu religion in its widest acceptation. The same may be said of the later reforming sects, such as the Arya Samaj and the Brahmo Samaj. The Sikhs occupy an intermediate position between the Muslims and Hindus, and number 3¼ millions, mainly in the Panjab. They will demand separate notice in the later history of India.

CHAPTER IV

THE MESSAGE OF BUDDHA

Significance of Buddha and Buddhism in History.—The life of Buddha (*d. circa* 480 B.C.) and the foundation and organization of the primitive Buddhist Church are important landmarks in the history of India. Its further extensions beyond the boundaries of India, to Ceylon (*circa* 246 B.C.), Kabul and Central Asia (first century B.C.), China (soon afterwards), Korea (*circa* A.D. 372), Japan (A.D. 552), and by way of Ceylon to Burma (*circa* A.D. 450), Siam (*circa* A.D. 638), and Java and the Eastern Archipelago (about the fifth to seventh centuries A.D.), belong to the general history of Asia. The developments and transformations undergone by Buddhist doctrine are part of the general history of human thought and religion. In Nepal and Tibet the introduction of Buddhism in the sixth and seventh centuries respectively marks the introduction of civilization. In Tibet Buddhism developed many fantastic doctrines, and it is the only Buddhist country ruled by an infallible head of Church and State (the Dalai Lama), supposed to be an incarnation of the Spirit of the Buddhas.

Dates in Indian History after Buddha.—The pre-Buddhist history of India has no dates. The learned researches of scholars can only establish approximate periods, with a margin of centuries. After Buddha it becomes possible to reconstruct approximate dates on account of the Ceylon Buddhist chronicles, which counted events from the death of the great teacher. His disciples collected a large body of literature in the spoken vernaculars of India, from which we can gather many facts about the political, social, economic, and intellectual condition of the country.

Buddha's Birth and Youth.—The facts of Buddha's life are briefly told. In the sub-Himalayan tract, about 130 miles north of the city of Benares, was the capital of a little kingdom, of the clan of Sakyas and the family of Gautama. The king's wife, expecting to become a mother, started, according to the Indian custom, for her parents' house to be confined; but her baby was born prematurely on the way, in the Lambini garden. This was the boy who was afterwards entitled the Buddha* ("the wise one"), after he obtained enlightenment. He grew up in his father's house, skilled in all manly sports, but also more observant than his fellows of the essential facts of life. His father, warned by soothsayers, is supposed to have shielded him from any knowledge of the evils of life, old age, disease, or death; but the moment came when his spirit had to face such facts, and to reason out their bearing on the ultimate destiny of man.

The Great Renunciation.—In his twenty-ninth year he abandoned his princely state and his happy home, and wife and child, beckoned by a vision of asceticism. Wandering into the night he was tempted by the spirit of evil, who offered him worldly good surpassing anything he had renounced. But the Buddha's mind was fixed on study and penance, and he passed on through city and forest, from one Brahman teacher to another, still dissatisfied with the solutions of the eternal problems which minor men offered. From Rajagriha (near the modern Patna) he passed on south to Bodhi Gaya, which still remains a centre of Buddhist pilgrimage. Six years of self-mortification failed to give him the great peace which he sought. At length he renounced self-mortification, and was abandoned by a few followers, who had been attracted by his asceticism.

The Enlightenment.—The key to the mystery was yet to come, and not without further inner spiritual struggles. The renunciation of the world may be a preparation; in itself it had no merit, nor had asceticism. Spiritual values had to be sought by spiritual means. Doubts could not be silenced by words, but must be faced honestly. The supreme moment of enlightenment came under a spreading pipal tree—the sacred Bo-tree of Buddhist tradition. It was the moment when he felt that all forms and ceremonies, all logic and learning, all

* "Buddha" is properly a title, but is used in Western nomenclature as a name. Where I use it as a title I prefix the definite article to it. Where I use it as a name I omit the article.

creeds and symbols, all deeds and hopes and fears, were vain; and that the one abiding fact in all life was the love that brings contentment within one's self and peace with all—freedom from passion, ignorance, and desire.

Teaching his Doctrine.—After this the Buddha entered on his mission. He left solitude, and went to Benares. There were many disputations about philosophy, but he preached his simple doctrine, the way of salvation for all men. His discourses in the Deer Park enquired into the cause of suffering and sorrow, and the way of salvation from sorrow. The true path was the Middle Path, free both from a desire for pleasure and from self-mortification. The eight principles which he enunciated have been elaborated as the "Noble Eightfold Path." He not only taught himself, but sent forth his disciples in all directions to spread his universal teaching about righteousness to all who cared to listen. He himself also travelled constantly, and built up a Brotherhood (*Sangha*), of which the members were to strengthen each other in virtue and right living. Now that he had successfully broken his earthly bonds, he visited his home and family more than once, but on the footing of a teacher.

Death.—For forty-five years he continued to teach and preach. Gentleness and good humour, infinite sympathy and infinite patience, were the corner-stones of his character. Like Socrates, he used the method of questions and answers to evolve his teaching. He also used parables and folk-stories for enforcing moral truths. In one of his last discourses he left this message to his order of poor friars: "Be earnest, mendicants, thoughtful, and pure! Steadfast in resolve, keep watch over your own hearts! Whosoever shall adhere unweariedly to this Law and Discipline, he shall cross the ocean of life, and make an end of sorrow!" If we add the twenty-nine years of his early life to the six years of meditation, and the forty-five years of his ministry, the Buddha's earthly life covered a span of not less than eighty years (roughly 560 to 480 B.C.).

Philosophical Teaching.—His own teaching was comparatively simple, and embraced the root ideas of Hindu folk-thought and Hindu philosophy, with a difference. He accepted the doctrine of Karma, or the universal chain of causation in the moral and physical world. He accepted the doctrine of transmigration, the constant births and rebirths, as the only reasonable explanation of the apparently unjust division of good and evil. The soul, as understood in Western theology, is not recognized; but the sum-total of an individual's good and evil deeds, words and thoughts, remains after the dissolution of his body, and this is Karma, which must be carried on in the next life. The chain can only be broken by "enlightenment," by realizing that the quest for happiness is a false and unmeaning quest. When that knowledge comes, false desire ceases to attract; the Eightfold Noble Path of right living is entered; all the shackles of individualized existence and Karma are broken; and this is NIRVANA, or the attainment of final peace or rest. This may sound metaphysical doctrine, but the Hindu mind has for ages dealt with abstract thoughts, and looks upon these as elementary approaches to the great problems of human destiny.

Practical Morality.—The practical morality of Buddhism teaches self-control, purity, humility, kindness to human beings and animals, stability of mind, and all the virtues held in universal reverence. "Never in this world," says the Dhammapada, an authoritative book of "Scripture Verses," "does hatred cease by hatred; hatred ceases by love; this is always its nature." There was one great social service which Buddhism attempted in India. It put men and women on a footing of social equality, and sought to destroy the tyranny of sacerdotalism and caste. In this it was before its time. Hinduism absorbed a great many of its theoretical doctrines, which were themselves a development of Hinduism, and even accepted Buddha as a divine incarnation. But it wholly rejected its social doctrines. The caste organization of Hinduism, aided by the Brahman monopoly of the means of knowledge and instruction, gradually made the Buddhist monasteries inert and powerless. Though we have no clear accounts of the persecution of Buddhists in India, it is probable that the cults of Shiva and Kali, in their militant phases, destroyed its monuments and expelled its votaries.

Later History of Buddhism in India : (*a*) *Doctrinal.*—Soon after the Master's death legends began to grow and be elaborated about his personality. He had himself laid no stress on the existence of God, and his teaching has even been described as atheistical. But an elaborate cosmogony and theology grew up in which he was described as one of a series of Incarnations, with what can only be described as a number of subordinate characters in a polytheistic Pantheon. Many Buddhist sects and schools of philosophy arose. Two permanent schools of Buddhist philosophy, the Lesser Vehicle (the Hinayana) and the Greater Vehicle (the Mahayana), may be referred to. The Lesser Vehicle is the simpler of the two, and closer to primitive Buddhism. The Greater Vehicle introduced the principle of adoration of the Buddhas, and in philosophy incorporated many subtleties, including the Vedantic doctrine that all the forms and events which we see are mere illusions, and not reality.

(*b*) *Social: Its Catholicity and Freedom from Race or Caste Organization.*—These developments of doctrine were aided and systematized by various General Councils and by the writings of Buddhist monks and laymen. But the social developments have left even a deeper mark on history. The idea of universality, as opposed to the power of a race or caste or tribe, gave an enlarged horizon to the political mind of Hinduism. The so-called "established" Buddhist Church of Asoka (see Chapter VI.), *circa* 260 B.C., two and a quarter centuries after Buddha's death, was the first organization we know of in Buddhism under which Imperial power was used for the dissemination of religion. But as it was coupled with a complete toleration of all sects and the preaching of ethical rather than sectarian doctrine, the term "Established Church" seems to be a misnomer in that connection. However, its strong ethical and universal character made it a world force and a leaven of civilization throughout Asia, and a factor in the development of Alexandrian philosophy.

Absorption of the Foreign Elements: Eventual Extinction in India.—When the momentous movements of population in Asia between the third century B.C. and the seventh century A.D. introduced on a large scale various strains of foreign population in India (see Chapter V.), the catholic faith of Buddhism received a fresh impetus. The foreign elements readily absorbed

Buddhism, and were absorbed by it. In the first century of the Christian era Buddhism was the prevailing religion in India, and it probably continued to be so till the fourth or fifth century A.D. A stream of Chinese pilgrims poured into India, the sacred land of Buddhism, beginning with Fa-Hien (A.D. 405-411), and a counter-stream of Buddhist Hindu teachers flowed into Eastern Asia. But already the reaction of Brahmanism had begun, and the cults of the gods Shiva and Vishnu were assuming new forms. By the time Hiuen Tsang visited India (A.D. 630-645), Buddhism was only one of many rival sects, whose worship, however, was not mutually intolerant. When the Muslims first invaded India (Sindh) early in the eighth century, Buddhism was still a power in the land, but it gradually waned, and it was absorbed into Brahmanism by the eleventh century. The great political anarchy of the centuries preceding Muslim rule had left the monasteries desolate and the Brotherhoods unprotected, and with their extinction passed away the separate existence of Buddhist doctrine in India proper. The rise of new and intolerant Hindu cults also hastened the process. Burma has had a wholly different history, and Buddhism remains still the prevailing religion in that province.

Jatakas and Pictures of Social Life and Institutions.—The value of Buddhist literature for the social and institutional history of India cannot be exaggerated. Buddha's teaching always appealed direct in the vernacular to the people, and it used folk-tales, parables, and pictures of the lives of the people for edifying illustrations. As the legends about the countless births and incarnations of the Buddha grew up, they enshrined every aspect of life. These stories of the Buddha's lives are called "jatakas," and though they deal ostensibly with previous ages, we can reconstruct from them a picture of society in the ages in which they were written—*i.e.*, mainly between the fifth and the third centuries B.C. We know that there were republics, oligarchies, and kingships, all on a small scale. The people's organization was mainly tribal. The village communities were autonomous, and based on the principle of peasant-proprietorship. There were few cities, but village arts and crafts were well developed, and common "civic" life was on a high plane. Craft guilds and trade partnerships had a vigorous life, and inland and maritime travel and commerce are mentioned as a normal feature in the people's mental landscape. With all this there was a simplicity and gentleness, a freedom from close organization or rigid law, a calmness and sadness, which fit in with the primitive message of the Buddha.

CHAPTER V

FOREIGN INVASIONS AND INFLUENCES

Indo-Aryan Civilization.—As we have seen, India has been the goal of foreign invasions from the earliest times. Traces of Sumerian and Babylonian culture are found in the north-west. The prehistoric stocks that poured into India received their last great accession with the arrival of the Indo-Aryan tribes, who soon moulded the literature and institutions of the country into forms which they either brought with them or developed in the land. They themselves were not unaffected by the influences that they found in India, and notably by the Dravidian culture with which they came into contact. The resultant systems and stocks of ideas have been described in a previous chapter under the heading of " The Roots of Hinduism."

Foreign Influences after its Crystallization.—But after Hinduism had begun to crystallize its political, religious, and social organization the process of foreign influences did not cease. It continued to act, either by foreign conquests of outlying parts of India, as in the case of Persia and Greece, or by cultural and diplomatic intercourse, as in the case of Buddhist pilgrims from China and Central Asia, or by means of fresh invasions and extensive conquests from Western or Central Asia, as in the case of the Parthians, the Huns, and the Scythians. It would be convenient to deal in this chapter with all such foreign influences which acted in India from the time of the Buddha in the beginning of the fifth century B.C. to the Muslim invasions which began in the eighth century A.D. These latter opened a wholly new chapter in the history of India.

Persian Conquest of the Panjab.—The events leading up to the Persian conquest of the Panjab in or before the fifth century B.C. are somewhat obscure. We know from Herodotus that the Persian King Darius (522-486 B.C.), whose general was defeated at Marathon, ruled over the whole country on the frontier of India, which now forms the kingdom of Afghanistan. The successor of Darius, Xerxes I. (486-465 B.C.), led his vast Asiatic hordes into Europe for the conquest of Greece. We find that this host included Indian infantry, clad in cotton, with bows and arrows of cane, and that Indian cavalry brought horses and chariots, while large numbers of Indian dogs accompanied the king's expedition into Greece. The Indus region was then included in the Persian Empire, and probably continued to be so included until Alexander the Great conquered the Persian Empire.

Alexander the Great: His Perso-Greek Army.—Alexander invaded India, 326-325 B.C., and marched across the Panjab at the foot of the hills as far as the river Hyphasis (modern Beas). The courses of the Panjab rivers have varied enormously in historical times, and it has been supposed that the extreme limit of Alexander's march was at the banks of the Satlaj, which the Beas now joins lower down; but the latest researches make it probable that the river referred to was the Beas, not far from its confluence with the Satlaj. Alexander had covered the whole length of the Persian Empire, including some of the rich lands of Central Asia, but his army refused to follow him further in India, and he had to retreat. He took the opportunity, however, of navigating the Indus, and sent a fleet, which he had had built in India, by way of the sea close to the coast, while he himself returned by the land route along the Makran coast in September, 325 B.C. His stay of a year and a half in the Panjab and Sindh was not in itself long enough to produce any remarkable historical results. But it formed the starting-point of new relations between India and the outer world. In the Persian Empire the north-west corner of India had been a remote province or satrapy When Alexander left India he left the tract which he had conquered partly in the hands of Hindu princes and partly under Greek or Persian officers. After Alexander's death in Babylon, 323 B.C., his empire broke up into fragments, and the fragments nearest India played an important part in Indian history.

Græco-Syrians: Seleucus Nicator.—We are not concerned with other successors of Alexander, but the kingdom of Syria under Seleucus Nicator, which inherited the Panjab satrapy of the Perso-Greek Empire, was unsuccessful in either extending its dominion in India or even consolidating or retaining what the great conqueror had acquired. It must be remembered that Alexander's army had included not only his Macedonian-Greek officers, but probably a large number of Persians as well. His conflict had been only with Indian local chiefs. The main power in Northern India at that time was the kingdom of Magadha, with its capital in the Ganges valley, near the modern city of Patna in Bihar.

Maurya Kingdom : Described by Megasthenes.—The kingdom of Magadha seems at that time to have suffered a revolution. Soon after Alexander left, we find a new dynasty established, the dynasty of the Mauryas, whose representative, Chandragupta (in Greek, Sandrakottos), gathered a large army, and came into conflict with the forces of Seleucus in the Panjab. Chandragupta was victorious (*circa* 305 B.C.), and the authority of the Syrian monarchy declined in the Panjab. But a treaty was concluded between him and Seleucus, which resulted in the residence of the Græco-Syrian ambassador Megasthenes at the Maurya court about 300 B.C. Megasthenes wrote an excellent account of that court and of India generally, which is preserved in fragments, and gives us a very favourable picture of the conditions then obtaining in India.

Asoka Maurya pushes back the Seleucids.—The grandson of Chandragupta was the famous Asoka (*circa* 273-236 B.C.), who extended his empire practically all over India, and the modern kingdom of Afghanistan. We must consider his reign and institutions a little more in detail in the next chapter. For the present it is enough to note that the strength of the Mauryan Empire meant the pushing back of the frontiers of Greek rule into the Oxus region in Central Asia. About 250 B.C. two provinces were separated from the Seleucid Empire of Syria, which subsequently played an important part in the north-west of India. One was the kingdom of Bactria, with its capital on the site represented by the modern town of Balkh. The other was the kingdom of Parthia further west, within the limits of modern Persia.

Rise of Græco-Bactrian Kingdom.—The Mauryan power began to decline after the death of Asoka, and the north-west frontier provinces fell away from it. Antiochus III. (the Great) of Syria attempted in 206 B.C. to lead an expedition to the East, and force Bactria to recognize his supremacy as well as to establish his authority on the north-west frontier of India. As regards Bactria he failed, and Bactrian independence was recognized. As regards the Kabul country, he imposed an indemnity and obtained some supplies from a Hindu prince, who seems to have become independent of the Mauryan Empire. But Antiochus had soon to turn his attention to the west of his kingdom, where he was involved in a disastrous war with the Roman Empire, and he did not trouble India any further. On the other hand, the Bactrian kingdom grew both in might and extent, and pushed forward south-eastwards. The fourth king of Bactria, Euthydemus, early in the second century B.C., carried his conquests so far as to include not only the modern kingdom of Afghanistan, but a great part of the Panjab.

More than One Indo-Greek (Yavana) Dynasty.—His own dynasty did not remain undisturbed in its power. Other lines of Greek princes seem to have at different times asserted their sway in portions of the territory comprising the Panjab, Afghanistan, Bactria, and the Oxus country. Their coins are found in great abundance in that tract of country, and show a considerable amount of artistic development on Greek lines. In the process of time, however, we can trace a gradual debasement of the coinage, as these dynasties were more and more affected by local influences. These lines of Yavana princes (as the Greek princes were called, Yavana being the Indian equivalent of "Ionian") held sway with varying fortunes in these regions between 200 and 53 B.C. One of the most famous names among these Græco-Indian princes was that of Menander, who, as King Milinda, figures prominently in later Buddhist literature as ruling on the site of the modern town of Sialkot. He probably led an expedition through the Jamna valley far down into the Middle Country, and came into contact with the kingdom of Magadha, which had always been a Buddhist stronghold. His reign may be dated somewhere between 160 and 140 B.C.

Parthian Kingdom.—The Parthian Kingdom was established about the middle of the third century B.C., also on the ruins of

Alexander's Empire. Parthian civilization at that period partook of the characteristics of both Greek and Persian civilizations, and the Parthian kingdom may be regarded in some respects as a rival to that of Bactria. But Bactria was more Greek. The Bactrian kingdom was practically overwhelmed by the invasion of the Sakas or Scythians, somewhere shortly before 135 B.C. The Bactrians had been cut off from their brother Greeks in the kingdom of Syria, on the west, by the wedge of the growing kingdom of Parthia, whose encroachments they were unable to resist. On the east the secular unrest of the nomadic races was sending forth wave upon wave of invasions, which ultimately submerged Bactria.

Chain of Nomad Movements from Eastern Asia, Second Century B.C.—It was under the Tsin dynasty in China, which ended about 210 B.C., that the Great Wall of China was built in order to keep out the Tartar invasions from the north. This may have stemmed the incursions of the barbarians into China, but it turned them westwards across Asia, and caused a racial convulsion which was felt not only throughout Central Asia, but in India, and further west in the countries over which the Roman Empire was extending its sway. The easternmost tribes which started the impulse were the Huns, who pushed forward and displaced the Yueh-Chi about 165 B.C. In their turn the Yueh-Chi pushed forward and displaced the Sakas, who had inhabited the country of the Jaxartes to the north of Bactria. The Sakas overthrew the kingdom of Bactria, and feeling the push from behind, moved further west, and came into conflict with the Parthians.

Sakas or Scythians.—Indian references mix up the Sakas, the Parthians (who are called Pahlavas in Indian writings), and the Yavanas, or the Greeks of Bactria. It is certain that the Sakas or Scythians were stopped in their westward course by the Parthians, and the contact of the two races produced a certain mixture in the Parthian country. A portion of the homeless Sakas, however, turned southwards, and appear to have entered India from the Persian side, through the Kandahar country, and by way of the Bolan pass. They established themselves in Sindh round the Indus delta, which was called Indo-Scythia for this reason. Gradually, however, they spread themselves to the Panjab in the north-east, and there destroyed the last remnants of the Indo-Greek princes who had looked to Bactria. The establishment of the Sakas in the Panjab may possibly be dated about 75 B.C.

Parthian Push into India.—Though the Parthians had established a kingdom in their own country before the homeless Sakas penetrated into India, their effective push towards India was later than that of the Sakas. The transition from the Sakas to the Parthians in India is very gradual, as the two races were associated together in Eastern Persia. But it is not a violent assumption to suppose that the conflict of Rome with Parthia in 53 B.C. helped in pouring the tide of the Parthians into India. The Saka-Parthians continued to rule as suzerains until between A.D. 45 and 64, after which they were overthrown by the Kushānas, who will be referred to later. As suzerains their kings used the title "Great King of Kings," and their viceroys and governors, who also issued coins, were called Great Satraps or Satraps. The Saka-Parthian coins are interesting, as showing the triple stream of civilization which they represent. Persian titles or Parthian names are represented in Greek words and letters (thus Βασιλέως βασιλέων μεγάλου), while the reverse has the Sanskrit equivalent, Maharaja or Rajadhiraj, in an Indian script.

Saka Satraps under Kushanas: The "Western Satraps" and their Era.—After the Saka-Parthians lost their supremacy, they continued to hold sway as tributaries to the Kushānas (see next paragraph) in Sindh. They even extended their sway (no doubt as Kushāna tributaries) over the peninsula now called Kathiawar and the province of Malwa, early in the second century A.D. These "Western Satraps" have left a complete series of coins and inscriptions, which use an era beginning in 78 A.D. This era is still used in Central and Western India, and is known as the "Saka" era, because it was used by the Saka Satraps, although the latest authorities suppose that it marks the establishment of Kushāna sovereignty at the accession of their King Kanishka. On the other hand, the Sambat era, commencing in 58 B.C., is supposed to mark the establishment of Saka suzerainty. This era is universally used in Northern India. The Saka Satraps continued to rule in Malwa (capital city Ujjain) and Western India till at least A.D. 388. The Sakas gradually merged among the people of India, and were absorbed in the Gupta Empire at the end of the fourth century A.D.

The Kushānas.—The Kushānas already referred to were a tribe of the Yueh-chi, who had ousted the Sakas from Bactria. They were a Turkish race, and soon spread themselves southwards into Afghanistan and the Panjab, westwards into Parthia, and eastwards towards China. Their supremacy was established in India by about A.D. 78, which probably marks the first regnal year of their King Kanishka.

Their King Kanishka: Gandhara Art.—Kanishka's capital was near the sites of the ancient city of Taxila and modern Peshawar. He is called in Indian literature King of Gandhara, which was the name of the north-western province of India. In religion he was a Buddhist. He called together a Buddhist Council to discuss and formulate doctrine, and the school of the Greater Vehicle of Buddhism owes much to the patronage of Kanishka and his successors. His Indian dominions extended over Kashmir, Panjab, and a part of the Jamna basin, while his supremacy was recognized in Sindh, Malwa, and Western India. His extensive dominions in Central Asia brought him into contact with China, Parthia, and the Roman Empire, and his cosmopolitan culture, based on Buddhism, included the influences of Chinese, Persian, Greek, and Roman civilizations. Gandhara art flourished during his reign, and though it inherited the Græco-Bactrian traditions, it evolved a school of wonderful originality, beauty, and vigour.

End of Kushānas.—It is difficult to fix precisely the duration of the Kushāna Empire. In India itself the Kushānas gradually merged into Hindus. Their influence probably extended over Magadha in the Ganges Basin, and the rise of the Gupta Empire early in the fourth century A.D. extinguished the last spark of their authority in India. The rise of the Sāsānian dynasty in Persia, A.D. 226, must have restricted their dominions in Central Asia.

Spread of Indian Culture in Asia.—It was during their supremacy that Indian civilization became supreme in Asia. The physical conditions in Central Asia have changed considerably since then. The desiccation of those lands probably gave rise to fresh world-movements of populations. Sir Aurel Stein's discoveries among the sand-buried ruins of Khotan show that an Indian language and alphabet were carried along with Indian culture to the country north of Tibet. Well has the region been named "Serindia," from the happy blending of the Chinese (Seres=Chinese) and Indian influences. The religion and philosophy of China and Eastern Asia continued to be influenced by Indian Buddhism for many centuries afterwards.

The Huns.—The Gupta Empire, in vigour from A.D. 320 to *circa* 455 (see Chapter VI.), was broken up by the Hun invasion about the end of the fifth century A.D. The Huns were a Mongolian race of Eastern Asia. We have seen that, after the construction of the Great Wall of China, their restlessness caused the great westward movement of the Turkish nations through Central Asia. The force of their push continued through subsequent centuries. One section pushed on to Europe in the fourth century A.D., caused a ferment in Central Europe, and under Attila (*circa* A.D. 406-453) threatened Rome herself in the middle of the fifth century. Another section, the White Huns, or Ephthalites, established themselves on the Oxus about the same time. From their bases in Bamyin (near the modern Herat) and Balkh, they attacked Persia, the Kabul country, and India. They were accompanied (as was the case in all such invasions) by other tribes, among whom we may mention the Gurjaras, after whom the province of Gujarat is called. The Hun chief Toramana penetrated as far as Malwa about A.D. 500, and established a kingdom, which was of short duration. His son Mihiragula inherited a large empire, of which the Indian provinces comprised the Panjab, Sindh, Gujarat, Malwa, Rajputana, and a great part of the Jamna valley. His cruelties have won him the title of the Attila of the Indian Huns. Within a generation he was driven out of Central India. The Hun Empire of Central Asia was also overthrown by the Turks by the middle of the sixth century. It left no impression on the history of India, but the various tribes it introduced into the population no doubt helped in the formation of the Rajput and other clans and septs.

CHAPTER VI

THE IMPERIAL IDEA IN HINDU INDIA

Periods of Internal Construction and Consolidation.—In the rapid review of the events of 1,200 years from the fifth century B.C. to the eighth century A.D., in the last chapter, we fixed our attention more particularly on the foreign invasions and influences which went to the making of India. In this chapter we shall cover mainly the same chronological ground, but dwell on the periods of construction and consolidation within India itself. The principal of these periods are: the reign of Asoka (273-236 B.C.), the Gupta Empire in its vigour (A.D. 320-455), the reign of Harsha (A.D. 606-647), and the conflict of some kingdoms of the Deccan with the north, and their grasp at imperial power between the seventh and the middle of the eleventh century A.D.

Conflict of Petty States.—From the earliest times tribal oligarchies, petty kingships, and village republics seem to have been among Indian institutions, in many cases overlapping each other. Some of the village republics may have been tribal oligarchies or family democracies, and petty kingdoms were not inconsistent with autonomous villages. The geographical unity of India, modified only by the division between north and south, made racial and cultural conflicts inevitable. As long as there were numerous petty States without a preponderating power to keep the peace, political and armed conflicts were also a normal feature of her history. But the dream of this preponderance, this Imperial idea, was woven in the very texture of Indian political thought.

Evolution of the Imperial Idea.—The doctrine of aggrandizement is stated in its crudest form by Kautilya, the Brahman minister of Asoka's grandfather, who wrote a treatise on politics about 300 B.C., which is comparable with that of the Italian Machiavelli eighteen centuries later. He contemplates a policy of peace, neutrality, or war as dependent wholly on opportunity or power. "If one king is inferior to another in power he shall make peace with him; if superior, he shall wage war; if he is strong enough to be safe from hurt, but not strong enough to destroy his enemy, he shall remain neutral." The great lawgiver Manu, who wrote some five to nine centuries later (the dates of early Indian books are generally conjectural), places prominently among the duties of the king that of augmenting his territory. "Let him be ever ready to strike; let his prowess be constantly displayed, and his secrets constantly concealed; and let him explore the weakness of his foe. Of him who is always ready to strike, the whole world stands in awe; let him therefore make all creatures subject to himself even by the employment of force."* One of the oldest of Hindu public rites was the Rajasuiya sacrifice, which was celebrated by a king who threw out a challenge of supremacy to the world, and made good his challenge. Such a king earned the title of *Chakravartin*—one whose chariot wheels passed through everywhere without obstruction. In the second book of the Mahabharat epic we have an interesting discussion of the merits which entitled a monarch to celebrate this imperial rite. The king must not only be victorious, but his victory must be against a powerful oppressor, and for the liberation of the oppressed; he must, besides, be endued with eminent virtue and wisdom, and must be able to promote the happiness and prosperity of his people. Self-seeking or reliance upon mere brute strength is deprecated; a high religious motive underlies the ideal. We shall see how far this ideal was pursued in concrete cases.

Merits and Weakness of Imperial Power in India.—The eras of anarchy and confusion were the eras of small States in mutual conflict. When a State established its supremacy on an Imperial basis, it usually organized public services on a large scale, and there was a period of widespread peace and prosperity. This gave opportunities for the development of the arts, for the cultivation of literature and the sciences, and for the advancement of those large ideas in religion and spiritual philosophy which leave their permanent impression on history.

* Manu vii., 102-103.

The weakness of Imperial power in India was that it rested generally on the character, energy, and benevolence of single individuals, and melted away almost as suddenly as it sprang up.

Asoka's Title to Fame.—The greatest and best-known of the Maurya emperors was Asoka, whose personality and achievements now claim our attention. His grandfather, Chandragupta, had doubtless profited by contact with the art of warfare and strategy which had established Macedonian supremacy in Western and Central Asia. Chandragupta used them to establish his own supremacy and Imperial power in India. The vast political and military organization which was inherited by Asoka was no doubt built up by his grandfather. Asoka himself extended the boundaries of the empire in the east and possibly elsewhere, until it included the whole of India north of the river Pennar (100 miles north of modern Madras), perhaps even further south. It also included the modern kingdom of Afghanistan and some territory in Central Asia won from the successors of Alexander. But Asoka's title to fame rests on his influence beyond the political bounds of his empire, for we shall see that his moral supremacy extended to Cape Comorin and the island of Ceylon in the south, and to the whole of Western Asia, Egypt, and Cyrene in Africa, and Epirus and Macedonia in Europe.

External Events of his Reign.—Before he ascended the throne Asoka had governed at least two of his father's provinces as viceroy. He had been fond of splendour, feasts, and hunting, which were no doubt looked upon as time-honoured royal virtues. Nor was his early career devoid of personal and dynastic ambition. He ascended the Imperial throne of Magadha, with his capital at Pataliputra (modern Patna), about 274-273 B.C. His coronation or consecration, a solemn rite which for some reason was postponed for four years, was in 270-269 B.C.* The events of his reign are counted not from his accession, but from his coronation. The conquest of Kalinga, the sea-coast tract adjoining and including modern Orissa, was in 262-261 B.C., and he died in 237-236 B.C.

* Some dates of Asoka's reign, as gathered from his inscriptions, are certain, but these are expressed in terms of the date of his coronation, which is uncertain. Latest research fixes it provisionally as correct within a year or two. Hence my scheme of double dates.

Extent of Power and Administration.—The extent of his power and administrative machinery may be judged from a few figures. He maintained a standing army of 60,000 infantry, 30,000 cavalry, 9,000 war elephants attended by 36,000 men, and many thousands of war chariots. The organization of his armed forces was entrusted to six Boards, one of which controlled the Admiralty. We have no clear evidence of the extent of his oceanic commerce or communications, but the traffic on the splendid river highways of Northern India and with Ceylon was very considerable. His dominions were traversed by great trunk roads, which were provided at intervals of a mile and a quarter with rest-houses and wells. On the roads were trees planted for shade and fruit, "for the enjoyment of man and beast," as one of his inscriptions puts it. There were, moreover, hospitals and "curative arrangements" for men and animals. The civil functionaries were numerous, scattered all over the empire, and towards the end of the reign included censors of morals.

Moral and Spiritual Zeal.—The turning-point in Asoka's life was the Kalinga war already referred to, in the ninth year after his consecration. It created a great impression on Asoka's mind, and turned it wholly to a spiritual outlook. In one of his inscriptions he expresses deep remorse, because the conquest of a country "involves the slaughter, death, or captivity of the people." Although the Buddhist religion had been preached in India more than 200 years ago, and had a well-knit organization, it had hitherto been a local sect. Asoka took it up and made it almost a State religion, but not an Established Church in the modern sense of the term. He was a lay disciple for two and a half years, and then became a monk. It is true he gave large endowments to the Buddhists, but he did the same for other sects. He is particularly careful to inculcate respect for all sects. In Rock Edict XII. on Toleration he inveighs against the false reverence to one's own sect by the disparagement of the sects of others, as calculated to inflict the severest injury on one's own sect.

Religious Missions to Foreign Countries.—He believed so zealously in the Law of Piety that he incorporated it in Edicts, issued them from time to time, inscribed them on rocks and pillars, and in caves, and addressed them to officials, subjects, and strangers. He sent out missions to Ceylon, Syria, Egypt, Cyrene, Macedonia, and Epirus. The seed sown in Ceylon produced a lasting harvest, and rendered possible the subsequent spiritual conquest of Burma, Siam, Java, and the Eastern Archipelago. The missions sent out to the seats of Greek culture in the West left a permanent influence on Western thought. Buddhist elements can be traced in many widespread schools of thought in Syria, Alexandria, and the Eastern Mediterranean for centuries afterwards. These missions did not merely send out preachers; they expressly disclaimed any political intentions, but they provided "healing for man and beast," and they introduced, apparently at Asoka's expense, some of the facilities and amenities of road travel in the form of rest-houses, wells, and trees. For Asoka esteemed above all conquest "the conquest by the Law of Piety; this it is that is won by Piyadasi* in his own dominions and in all the neighbouring realms as far as 600 leagues."

Asoka's Inscriptions.—We gather all this from the wonderful inscriptions of Asoka upon stone, which have been found in all parts of India. The same inscription has been found in more than one place, with local or dialectic variations. The language is the language of the people, not the highly sanskritized idiom of the Gupta Empire, which we shall notice later. The religion which the inscriptions preach is unsectarian. The morality they inculcate is severely practical, without metaphysical argument. The Law of Piety is presented as one for the good of all, high and low. Obedience to father and mother, respect for all living creatures, truth and fidelity, reverence for teacher, kindness to relatives—such are the virtues in the Law of Piety. Asoka's name is itself never mentioned; his earthly power and might are ignored; the only reference to a military or political adventure is that to the Kalinga war, for which he expresses sincere remorse. The title which Asoka uses for himself is Piyadasi (beloved of the gods). It may have been used by his predecessors as a ceremonial title; but it acquires a new meaning in Asoka's Edicts, and Asoka himself evidently dwells on its spiritual flavour. The chief motive to his untiring work is, in

* A title of Asoka.

his own words, that he may make some happy here as well as in the next world.

Interval between Asoka and the next great Imperial Experiment in Hindu India.—This gentle, non-sectarian, non-racial, practical Buddhism underwent many changes in the centuries following Asoka's period. The welter of races from Central Asia broke up the political organization of the Maurya Empire, but these races became the champions of Buddhism when Buddhism again became a mere sect in India, and its influence receded before the advancing tide of the new Hinduism. The last chapter has detailed the stages which bridged the interval between Asoka and the Gupta Empire, the next great experiment in Imperialism in Hindu India. During this period the centre of power and authority had passed from the central position of Pataliputra to places in the north-west frontier from which the foreign tribes came, or places in Western India or Malwa, to which they spread themselves, avoiding the obstacles which the prestige of the once-glorious Magadha Empire interposed in their path. When the Gupta Empire reared its fabric in Magadha, the centre of authority came back to Pataliputra, although the now established position of Ujjain in Malwa, together with its obviously more favourable position for the maritime trade of the West, made that city a serious rival to the imperial position of Pataliputra. Later the capital itself seems to have been removed from Pataliputra to Ajodhya, possibly as the national capital of the ideal hero Rama.

The Gupta Empire: Contrasted with Asoka's Empire.—The Gupta Empire was in its vigour for only three or four generations. It had three kings of remarkable capacity—viz., Samudra Gupta, Chandra Gupta II., and Kumara Gupta, whose long reigns cover the period from A.D. 320 to 455. After that date the Huns came in great force and shook the foundations of the empire, as we have seen in the last chapter. The Gupta dynasty did not cease to exist, but it became a local power among the many conflicting powers in India, even as the last of Asoka's descendants was known to exist in Western Magadha as late as A.D. 590. In its extent the Gupta Empire was less far-flung than Asoka's Empire, especially in the north-west, where Central Asia was pouring wave after wave of invasions.

It had also less of the universal character of Asoka's Empire, and less of that gentle benevolence which we associate with Piyadasi. But it had more of a national character. Hinduism assumed the shape of a national religion. The Sanskrit language was perfected, and came into general use in polite society. The inscriptions of the Gupta period are in a highly artificial form of Sanskrit, while those of earlier periods are in Pali. For the first time the coins also bear Sanskrit legends. There was an enormous amount of literary, scientific, and artistic activity, whose results remain as the heritage of the Hindus to the present day. The old scriptures, lawbooks, and epics were edited; the science of grammar, which had been systematized at least three centuries before the Christian era, received a new impetus in comprehensive commentaries; and great original works of all kinds were produced in abundance. In particular, the romantic drama was perfected, and Sanskrit literature was secularized. Very little Sanskrit literature of any merit was produced after the Gupta era, if we extend the era for literary purposes to about A.D. 800. The beautiful gold coinage of the Guptas, originally imitated from Kushāna coinage, but subsequently developing a variety of designs and a skilful representation of national emblems, is deservedly popular among numismatists. The remains of Gupta architecture and sculpture testify to a high sense of refinement, and their influence persisted through many centuries and extended far beyond the boundaries of the political empire.

Political and Social Aspects.—Returning to the political and social aspects of the Gupta Imperial power, we may dwell a little on the reign of Chandra Gupta II. (Vikramaditya), A.D. 375-413. It was during his reign that the famous Chinese Buddhist pilgrim, Fa-Hien, came to India by land, and returned to China by sea, visiting Ceylon and Java. He found great prosperity and contentment in the country. Asoka's buildings were still standing in Pataliputra. Medical and other endowments were common, and the facilities provided on the roads were similar to those we mentioned in speaking of Asoka's reign. The government was efficient and tolerant, and though the king professed the cult of Vishnu, Buddhism seems still to have been the prevailing religion. But the free social atmosphere of Buddhism seems to have gone. The lower castes were segregated, and had no freedom of movement. Apart from that, however, for ordinary men of culture, whether Hindu or foreign, there seems to have been great individual freedom.

Harsha's Empire: New Factors.—The next great Imperial power was that of Harsha Vardhana, who reigned from A.D. 606 to 647. For his reign we have excellent material for filling in the details in a romantic life (or panegyric) of him by a famous Sanskrit author (Bāna), and in the account of the Chinese Buddhist pilgrim Hiuen Tsang, who visited the country. The family of Harsha had originally ruled a small kingdom in the Panjab, with its capital at Thaneshwar, fifty miles north of Panipat, the historic battlefield of India. That tract may well be called the gateway of the rich Gangetic plain from the north-west. A king successful in that tract against protracted foreign invasions would be able to measure his strength against the powers of the interior. Harsha's family had also had frequent matrimonial alliances with the Guptas of Magadha. In a sense, therefore, his empire was a continuation of that of the Guptas, and in its essential features, artistic, literary, and cultural, it continued the Gupta tradition. Three new factors, however, now appeared, which fundamentally altered the current of India's history. First, the powers of Southern India began to make a bid for Imperial supremacy. Secondly, the foreign intercourse of India became sustained and continuous instead of spasmodic. And thirdly, before Harsha died, the Muslims had invaded Broach, a port on the western coast of India, A.D. 636, and the province of Sindh, A.D. 643.

Northern India brought to Unity and Order.—At his accession King Harsha is represented by his panegyrist as a young man of eighteen, who accepted the throne not in fulfilment of a personal ambition, but as the hero of destiny, who yielded to the solicitations of his people to take up the strenuous task of establishing order out of chaos, and restoring unity in the country. For over five years he was constantly on the move, fighting and subjugating: "the elephants were not unharnessed, nor the soldiers unhelmeted." He reduced all Northern India to order, from the extreme east of Bengal to the marches of the Eastern Panjab. But he suffered a check in his conflict with the southern kingdom of the Chalukyas.

A Glance back at South Indian History.—The early history of Southern India (using this term for India south of the Narbada) pursued a course independent of that of North India. Prehistoric archæology tells us that there was no Copper Age interposed between the Stone Age and the Iron Age in South India, as there was in the north. Before the time of Asoka there are few historical facts known of Southern India. We have already seen how Asoka's influence reached to the extreme south, and also embraced the island of Ceylon. But the intercourse of the south with the outer world was by sea, while that of the north was mainly by land, through the north-western passes. The alphabets of the Aryan languages of the north, as well as the Dravidian languages of the south, are derived ultimately from Semitic sources; but they are derived independently of each other. The Jewish and Christian religions came to the south long before they were known in the north. Roman coins of the empire are found in great abundance in the south, but hardly any in the north, owing to the maritime character of Roman commerce. The Aryan penetration from the north was not in any great numerical force, owing to the barrier of dense forests in Central India and the river and mountain barriers dividing north from south. The Aryan penetration left the Dravidian system intact, but merely imposed a coping on the political, social, and religious fabrics. On the other hand, the south was not subject to the sudden and sweeping changes produced by constant invasions in the north, and its cultural reactions in the north were much greater than is generally recognized.

Kingdoms of the South: Their Varying Importance.—From very early times in history we know of the Cholas of Tanjore, the Pandyas of Madura, the Andhras of the Godavari and the Krishna, and other tribes or communities which we need not detail. These remain on the stage of history from the third century B.C. to the thirteenth century A.D., with some additions and modifications from time to time. But their relations among themselves were constantly changing. Now one and now another was more powerful than the rest. Sometimes one was absorbed in another. Sometimes a new kingdom was created by the regrouping of some of the old ones under a fresh impetus received from outside. The Pallavas of Kānchi (modern Conjeeveram) are heard of as early as A.D. 150. They were probably a foreign tribe, and are possibly to be identified with the Perso-Greek Pahlavas, whose invasions we referred to in the last chapter. In any case, we know that the "Western Satraps" and Scythians played a large part in Malwa and the west coast of India as late as the fourth and fifth centuries A.D., and formed a link in the western route between north and south. The Pallavas spread themselves out from Conjeeveram to a great part of Southern India, and were in their turn absorbed by the Chalukyas, who became supreme in the south, with their territory extending from sea to sea across the peninsula of India.

Conflict of North and South.—In the time of Harsha the Chalukya king was Pulikesin II., a great conqueror who had reached as far north as Puri on the east coast. His capital was at Vatapi (modern Badami, in the Bijapur district). Meanwhile, King Harsha had consolidated his conquests in the north, and tried conclusions with Pulikesin II., but was driven back. Pulikesin himself found his southern empire too large to rule as one unit, and the Chalukyan Empire broke up into two branches, Eastern and Western, which remained with varying fortunes on the stage of history till the thirteenth century. The Chalukyas have left great buildings in Southern India, and their name is associated comprehensively with more than one style of noble architecture to be found in Southern India.

Sustained and Continuous Foreign Intercourse.—In this conflict of north and south it is interesting to note that the southern monarch invoked the aid of Persia, with which he had direct relations by sea, while Harsha invoked the aid of China, to which India was the classic land of Buddhism, which attracted learned Buddhists from all over the world. Nothing came of the invocation on either side. The Chinese envoy to Harsha reached Harsha's court after Harsha's death, but he interfered with a usurping minister at Kanauj, and sent him captive to China. The Persian Empire was too effete to send aid to

India, and was itself on the brink of extinction. The Persian alliance of the Chalukyas is pictorially represented in the caves of Ajanta, one of the most important monuments of India, in the north of the Nizam's dominions. Among the Indian imports of the period are mentioned Persian horses and Chinese merchandise, not as articles bought as curiosities, but as articles of regular commerce. The birth of the religion of Islam released new forces, whose results we shall study in the story of Muslim India. India was now no longer isolated. Her history links itself closely and continuously with that of Western, Central, and Eastern Asia.

Harsha's Religion.—Harsha's religion was the cult of Shiva. The religion of the people in Northern India was Buddhistic and Brahmanical in about equal numerical proportions. Harsha's mother immolated herself by fire on her husband's death; the rite of *Sati* was therefore well established, at least in royal households. Buddhists were endowed and protected. There is no contemporary evidence that Harsha came into contact with the new religion of Islam. But a late Hindu writer attributes to him the extirpation of the Muslims and the destruction of their mosques in India.

Administration and Social Life under Harsha.—His administration is praised by the Chinese pilgrim as patriarchal and not too complicated. Labourers were not oppressed with taxes, or subjected to forced labour. The produce of Crown lands was used for the king's expenses only as to a fourth portion. The other three-fourths were used for the expenses of his ministers, the support of men of intelligence and learning, and works of charity. Travellers and merchants were well treated. Official salaries were paid from grants of land. The officials were honest, and the people had polite and easy manners. The law was not harsh; but no new code of laws was introduced. The whole machinery of government depended on the personal exertions of the king. Poetic contests were held, and the king himself was admired as a poet and author. Music was in fashion. Every day the king awoke to the sound of music, instrumental and vocal. The capital was established at Kanauj. The westward move from Pataliputra to Ajodhya (with a secondary capital at Ujjain) and now to Kanauj is in accordance with the shifting of the political centre of gravity. When the Magadha Empire included much territory in the south, Pataliputra was appropriate. But Gupta national sentiment found a better rallying point in Ajodhya, the sacred city of Rama. When the Gupta dynasty was absorbed in a Panjab dynasty, Kanauj, midway between Ajodhya and Thanesar, was found more convenient, especially as new dangers were now looming ahead from the north-west.

Three Centuries and a Half of Anarchy, A.D. 647-1000—Harsha left no heir, and his kingdom broke to pieces. The three centuries and a half between his death and the commencement of the eleventh century were a period of political anarchy and social regrouping in India. The Mongolians from the north, under the influence of China, tried to assert their supremacy in the plains of Northern India, but without success. The kings of Kashmir received their investiture from China. The powers of the south continued their internal struggles, and the Chola Empire, as we shall see, penetrated both to Northern India and to the oversea countries east of India. The Muslims spread out west and east, and Sindh became an Arab province in 712. The Arabs continued to advance in Central Asia, and having subjugated the Turks, who were under Chinese influence, met and defeated Chinese forces in 751 in the region of the Pamirs. This relaxed the pressure on India from the north, but prepared the way for the eventual Muslim conquest of India from the north-west.

The Cholas from the South Reach the Ganges on the North, and Tighten their Grip on Ceylon.—The supremacy of the Chola kingdom of the south (which absorbed the eastern Chalukyas), about A.D. 1000, was aimed not only at Northern India, but at the Malay Peninsula and the Indian Archipelago. In 1023 King Rajendra Chola, after having subjugated Southern India, sent his forces to Bihar and Bengal, and brought the sacred water of the Ganges to mingle with the water of the Kaveri (Cauvery) and run into a splendid irrigation tank which he constructed round his new capital. The invasion of Ceylon from Southern India and the counter-invasion of Southern India from Ceylon were known from centuries preceding the Christian era, and recur as frequent episodes in the ninth, tenth, and eleventh centuries; but the Cholas possessed sea-power, and they tightened their grip on Ceylon. The kingdom of Ceylon was not consolidated under a native dynasty until the reign of the famous Parākrama Bāhu (1164-1197).

Their Sea-Power: Conquests in Malay Peninsula and Sumatra.—Previous to the Muslim period, such sea-power as existed in India was located on the east coast, from which large vessels sailed through the Bay of Bengal, north to the Ganges, or further east to the Malay Peninsula or the Malay Archipelago. The history of Java knows of an era beginning with 75 B.C., established by the Hindus in that island. In the fourth century Java was a Hindu colony, professing the Brahmanical religion, though, within two or three centuries, the Buddhist religion became the dominant religion, which has left its splendid sculptures in Boro Bodur. The Cholas in the eleventh century, profiting by their sea-power, tried to obtain a footing in Sumatra, and Hindu influence continued to be active in the Malay Archipelago till the end of the fourteenth century, when it was superseded by Islam.

Chola Public Works, Art, and Administration.—We have records of the magnificent public works and endowments constructed and maintained by the Cholas. Among these are great irrigation works, fine educational and theological institutions (the latter devoted to the cult of Shiva), students' hostels, and endowed hospitals. The temples and sculpture show high craftsmanship and artistic merit. They continue the traditions of Pallava art. The chief merit of Chola administration was that it was well decentralized, and used the village or group of villages for administrative units. Each group was governed by an elected assembly with adequate powers. The term of office for members was a year. Each local authority had its own local treasury. The currency was on a gold standard, and, in fact, very little silver coin was used in Southern India. To the present day the production of gold is confined to the south of India.

Influence of Southern India on the North.—In art and literature, in religion and philosophy, the Dravidian south exercised enormous influence on Hindu institutions. Northern India owes more to them than is ordinarily recognized. Stone temples were practically unknown in Central and Northern India until the south invaded the north—*i.e.*, mainly from the seventh and eighth centuries A.D. onwards. The hymns of the Tamil saints, of the Shiva cult, between A.D. 600 and 800, show an emotional fervour and a catholicity which paved the way for the best devotional literature in the vernaculars of Northern India. The two great philosophies which dominate modern Hinduism were developed by teachers from the south, who taught in the north. Shankara (eighth century), through his commentaries, is the high-priest of modern Vedantism, and the doctrine of one universal Being, with the illusion which produces the appearance of many. Rāmānuja (eleventh to twelfth century) lived when the Muslim saints and Sufis were spreading themselves over India. He is responsible for the doctrines of a personal God, and salvation by faith. He was the precursor of the great Vaishnava saints. Coming from the south, the vernaculars of the north were closed to him, and he wrote in Sanskrit. But his successors used the northern vernaculars, whether (like Kabir and Nanak) they tried a synthesis of Hinduism and Islam, or (like Tulsi Das) they attempted a restatement of doctrines in purely Hindu terms.

CHAPTER VII

MUSLIM INVASIONS, 1000–1206

"Islam," "Muslim," "Muhammadan."—Soon after A.D. 1000 the relations of Islam with India began to assume a new character. It will be desirable now to take a short retrospect, glance at the life and work of the Prophet Muhammad, the basic ideas of his mission and its results, and the spread of his religion geographically and ethnically, in order to understand the new races and ideas which it poured into India, and the consequent profound modification in the current of Indian history. The religion which he preached is properly called Islam, and the people who profess it are Muslims. The terms popularly used in Europe are "Muhammadanism" and "Muhammadans" (also spelt "Mohammedans" or "Mahometans").

Muhammad's Birth: State of Arabia.—The Prophet Muhammad (the name is also spelt "Mohammed" or "Mahomet") was born in Mecca about the year 570-571. Mecca was the holy city of Arabia. The Arabs were a loosely knit aggregation of tribes, without a centralized form of civil government. They were proud of their racial purity, and the beauty, flexibility, and richness of their language. Four tracts may be distinguished in the Arabian Peninsula with reference to the cultural influences which went to the building up of the Islamic nations. The most important was the Hijaz, with its sacred city of Mecca, to which the desert and nomad Arabs resorted every year, and from which cultural influences spread in all directions over the Arabian Peninsula. Secondly, Rocky Arabia, the corner to the north-west, included the sacred mount of Sinai, and was full of Christian monasteries. This was in contact with Palestine and Syria on the east, and Egypt on the west, all portions of the Byzantine Empire. Thirdly, the cities of fertile Yemen, in the south-west corner, the home of coffee, which had a maritime trade with the Red Sea, the Persian Gulf, and the western and eastern coasts of India and the lands beyond as far as China. This portion was also in intimate contact with Abyssinia, from which it is divided by a narrow strait. Lastly, the Persian Gulf tract was under the influence of Persia. The Eastern Roman (Byzantine) Empire and the Persian Empire were on the land frontiers of Arabia, but both were in a tottering condition, ready to fall before the first vigorous onslaught of a young nation united by religious and moral fervour.

Religions then Known.—There were four distinct religions known in Arabia. The national Arabian religion was a free-and-easy paganism, in which idol worship was combined with the worship of the heavenly bodies (Sabæanism) and a number of time-honoured superstitions. The tribe and family to which the Prophet belonged were connected with a powerful vested interest that centred round the 360 idols of Mecca. There were some Jewish villages and tribes in Arabia. The Jews were already a scattered race, but they played an important part in religious controversies, and the intimate connection of their religion with the foundation of Christianity placed the two religions in association in the Arab mind. The forms of Christianity best known to the Arabs were the Abyssinian Church, the Byzantine Church, and certain heresies, like the Nestorian, which were strong in Arabia, Syria, Mesopotamia, and Central Asia. They were all divided by creeds and metaphysical formulæ, and there was little practical or spiritual life. The Persians had the cult of Zoroaster, which in its origin inculcated high moral doctrine, but which had been debased with the decay in Persian national life. There were two other religions over which Islam gained considerable victories in its later expansion, but they were not then known in Arabia. These were Buddhism and Hinduism, whose main features we have already examined.

Muhammad's Life and Ministry.—Muhammad was born an orphan, and his mother died when he was only six years of age. He grew up in solitude, but the forces of nature stirred the depths of his soul. His own moral and spiritual promptings led him to enquire into and feel every kind of religious experience. Among those who knew him he soon acquired the sobriquet of the "True," the "Trustworthy." In his commercial journeys to Syria, as agent for his future wife Khadija, he enquired much and heard much of Jewish and Christian controversies. As he grew older his contemplative nature dwelt more and more on the mysteries of life. At forty years of age he felt the call to the Prophetic Mission, and announced it. His wife, Khadija, and his cousin, Ali, who knew his most intimate life and thoughts, were among his first disciples. But his other kith and kin, whose material interests were threatened by his preaching against idolatry, began to persecute him and all those who listened to his message. However, the little community of earnest men and women grew in spite of persecution. This enraged his enemies the more, and they took counsel to slay him. Meanwhile, the neighbouring city of Medina had heard his message, and coveted the honour of his stay in their midst. His adherents arranged that he should emigrate thither, and the date of emigration (Hijra, incorrectly *hegira*), July, A.D. 622, forms the starting-point of the Muslim era, which is used in all Muslim countries to the present day.* During ten eventful years he lived in Medina, not only preaching and teaching, but organizing his community until it became a nation, and building up a social and political system which is one of the great landmarks in the world's history. He then visited his native city of Mecca, the city which had persecuted and cast him out, now the acknowledged spiritual and temporal head of Arabia, to put the coping-stone to his ministry. A year after his return to Medina he died, in the eleventh year of the Hijra, A.D. 632 (June).

Essential Features of Islam.—The essential features of Islam may be stated briefly. It preached the unity of God with a fervour and emphasis unknown since the time of the Hebrew prophets. It abolished priesthood and monasticism, and brought home the direct responsibility of man's spirit to his Maker, and the intrusive concern of religion and morals with every phase of man's life, collective or individual, and with our daily experience as well as the experience which comes in moments

* The Muslim year is lunar, consisting of 354 days, and therefore adjustments have to be made in converting dates from the Muslim era to the Christian era, and *vice versa*.

of great crisis or exaltation. It placed reason and common sense above obscurantism and mysteries. It regulated many evils, such as infanticide, gambling, self-indulgence in drink, food, and luxuries, sex domination, slavery, etc., by an appeal to the moral sense. No less than the unity of God, it emphasized the unity of mankind. It abolished the false barriers of race, tribe, or caste, and introduced the spirit of brotherhood and discipline.

Extension of Islam from the Atlantic to the Oxus.—It was this spirit which seemed to conquer in all the early wars of Arabia, united together for the first time under the banner of Islam. To the Muslims they were wars of liberation, the liberation of mankind. The Byzantine Empire and its Christianity lost province after province in Asia and Northern Africa. In fact, these provinces became the centre of gravity of Muslim power, and Egypt became, as it still remains, a great centre of Arabic learning. The Goths in the eighth century lost Spain, which became a flourishing outpost of Western Islam. The Persian Empire of the Sasanians was crumpled up with but feeble resistance, and the priest-ridden temples of fire-worship gave place to the mosques of the reformed religion. With Persia went the Turkish regions in Central Asia, on the borderland of Persian and Chinese civilization. Within sixty years of the Hijra the Islamic banner, with all its social and political implications, flew from Morocco to the Oxus.

Arab Dispersion and Decay.—Among the successors of the Prophet, called Caliphs, or more properly, Khalifas, were men whose selfish ambitions caused civil wars, and introduced a blight into the Arab nation. Among these was Moawiyah (A.D. 661-680). He was the first ruler in Islam to throw aside the dignity of democratic simplicity and religious conviction and assume the title of king. His capital at Damascus became the seat of pleasure and vice. His selfish ambition dreamed of the splendours of the Byzantine Empire, but its corruption and luxury demoralized the Arab nation, and drove into retirement or rebellion many of its choicest spirits. The great moral impulses which had raised the Arab nation in so short a time to its pinnacle of greatness were not spent for some centuries to come, but the final Arab dispersion and failure transferred the leadership of Islam to other nations, notably the Turks, from about the tenth century A.D.

Arabs in Sindh.—The Arabs had long been connected with India as seafarers and merchants. Islam gave them also missionary zeal, and Muslim Arabs were probably to be found on the coasts of India, if not during the lifetime of the Prophet himself, at least soon afterwards. The record of the early Persian and Central Asian connection with India is more specific and detailed, as we have already seen.* When, therefore, the Arabs established a strong centre of government in Persia, the question of India was forced on their attention. The Arabian Sea was infested with pirates from Sindh and the west coast of India. Attacks were made by these pirates on Muslim vessels. The Governor of Iraq complained, but no satisfaction could be obtained. The honour of Muslim women was also involved, and it was resolved to send an expedition to Sindh. The expedition consisted of no more than 6,000 men, and was under the command of Muhammad Kāsim, a youth of twenty. With his small forces reinforced from time to time, he conquered and reorganized the whole of the country from the mouths of the Indus to the borders of Kashmir, a distance of 800 miles, in three years (712-715). The country of Sindh in those days included not only the modern province of Sindh, but also the Panjab.

Arab Policy in Sindh.—Muhammad Kāsim had probably better weapons of war than the Hindus whom he subjugated, but he was very inferior in numbers, and he was very far from his base. Muslim sea-power was not very strong, and his troops had to march from Shiraz along the inhospitable Makran coast, where Alexander the Great's army had fared so badly a thousand years before. The secret of his success was twofold. The Hindu power against which he fought was disorganized and disunited; and Muhammad Kāsim's policy was one of conciliation and statesmanship. When once his supremacy was established, he employed local agency in the administration, and he gave the mass of the people better government than they had enjoyed before, and scrupulously kept faith

* See above, Chapter V.

with them. The dispatch from the Governor of Iraq, under whose orders the expedition had been organized, after praising his military conduct, commended " the pains you have taken in protecting the people, ameliorating their condition, and managing the affairs of the Government. The fixing of the revenue upon each village, and the encouragement you have given to all classes of people to observe the laws and their agreements, have brought much vigour to the Government." It added, " Show kindness, that your enemies may desire to be submissive; comfort them." That policy, combined with the free reception as brothers of all Hindus who accepted Islam, carried the victorious banner of the Arabs rapidly from the sea to the foot of the Himalayas. Muhammad Kāsim contemplated a further trial of strength with the Kanauj dynasty, the next great power in Northern India, when he was recalled in disgrace, and executed out of personal jealousy.

Later Developments in Sindh.—While young commanders and vigorous soldiers of Islam were thus carrying the successful Muslim arms forward in all quarters of the globe, the Arab civil wars, and the corruption at the seat of authority in Damascus, produced symptoms of decay at the core. By 750 the power in Islam was transferred from Damascus to Baghdad, from the Arabs to the Persians. But the Persians of that day were no less a decaying nation than the Byzantines, and they needed racial invigoration from their eastern neighbours, the Turks and the Afghans, both of whom play a large part in future Indian history. The Muslim power in Sindh soon got cut off from the Khalifate. But local Muslim dynasties, with occasional Afghan incursions, continued to rule in Sindh until the eleventh century, when the Afghan invasion may be said to have begun in full force—not directed merely at the frontiers of India, but penetrating through the centre to its remote corners. History thus explains why the population in Sindh and the Panjab is predominantly Muslim.

Subsequent Muslim Invasions: Who were the Afghans?—The Arab invasions had been mainly cultural. The Arabs came to India in very small numbers, and they rarely brought their women with them. The Afghan invasions were in force, and were mainly for conquest of arms. Their cultural effects, though important, were secondary. Afghan culture was but Muslim culture, only recently derived by the Afghans themselves from Arab and Persian sources. Racially the Afghans were a mixture of Turkish and Persian stocks, superimposed upon an earlier mixture in which various Central Asian elements, with some Greek, Parthian, and Indian blood, participated. According to their own traditions they are Semitic; they claim to be one of the lost tribes of Israel. Until the eighteenth century their country was merely the debatable land between Persia, Turkestan, and India. Sometimes they were partitioned among the adjoining countries. At other times they became masters of the adjoining countries. Their mountain fastnesses have welded them into a young and vigorous nation, though composed of different racial and linguistic elements, as is the case with Switzerland. Three languages—Persian, Turki, and the native Pushtu—are spoken in the country, but the polite language is recognized to be Persian. In the eleventh century the Turks were coming to the top among the Eastern Muslim nations. Tribes like the Ghilzai were almost wholly Turkish, though an integral part of the Afghan people. Turks fought in the armies of Islam in Central Asia, Afghanistan, Persia, Asia Minor, and Syria. The royal bodyguards were everywhere Turks, as they were both brave and reliable. Emancipated Turkish slaves carved out kingdoms and ruled peoples. In this sense the eleventh-century local dynasties in Eastern Persia and Afghanistan may be described as Turkish principalities. The period from 1000 to 1206 in India is described as the period of Afghan invasions, and that from 1206 to 1526 as the period of Afghan rule. In both cases "Afghan" must be understood in the sense just explained. Both periods would just as well be described as Turkish. In the period 1000 to 1206 the seat of authority remained in Afghanistan, but Muslim rule was firmly established in the Panjab. At the same time Muslim rule was being gradually extended in India; but the Indian Afghans or Turks were still part and parcel of the system of Muslim States beyond the Indian frontier. After 1206 they were cut off from the main current of Muslim political history outside India, although free intercommunication continued.

The House of Ghazni and the House of Ghor.—The two dynasties which cover the period of what we have called Afghan invasions were the house of Ghazni and the house of Ghor. Ghazni is the name of a city 140 miles to the south-west of Kabul. Ghor is the name of the tract of Central Afghanistan between Kabul and Herat. For a certain period these powers co-existed. For Indian purposes, the Ghaznavi period may be taken to be from 1000 to 1186, and the Ghori period from 1186 to 1206.

Mahmud of Ghazni: Indian Invasions, 1000-1026.—The most masterful personality of the Ghaznavi period, and the only one we need consider, was Mahmud of Ghazni. He played a large part in general Muslim history outside India, but his Indian period may be taken to be from 1000 to 1030. He was the first ruler in Islam to adopt the title of Sultan. His grandfather, a Turk, had established an independent principality at Ghazni. In his father's time the Hindu Raja of Lahore had tried to invade the territory of Ghazni, but had been defeated, and Peshawar had already been annexed to Ghazni. Mahmud increased his ancestral kingdom in all directions. India did not escape his attention. Between 1000 and 1026 he carried out at least twelve expeditions into India, destroying idol worship, and carrying away enormous wealth to his capital in Ghazni. Among the famous Indian cities which he took were Lahore, whose Raja had previously attacked the Ghaznavi territory; Multan, then the chief Muslim city of India, under an Afghan ruler who was accused of heresy by orthodox Muslims; Thaneshwar, on the Jamna, the home city, as we have seen, of the Imperial house of Harsha; Kanauj, Harsha's later capital, and now (eleventh century) the most important kingdom of Northern India; and Somnath, on the peninsula of Kathiawar, where there was a famous idol endowed with the revenue of 2,000 villages, to whom were dedicated 500 dancing girls and numerous attendants, male and female, including the daughters of high-born Hindu princes. Mahmud also made two incursions into Kashmir. His ambitions included the conquest of Ceylon and Burma, but he had rougher work closer to his home, against the Seljuk Turks, who were marching westwards across Asia—the same who eventually established a vigorous kingdom on the Asia Minor littoral of the Mediterranean, and paved the way for the conquests of their successors, the Ottoman Turks, farther west. Mahmud established his supremacy over an undefined area in the interior of India, but his effective occupation did not reach farther east than the city of Lahore. His descendants continued their eastward advance in India, but without notable results. They gradually lost ground in Ghazni itself, which was destroyed by the house of Ghor in 1152. The Ghaznavis were finally extinguished in Lahore in 1186.

Mahmud's Character.—Mahmud's character has been described as fanatical, avaricious, blood-thirsty, and destructive, with no redeeming features. Such a picture would be very far from the truth of history. He was a professed warrior of Islam, and there is no doubt about his iconoclastic zeal. But the story of his father's dream illustrates the ideas in the minds of those rough and hardy warriors. In that dream the Prophet Muhammad appeared, and said that the kingdom of Ghazni was assigned to him as a reward for a kind deed: "Let not thy power," added the Prophet, "undermine thy virtue, but continue the exercise of benevolence towards mankind." Mahmud's largesses to the great Persian poet Firdausi were short of the poet's covetous expectations. But Mahmud gave generously to men of learning in his court, and was even more generous in endowing a library, a museum, and numerous mosques and public buildings in his capital. The spoils of his conquests he displayed to his people, and in a large measure shared with them. About Mahmud's unbending justice many anecdotes are narrated, of which one may be told here. A man complained to Mahmud against Mahmud's nephew for forcible invasion of his house and unseemly conduct therein, adding that his complaints to subordinate authorities had borne no fruit on account of the offender's rank. Mahmud was angry, and promised him impartial justice. Having caught his nephew in the act, he extinguished the light, and slew him. He then called for a drink of water. In explanation of his conduct he said that he tenderly loved his nephew, and put out the light that pity might not arrest his hand in the execution of his duty. From the moment he had heard the complaint he had made a vow to God that he would neither eat nor drink till he had brought the criminal to justice, which was the cause of his intense thirst.

Study of Hindu Thought.—One of the learned men whose cultural work was a factor in the Muslim conquest of India was Abu Raihan Al-Biruni (973-1048). Born in Central Asia, he travelled over Muslim countries for forty years. He travelled in India under the protection of Mahmud, and dedicated his books in Arabic to Mahmud. He learnt Sanskrit, with a view to getting a first-hand acquaintance with Hindu thought and Hindu science, including Hindu astronomy, philology, and philosophy. His object was to bring Sanskrit learning within the reach of the Muslim world, and Arabian learning within the reach of the Hindus. The account of India which he has left is full of critical insight, and in accuracy and erudition challenges comparison with similar works written in any country or age. Greek and Chinese observers had previously written accounts of India, but according to Dr. G. Bühler, the great Sanskrit scholar, they read, by the side of Al-Biruni's work, "like children's books or the compilations of uneducated and superstitious men." The presence in the court of Mahmud of men like Al-Biruni shows that even the early Muslim conquests in India went hand in hand with a serious attempt at understanding the mentality of the highest Indian minds, and explaining the point of view of the new people who came with a new gospel and a new social and political message.

State of India.—The writings of Muslim historians, geographers, and travellers throw a vivid light on the conditions in India during the tenth and eleventh centuries. As we have seen, the north and south were coming into more habitual contact, whether by way of conflict or otherwise. Buddhism had not yet died out, but it was dying, or being absorbed into Brahmanism. The yoke of caste was fastened strongly on the neck of the people. The Rajput clans and tribes had been organized, and had become everywhere the ruling and fighting classes. Their own social system was on a clan basis, so different from the caste system of Brahmanism. But though of different foreign stocks, the Rajputs had been absorbed into the Hindu system, and fitted into its classical frame-work as the warrior caste. There was, however, little cohesion, either between the rival Rajput clans, or as between the Rajput rulers and their subjects. Mahmud found, in the important kingdom of Gujarat, which he conquered, internecine differences in the ruling family. The Muslims found no national spirit against themselves, and the lower classes often looked upon them as liberators. Sindh and the Panjab were Muslim provinces, but Muslim missionaries, travellers, merchants, and sailors had spread themselves all over the country, and especially on the southern coasts of India, where indeed they were welcomed and treated with honour. The shipping and foreign trade were in their hands, and a Muslim usually held the dignity of *Marzban* or Chief (of maritime affairs). A Muslim saint named Nathar Shah (or Nadir Shah) (969-1039) settled in Trichinopoly, where he has left a tomb and the memory of his prayers and works of charity.

Mas'udi's Picture.—We may supplement this composite picture with a picture from Mas'udi, the Arab historian, who wrote about A.D. 944. He recognizes that India is a vast country, extending over sea, land, and mountains. He reckons its eastern boundary to be Java. The dominions of the King of Java, "the Maharaj," the king of the islands, separated India from China, but were considered part of India. He noted the enormous differences in language and religion in India, and the constant internal wars. In his view the greatest of the kings of India was "Balhara," wrongly identified with Vallabh Rai, the supposed title of successive kings of the Vallabhi kingdom in Kathiawar. But the Vallabhi kingdom seems to have been overthrown by the Arabs in the eighth century. The real Balahra (Balhara) of the Arabs, with his capital at "Mankir," must have been the ruler of Malkhet in Eastern Deccan. Malkhet was the capital of a Chalukya kingdom (500-753) and a Rashtrakuta kingdom (753-972), the kings bearing the title of Vallabha. Other powerful kingdoms which Mas'udi mentions are those of Kanauj and Kashmir. He notices that the office of minister and other offices of state were hereditary. The part of elephants in Indian warfare is frequently referred to. The King of Kanauj is credited with four enormous armies of at least 700,000 men each, constantly warring towards the four points of the compass; but as he says in another connection, Indian forces are generally exaggerated. Of one Indian king he remarks: he "is brave, haughty, and proud; but to tell the truth, he has more haughtiness than power, and more pride than courage."

The House of Ghor: Conquest of Ajmir and Delhi.—The house of Ghor had only a short lease of power in India (1186-1206). Its most important king was Muhammad Shahab-ud-din, who began his long series of conquests in India in 1176 while he was still a prince, in the reign of his brother. He overran Sindh, but received a check from the Hindu Raja of Gujarat. In 1186 he deposed the last of Mahmud's descendants at Lahore, and then prepared to meet the coalition of powerful Rajput kings, who were now thoroughly alarmed at the progress of Muslim arms. The chiefs of the coalition were the famous Prithwi Raj of Ajmir, and his brother, the Raja of Delhi. The armies met in 1191 about 100 miles north-west of Delhi, the Hindu host numbering 200,000 horse and 3,000 elephants. Outnumbered and outflanked, Shahab-ud-din continued to fight with the greatest personal bravery though his army had given way. A faithful servant carried him off from the field, wounded and faint from loss of blood. He retired for a time to Ghazni, but he disgraced the officers who had deserted him in battle. He was determined to recover his lost honour or die in the attempt, and never slept in peace until he had collected a powerful force of 120,000 Turks, Persians, and Afghans to meet Prithwi Raj again. Before starting, he gave a chance to his disgraced officers to recover their honour, and they all joined his camp with enthusiasm. The opposing armies again met in the same tract near Delhi in 1192, the Hindu forces consisting of 300,000 horse and 3,000 elephants. As many as 150 Rajput princes had sworn by the water of the Ganges that they would conquer or die. The Ghori tactics were cautious this time, and the struggle was obstinate and prolonged. At length a desperate cavalry charge, led by Shahab-ud-din himself, broke the Hindu army, whose leaders were slain or captured. Ajmir fell to the conqueror, who appointed as governor a former Turkish slave, Kutbuddin. Shahab-ud-din himself ascended the throne of Ghazni in 1202.

Rapid Muslim Conquest of Northern India: Rajput Bardic Literature.—After the conquest of Ajmir and Delhi and the rout of the Rajput confederacy, the Muslim arms marched rapidly into the interior of India. Kutbuddin played a very important part in this conquest. The forts in the neighbourhood of Delhi were all subjugated. Before Shahab-ud-din's death in 1206, Gwalior, Kalinjar, Kalpi, Budaun, Kanauj, and Benares, as well as the distant kingdoms of Gujarat in the west and Bihar and Bengal in the east, had been reduced. All Northern India had been brought under Muslim influence, and most of it under direct Muslim rule. The strongholds of lingering Buddhism in Bihar were merged in a less gentle form of Hinduism. There was a dispersion of the Rajput princes from the fertile lands of the Gangetic tracts, and their concentration in the deserts of what has since been called Rajputana. The Rajput bardic literature, celebrating the exploits of Rajput heroes, looks back to this period, just before the Muslim conquest. Chand Bardai's great poem on Prithwi Raj is the earliest specimen of the Hindi language we possess.

CHAPTER VIII

ESTABLISHMENT OF THE MUSLIM EMPIRE IN INDIA, 1206–1526

Separation of India from the Main Currents of Muslim History.—On the death of Shahab-ud-din Ghori, his line was not extinguished at Ghazni, but its power came to an end in India. His feeble successors were caught in the great Turkish and Mongol vortex which turned the whole of Asia (outside India) upside down, and sent its waves into Africa and Europe. His Indian possessions were now separated from the main currents of Muslim history. They had been won chiefly through the exertions of his Turkish slaves, of whom Kutbuddin was easily the first. He held the important centres of Delhi and Ajmir, and proclaimed himself Sultan. Shahab-ud-din in his lifetime had recognized his genius, and called him "his son." The Delhi Sultan's title was now recognized by Shahab-ud-din's Ghori successors. But it rested chiefly upon the Prætorian Guards, who on the death of each Sultan raised military commanders to the throne, without any strict rules of succession.

Dynasties of the Sultans of Delhi.—The Sultans of Delhi are usually grouped into five so-called dynasties. The "Slave" Kings were usually those chosen from among the slaves of the Ghoris or the slaves of such slaves, and ruled from 1206 to 1288. Then followed a succession of Sultans of the Khalji or Khilji tribe (Turco-Afghan), 1288-1320, and then of the house of Tughlak (1321-1414). The power of the last of the Tughlaks was reduced to a mere shadow by the invasion of the Mughal Timur or Taimur (Tamerlane) in 1398. From the succeeding welter there emerged a successful general who was a descendant of the Prophet, and hence styled Saiyid (Syed). He had strengthened his position by accepting Timur's suzerainty and ruling on his behalf. The Saiyid line ruled from 1414 to 1450, after which another line was established by an Afghan general belonging to the tribe of Lodi, which held power at Delhi with varying fortunes from 1450 to 1526. The year 1526 opens a new epoch in the history of India by the establishment of the Mughal Empire.

Leading Features of the Period.—It would be an unprofitable task to follow even in outline the wars, conquests, intrigues, rebellions, massacres, and revolutions which mark this period of three centuries. We shall only review those salient facts which went to the making of India and left a permanent impress on her history. The outstanding features were: the constant fear of Mongol invasions from the north-west; the definite establishment of the Muslim Empire with its base in India instead of outside India; the steady expansion of Muslim dominion by the establishment of local Muslim kingdoms at the expense of the Sultanate of Delhi; the increasing importance of India in the estimation of Muslim eyes, and its comparative security, especially when contrasted with the devastation and havoc wrought in other Muslim kingdoms prior to the consolidation of the vigorous empire of the Ottoman Turks in Western Asia and South-eastern Europe; and the permeation throughout India of Muslim saints, whose preachings caused reactions in the form of new sects and new movements in Hinduism. The political rapprochement of the Muslims and Hindus was not yet either achieved or aimed at; that was the task and mission of the Mughal Empire. But we already discern in the Indian Muslims the invasion of luxury, and the decay of those virtues, military and moral, which had given them dominion. It was necessary in the sixteenth century to replenish these from a fresh and vigorous stock of the hardier races of Central Asia.

Mongol Invasions.—Mongol invasions occurred in almost every reign. They were merely continuations of the secular invasions from Eastern and Central Asia, which we have noted from the beginning of history. But now there were new factors which deflected the invasions differently. Islam had established new centres of culture and wealthy cities all over Central Asia, Persia, and Western Asia. Some of the hoarded wealth of India had gone out to those lands, while productive and artistic wealth was not much developed during these centuries of racial and religious conflicts. The richest spoils were now to be had without crossing the Hindu-Kush. The north-western corner of India was inhabited by warlike races, akin in blood, but protected by their position from the main currents started by the maelstrom. The very expansion of China northwards under the great Tsang dynasty (618-907) had familiarized the Tartars and Mongols with the rich lands within the Chinese Walls. Jenghiz Khan the Mongol (1162-1227) conquered North China and the whole of Central Asia, and passed on to Southern Russia; the Sultan of Khwarizm (Central Asia), though driven from his kingdom to India, acted as a buffer between Jenghiz Khan and India (1221). An irruption of Mongols is, however, recorded into India as far east as the walls of Lakhnauti, the capital of Bengal. Jenghiz Khan's grandson, Hulaku, and his hordes were similarly deflected northwards and westwards; he sacked Baghdad and practically destroyed the Abbaside Khalifate in 1258, but he sent an embassy to one of the Slave Kings in Delhi (1265-1266).

"Mongols," Mughals, and the "Great Mogul."—The Mongols had hitherto been barbarians, without any religion, but from this time onwards they mingled with the Muslim nations and became Muslim themselves. The Western Turkish tribes were pushed on towards Europe, but the Turks in the neighbourhood of the Mongols were allied with the Mongols, and the Turkish and Mongol armies were manned by both races. Their ruling families also contracted matrimonial alliances with each other, and ruled over mixed populations of Mongol and Turk. In this way the two came to be confused, and Turkish rulers, speaking a pure Turkish dialect and with Caucasian features, came to be called Mughals. "Mongol" and "Mughal" are variants of the same word, but it is convenient to restrict the term "Mongol" to the men with "goat-beards," high cheek-bones, and slanting eyes, while the term "Mughal" may be used for the Turkish or predominantly Turkish princes (and their following), who soon reacquired the ascendancy in Central Asia, and whose armies included a large proportion of Mongols. Such a prince was Timur, Taimur, or Tamerlane (1336-1405), whose invasion of India in 1398 broke up the Turkish Sultanate of Delhi, and plunged India into an anarchy from which she did not recover until the establishment of the Mughal Empire by Babar in 1526. Babar was a direct descendant of Timur, and his line is known in Western history as that of the "Great Moguls." The Mughal invasions were, however, a factor that influenced the history of India throughout the period which we are now considering. In 1293 the Mughals were specially assigned a suburb of Delhi for settlement, which became known as Mughalpura.

Muslim Base now in India: Coins, Architecture, and Public Works.—The city of Delhi became from 1206 onwards the Imperial City of India. It was adorned with mosques, colleges, and public buildings. The first Muslim mint had been located at Lahore before the Slave Kings established their capital at Delhi. But the Delhi mint soon became the central Muslim mint of India. It is true that the coinage of the early Delhi Sultans long retained the name of the Khalifa at Baghdad, but it implied no control from Baghdad, and, indeed, Baghdad had already become moribund before the Delhi Sultanate was born. A good deal of silver and gold was imported into India from the lands of the Khalifate when the native Indian currency showed signs of depreciation, and a popular Muslim anecdotist of the thirteenth century laments the fact that the wealth of the Muslims was drawn to Hindustan. Though this was a temporary flow, it replenished the silver in the currency of India. With the Tughlak conquest of the Deccan in the beginning of the fourteenth century, gold, which was scarce in Upper India, was brought in large quantities from Southern India, where it was (and is still) produced. Gold coinage in great variety was struck in the time of the Tughlaks. India soon became self-contained again both politically, administratively, and economically (except in the matter of horses). Her Muslim architecture developed on original lines, and paved the way for those masterpieces of surpassing beauty which were constructed later under the Mughal Empire. Her public works won the admiration of travellers from other lands. In the single reign of Firoz Tughlak (1351-1388) we have a record of the construction of 150 bridges, 100 public baths, 100 hospitals, 200 towns, 100 caravanserais (free public inns for travellers),

30 colleges with mosques attached, 40 mosques, and 50 irrigation dams, besides the repair of numerous public works of that kind.

Administration: Law, Public Service, Finance.—In the matter of administration the same king has left a very creditable record. He abolished the practice of mutilating criminals, which had been prevalent hitherto. As he says in an inscription which he caused to be engraved on a mosque in Delhi for the information of the public, "God in His infinite goodness having been pleased to confer on me the power, has also inspired me with the disposition to put an end to these practices." The Criminal Law was applied uniformly to his subjects, whether Hindu or Muslim. He also tried to root out corruption from the public services. In the matter of public revenue and finance the regulations apparently were far-reaching, and it would be most interesting if we had had fuller details than we possess. But we know that he abolished a large number of small and vexatious taxes on trade, arts and crafts, and grazing. As he says in the same inscription, "It is better to relinquish this portion of the revenue than realize it at the expense of so much distress, occasioned by the discretionary power necessarily vested in tax-gatherers and officers of authority."

Land Revenue, Army, and Public Instruction.—The Land Revenue administration, under which term is included the demand which the State makes upon cultivators of the soil—this demand having formed the mainstay of the receipts of the Public Treasury in India until quite recently—was greatly improved and systematized. In India the merits of a Government administration as concerned with the lives of the people can fairly accurately be judged by the efficiency, justice, and moderation of the Land Revenue administration. A good system means both increase of cultivation and of population, and eventually an increase in the public revenue. Both these points were carefully held in view in Firoz Tughlak's system. When the Muslims penetrated to the Deccan they studied the local customs and conditions, and systematized a code of settlement with the cultivators of the soil, which still forms the basis of what is known as the Ryotwari Settlement (settlement with ryots or cultivators) in the Bombay and Madras provinces. In regard to the army, Firoz Tughlak laid down the same essential principle for good government—namely, moderation of the demand of the Crown as against the needs of the public services, or of the citizens at large. Before his time the property taken in war was divided in the proportion of four-fifths to the Crown and one-fifth to the troops. He reversed the proportion, and reserved only one-fifth for the Crown, and four-fifths for the troops. But the most far-reaching reform of his reign was the organization of a system of public instruction. He encouraged men of learning, as had been done by many kings before him, but he sent them out to reside in different parts of the empire for the sake of imparting instruction to the people. This glimpse into the administration of Firoz Tughlak is valuable as showing the constructive statesmanship of the best of the Muslim rulers, although it must be confessed that in the period of chronic anarchy, wars, disputed successions and rebellions, these ideals were apt to be very much obscured by the immediate needs of the moment.

Rapid Muslim Expansion.—The rapid expansion of the Muslim dominion in India has frequently been noted with surprise by historians. Unsympathetic writers have not hesitated to ascribe this to the prevalence of brute force over a gentle population. But it must be remembered that in most cases, from the Arab invasions onwards, various sections of the population welcomed the conquerors, who also brought better organization and a manlier culture into India. When Bakhtyar Khilji invaded Bihar on behalf of Kutbuddin, who afterwards became the first Sultan of Delhi, about 1197, his dash was made with only 200 horsemen. In the following year he invaded Nadia, then the capital city of Bengal (about seventy miles north of modern Calcutta). He had only eighteen horsemen with him, and the people thought that he was a merchant who had brought horses for sale. The invasions were usually with very slender forces, and were often repelled, but they went steadily on. There was some planning, but in most cases it was deeds of individual valour and audacity which won. The rush tactics usually took the Hindu rulers by surprise. As their rule itself was not broad-based on the people's will, there were always local feuds and local discontent to lend a powerful aid to the invaders.

Whole Continent under Muslim Sway by 1309.—Delhi was only captured in 1193, but before Kutbuddin died in 1210, the Muslims had spread over the whole of the Jamna-Ganges Doab (tract of country between the two rivers), and the provinces of Oudh, Bihar, and Bengal, right up to Assam and the river Brahmaputra (a distance of over 1,200 miles from west to east). In a south-westerly direction they mastered Ajmir, Rajputana, Malwa, and Gujarat. The tract now called the Central Provinces was mostly forest country inhabited by aboriginal tribes, and even in later Mughal times remained more or less a *terra incognita*. But the masters of Northern or Southern India always claimed its overlordship. In 1294, Ala-ud-din Khilji, on behalf of his uncle who was then on the throne, penetrated into the Deccan with only 8,000 horse from the neighbourhood of Allahabad, and conquered Deogiri, the capital of the most powerful Hindu king of the south. It was an expedition of over 600 miles through mountains and forests, with no supplies, and by unknown routes into a hostile country, and was wholly unauthorized by the reigning Sultan of Delhi. But it succeeded beyond measure, and immediately established Muslim supremacy throughout the continent of India. For it was followed in succeeding years by the spread of Muslim forces to the east and west coasts of the peninsula of India, and by the year 1309 Malik Kafur, a Muslim general, had built a mosque at Cape Comorin, the southernmost point of India. Thus, in a period of a little over a century the whole of the Indian continent had fallen under the sway, and the greater part under the direct rule, of the Muslims.

Southern Muslims not United with Northern Muslims.—We have already seen how at various points in her history South India and North India have been completely isolated from each other, and how during other periods they have been brought into contact either by way of war or by means of cultural influences. The same statement applies to the relation of the Muslims with India. The first Muslims to come to the country were Arabs in the south, either as merchants, sailors, or missionaries. As they did not come for conquest, their relations with the Hindus were excellent. In many cases they attained great influence, material and moral, and some of the Arabs or mixed

Arab populations enlisted in the armies of the Hindu States. The first Muslim arrivals in Malabar even talked of the conversion of the rulers of Malabar to Islam in the same way as the Portuguese missionaries to the court of Akbar dreamed of the conversion of the Grand Mughal, and through him of the whole court, to Catholicism. The tombs of some of the Muslim saints in the south were converted into objects of worship among the lower classes of the Hindus, and the saints themselves became local godlings in the scheme of popular as opposed to book Hinduism. But these southern Muslims knew nothing of the events that were taking place in the north. On the other hand, the northern Muslims, who came as conquerors, knew very little of the Muslims already settled in the south.

Break-Up into Local Dynasties.—The northern historians speak of Ala-ud-din's raid into the Deccan in 1294 as if "the people of that country [the Deccan] had never heard of the Musalmans." They soon, however, found out their mistake. Their warlike expeditions, the rich booty that they carried away to Delhi from Southern India, and the wholly different attitude they adopted towards the Hindu populations, introduced elements of hostility to Islam which were new to the Deccan. Racially the Muslims had hitherto been represented in the Deccan by Arabs and Persians. From the fourteenth century onwards the Turkish element came into the upper layers of population, not only from Northern India, but from the growing Turkish Empire of the west. After the Northern Muslims (frequently referred to as the Turks) had been established in the south, they had not only to meet the hostility of the Hindus, but also of the Muslims of the south, who constantly formed "country parties" composed of Muslims and Hindus. The distance from Delhi to Cape Comorin would be more than 1,400 miles along rough roads. The ordinary journey from Delhi to Daulatabad took forty days, and that must have meant rapid transit, as the distance travelled must have been 700 to 800 miles. With the means of transport then available, the supremacy of Delhi could not be rendered effectual at these enormous distances. The Muslim Empire soon broke up into little kingdoms, especially when there was any weakness in the sultanate of Delhi.

Zenith of Delhi Sultanate under Muhammad Tughlak, 1338.—The expanding phase of the sultanate of Delhi lasted from 1206 to about 1338, when Bengal in the east and the coast provinces in the south began to rebel. Muhammad Tughlak (1325-1351) had actually proposed the transfer of the capital from Delhi to Daulatabad (the old Deogiri) in the Deccan. Muhammad Tughlak's plans were very grandiose, and included the conquest of China when the Mongol power was in its dying stages, before the establishment of the Ming dynasty. In the matter of currency and internal administration he had very large ideas, and was distinctly before his time. He has often been called a mad and ruthless king. Certain it is that his policy ran counter to all the prejudices and traditions of the time, and while the Muslim Empire attained its zenith in the middle of his reign, a decline soon set in on account of the general discontent. The disruptive forces made headway in all directions, and province after province set up independent kingdoms, mostly under Muslim rulers.

The Bahmani Kingdom and its Five Offshoots.—In the Deccan the discontented elements formed the famous Bahmani kingdom about 1347. This Muslim kingdom of the Deccan was proclaimed at Daulatabad. Its capital was at first (1347-1422) at Gulbarga, a beautiful city of white domes in an undulating plain, the last resting-place of a Muslim saint of some celebrity. The capital was removed later (1422-1482) to Bidar, an ancient town in the hilly tract in the centre of the modern State of Hyderabad. This local Muslim kingdom itself was too unwieldy in area to hold together, and broke up into five separate Muslim kingdoms. The first to rebel was the military governor of the strong fortress of Gawilgarh in Berar, who founded a dynasty (1484-1574) that lasted for four generations. Another dynasty was established at Bidar (1492-1609) by a minister of the old Bahmani kingdom. The kingdom of Ahmadnagar (1490-1600) created its own capital (Ahmadnagar), and is remarkable for the heroic resistance offered by its romantic Queen Chand Bibi before it was practically extinguished by Mughal arms under Akbar in 1600. The Bijapur kingdom (1489-1673) was founded by a son of the Ottoman Sultan Murad II. of Turkey, and a brother of the conqueror of Constantinople. This dynasty has left some splendid architectural remains. The Golkonda kingdom (1512-1687) succeeded to the territory of what had been the Hindu kingdom of Warangal, but moved its capital to Golkonda, near the modern Hyderabad, the capital of the Nizam's dominions. Its territory extended on the east to the sea, and included on the south the famous diamond mines of the valley of the Krishna, from which both the Koh-i-nur and the Pitt diamonds seem to have been derived.

Empire of Vijayanagar.—The establishment of the Muslim power or powers in the Deccan also gave rise to a Hindu reaction, which ended in the consolidation of Hindu forces, from which emerged the powerful Hindu empire of Vijayanagar. The territory of this empire was mainly to the south of the river Tungabhadra. It rallied around it the fragments of the Hindu principalities of Southern India, and was already in a strong position in 1346. Perhaps its period as an empire may be dated from 1379 to 1565, when it was destroyed at the battle of Talikota. This was a trial of strength between a combination of Muslim forces pitted against Hindu forces in the south. The Southern Muslim coalition won against the Hindu coalition. But it was in its turn overwhelmed by the expansion of the Mughal Empire from the north in a little more than a century.

Contribution of Local Southern Powers to General History.—The history of all these local dynasties is very interesting, and their contribution to the general history of India is considerable. But we can only pause to notice a few prominent facts connected with them. They were nearly always at war with each other, either singly or in varying combinations. The Hindu kingdom of Vijayanagar stood as a bulwark of southern Hinduism, and added to its cultural heritage. Its capital city was large, well built, and prosperous. It developed a system of decentralized local government, and fostered architecture and the arts. But its social life seems to have broken away from orthodox Hindu standards. Amongst the five Muslim kingdoms of the Deccan the most important were those of Ahmadnagar, Bijapur, and Golkonda. Ahmadnagar, being the most northern kingdom, had constant wars with the neighbouring Muslim kingdom of Gujarat, and absorbed the Berar kingdom. It was the first to enter into friendly relations with a European power. The Portuguese had in 1510 occupied Goa, which had been an important Muslim port in Bijapur territory. They played off Ahmadnagar against Bijapur, until these two Muslim powers joined forces against the Portuguese in 1570. In spite of the co-operation of two Hindu powers with them against these foreigners, they failed to dislodge the Portuguese, whose sea-power enabled them to hold their own on the coast.

Architecture of Bijapur.—Both Bijapur and Golkonda have left some splendid architectural remains. The Gol Gumbaz at Bijapur, a mausoleum of one of its kings, is described by James Fergusson, the historian of Indian architecture, as "a wonder of constructive skill." Its dome (built in 1659) is 124 feet in diameter, which may be compared with the 108 feet diameter of the dome of St. Paul's Cathedral in London (built in 1675-1697). A broad gallery runs inside the dome, so wide that a carriage might pass round it. The whispering gallery so magnifies the echoes that, according to Mr. H. Cousens, who has described Bijapur architecture in detail, "one pair of feet is enough to awaken the echoes of the tread of a regiment." The hall which the dome surmounts is 135 feet square, one of the largest domed spaces in the world. The water-works, baths, and cisterns of Bijapur formed an elaborate system, combining elegance and refinement with utility.

More Order and Prosperity in Southern than in Northern India in the Fifteenth Century.—In spite of the constant mutual conflicts of the southern kingdoms (among which we may include the Hindu empire of Vijayanagar and the Muslim offshoots of the Bahmani kingdom) and the Muslim sultanates of Gujarat and Malwa, there was a sort of balance of power established in the south in the latter part of the fourteenth and throughout the fifteenth century. As between Northern and Southern India, the advantage lay with Southern India. While the north was again enveloped in anarchy, the south showed considerable prosperity. The numerous ports of the south admitted the shipping and commerce of all the nations. In the reign of the Bahmani Sultan Mahmud (1378-1396) schools and colleges were established in the principal towns. The most striking of the architectural remains of Bidar is a great college founded by Khwaja Mahmud Gawan, who died in 1481. He had also collected a very extensive library, and carried on a regular correspondence with the famous Persian poet Jami. The poet Hafiz was actually invited to the Bahmani Court at Gulbarga (*circa* 1380), and has left an ode in which he describes humorously his reason for declining the invitation.

Isolation of Bengal and Kashmir.—In Bengal, with which must be included Bihar, the local Muslim dynasty was, after its revolt from Delhi, thrown on its own resources, without much intercourse with the outer world. The Muslims and Hindus therefore established more intimate relations among themselves. The names of the Muslim kings, Husain Shah (1493-1518), and his successor, Nusrat Shah (1518-1531), are held in deserved respect by the Hindus, and the Muslims have attained in Bengal a numerical majority. The patronage and favour of the Muslim emperors and chiefs, says a Bengali historian, gave the first start towards the recognition of the vernacular Bengali language in the courts of the Hindu rajas, who had been inclined to favour Sanskrit under the influence of their Brahman advisers. Similarly, the local Muslim dynasty in Kashmir was isolated in its mountain valleys, and the conciliatory policy of Sultan Zain-ul-Abidin (1417-1467) drew the Hindu population to him, and favoured the almost universal acceptance of Islam. At the present day over 74 per cent. of Kashmiris are Muslims.

India's Importance in the World of Islam.—There are many evidences of the large part filled by India in the world of Islam between 1200 and 1500, when the rest of the Muslim world was shaken to its foundations by violent convulsions and revolutions. We have seen glimpses of it in describing the position of the southern kingdoms. The Delhi sultanate in its more vigorous days was the resort of many kings in exile. Ghayas-ud-din Balban (1266-1286) was proud of giving honourable asylum to upwards of fifteen unfortunate sovereigns from Muslim Asia. As they brought in their train some of the most illustrious men of learning, the Delhi Court became celebrated as the most polite and magnificent in Islam. Societies for the cultivation of literature, music, and the arts were formed under royal patronage in Delhi, and attracted distinguished travellers from distant parts of the world. Learning commanded high esteem, and led to honours and emoluments. The poet Amir Khusrau (*circa* 1290) was made the royal librarian, granted a State pension, and elevated to the rank of the highest Amirs, or nobles, of the court. He was equally at home in Persian, Turkish, and Hindi, and may be called the father of the new vernacular which spread all over India, and is called Hindustani, or Urdu.

Account of Ibn Batuta in the Fourteenth Century.—One of the illustrious travellers to India during this period was Ibn Batuta, a native of Tangier. He has left in Arabic a spirited account of his travels. He was in India from 1334 to 1337, and travelled by way of Constantinople. As soon as he entered at the north-west frontier, information of his arrival was sent to the King in Delhi. He found the postal arrangements efficient; there were mounted relays, as well as foot relays, according to the urgency of news or travel. He bears out the fact (which appears from biographies of the time) that the Muslims in India lived long and healthy lives, and centenarians were often met with. He gives a list of the fruits, trees, and grains produced in India, but was disappointed to find few fruits with which he was familiar. The practice of the self-immolation of widows (*sati*) was frequent among the Hindus, but it was not compulsory. When he reached Delhi, the sultan was in Kanauj, which he describes as at a distance of ten days' journey. As the distance is about 250 miles, travel with heavy baggage at the rate of twenty-five miles a day implies efficient road arrangements. The roads in the neighbourhood of the capital were planted with trees, and looked like gardens. They were furnished with all conveniences for travellers.

The City of Delhi.—He calls Delhi not only the first city in India, but in all the East. The citadel had two strong broad walls, over which two horsemen could trot side by side with ease. It was well stored with grain and provisions. The mosque was built of marble fixed with melted lead; no wood was used in its construction. Many learned and holy men lived there; one who preached every Friday effected many conversions. In the absence of the sultan the traveller was received with distinction in the house of the Sultan's mother, who personally received his wife. The State minister was a man from Rum (Anatolia). It was a part of his hospitality to offer honourable employment to strangers of distinction, and Ibn Batuta was appointed Kazi (judge) of Delhi. His daughter died in Delhi, and he seems, later on, to have been uncomfortable with the king, and was glad to get away on an embassy to China, whose emperor had sent presents to the sultan at Delhi. He went through Southern India and embarked from Calicut in a Chinese vessel manned by a thousand sailors, and escorted by three smaller vessels.

Influence of Muslim Saints and Sufis.—The period 1200-1500 was remarkable for the permeation of Muslim saints and Sufis throughout India. Their influence and teaching are important not only in the history of the Muslims or in the formal conversion of Hindus to Islam, but in the indirect influence which they had in the further development of Hinduism itself. New sects and movements arose midway between Hinduism and Islam, and orthodox Hinduism itself evolved new doctrines which have gained in vitality through succeeding centuries. The Sufis are religious Orders or Confraternities in Islam. From the beginning of Islam they have played an important part in propaganda work and in the development of mystical doctrine. They still constitute the most living spiritual forces in Muslim countries. Each Order has a discipline and organization of its own, and traces its history in unbroken succession to its founder, who himself must show a similar spiritual link with the fountain-head of Islam. A saint with such a spiritual commission or credentials may found a new Order or establish new centres. Many such saints spread themselves over all parts of India during the period we are considering. We shall notice three whose foundations still exert living influence.

Chishti, of Ajmir.—Khwaja Moin-ud-din Chishti, of Ajmir, is perhaps the most important of them all. He was born in Central Asia about 1142-1143. Heir to lands and possessions, he resigned them at the call of religion. He wandered in search of spiritual knowledge to Samarkand, Baghdad, Jilan, Hamadan, Tabriz, and Mecca—in other words, to all the renowned cities of Islam where Sufi teachers were to be found. Among his masters was the famous Sufi, Shaikh Abdul-Qadir Jilani, who holds a pre-eminent position among the Sufi Orders. In 1165 the Khwaja succeeded to the position of head of the Chishti Order, and soon afterwards he received his commission of propaganda for India. Other Sufis had preceded him, but he seems to have worked on a very large scale, and started his work in the most powerful centre of Hinduism. He arrived in Ajmir in 1166. This city was then the capital of the Chauhan kingdom, the most important Rajput kingdom in India, for after its fall to the Muslims in 1192-1193 they practically became masters of the whole of Northern India. The Chishti established himself near the beautiful Ana Sagar (lake), and laboured for seventy years until his death in 1236. He converted the local Hindu mahant (abbot), who became a zealous disseminator of his doctrines. He also appointed sixty-six khalifas, or deputies, to go and establish lodges in all directions. He married a raja's daughter, and his daughter, Bībi Hāfiza Jamāl, was one of those appointed khalifas; her influence reached out among thousands of women. She lies buried near her father in Ajmir. The saint's tomb is held in much reverence, and scores of thousands of Muslims and Hindus visit it every year.

Baba Farīd, of Pāk Pattan.—About 110 miles east of Multan stands Pāk Pattan, the "holy city," containing the shrine of another saint, Baba Farīd-ud-din Shakar-ganj (1173-1265). He was descended from a king of Kabul, but his family had settled in Multan in the time of his grandfather. He resigned his family estates, travelled in Muslim lands, and studied under the greatest Sufi masters of the age in Baghdad. He established his seat at a ford on the Satlaj river, on the main road from Multan to Delhi, a well-chosen position for a missionary of a new culture, whose representatives were now sovereigns of Hindustan. Out of respect for his memory the city of Pāk Pattan was spared by Timur in 1398. His mystical verses contain some sublime passages, from which the following is an extract:

> "Man, what thou art is hidden from thyself.
> Know'st not that morning, noon, and eve
> Are all within thee? The ninth heaven art thou,
> Though from the spheres into the roar of time
> Thou didst fall ere-while. Thou art the brush that painted
> The hues of all the world—the light of life
> That ranged its glory in the nothingness."

Gesu-daraz, of Gulbarga.—With the conquest of the Deccan came the patron saint of the Deccan, Khwaja Bande Nawaz, surnamed Gesu-daraz (long-haired), of Gulbarga (1321-1422). We have already spoken of the city of Gulbarga in our account of the Bahmani kingdom. He was born in Delhi when the Delhi sultanate was over a century old. He was only five years of age when Muhammad Tughlak ordered the evacuation of Delhi and the march of its inhabitants to Daulatabad in the Deccan. His father moved with him to the Deccan capital. But the boy hankered after the established learning of the north, and it is said that he chose his own *Pir* (religious preceptor). He studied and lived for many years in Delhi, and worked among the plague-stricken when plague invaded that city, about 1356, contemporaneously with its ravages in Europe. In the panic preceding the sack of Delhi by Timur in 1399, he played the part of prophet, warner, and friend; then he went on an extensive tour through the country, eventually arriving at Gulbarga at the invitation of Sultan Firoz Bahmani (1397-1422). He died in 1422, and left 105 books from his pen. His tomb is an object of great veneration all over the Deccan.

Hindu Seers and Reformers.—While this great religious and intellectual activity was going on, on the part of the Muslims, its reaction on Hinduism is full of interest. The great southern teacher, Ramanuja, wrote in Sanskrit in the latter half of the twelfth century, and is esteemed a seer and prophet by the most orthodox Hindus, as he made no attack on caste or other Brahmanical usages. But he worked out a doctrine of the Vedantist school, which is very like Sufism; with its central figure of a personal God and its insistence on salvation by faith and adoration (*bhakti*). There are writers who perceive in this some influence of Christianity, but there is no evidence of any trace of Christianity in India in those days, while there is abundant evidence of a strong Sufi propaganda before, during, and after his time. He clothed his doctrine in Hindu terms, and concentrated his worship on the Rama incarnation of Vishnu. The foundation which he thus laid had far-reaching influences on the subsequent development of Hindu religious thought.

Development of Theism.—The line of spiritual succession which he established led logically to results which Sufism itself was aiming at—viz.: (1) the elimination of all distinctions of caste; (2) the test of faith rather than works for the salvation of man; (3) the unity of God and the brotherhood of man; (4) the possibility of approach to God through living human teachers rather than through a priestly caste; (5) the preaching of the truth to all who cared to listen in their own vernacular, rather than its "protection" and preservation in a sacred tongue in the hands of a close and privileged caste; (6) the appeal to emotion for spiritual experience more than to dialectics and arguments, music and folk-hymns being prominent features of worship and praise; and (7) the abandonment of the worship of idols. This movement towards theism is a living force in modern Hinduism.

Ramanand.—These points attained their best development in Northern India, and in the teachings of Ramanand, Kabir, and Nanak. Chaitanya of Bengal (1485-1527) is of the same spiritual kinship, but his teaching is of more importance for Bengal than for India generally. Ramanand's dates are not precisely ascertained, but he died in the fifteenth century. His laxity in caste observances and his appeal to the lowest castes drove him from his home in Southern India. He wandered about in the north, and his teaching prepared the way for the fuller teaching of Kabīr and Nānak in Hindi. One of his hymns, on being invited to worship in a temple of Vishnu, runs as follows:

> "Whither shall I go, Sir? I am happy at home.
> My heart will not go with me; it hath lost its limbs.
> One day I did feel inclined to go;
> I ground sandal, took distilled aloe wood and many perfumes;
> And was proceeding to worship God in a temple,
> When lo! my Master showed me God in my heart!"

Kabir.—Kabir was a disciple of Ramanand. His dates are also uncertain, but we know that he flourished in the reign of Sikandar Shah Lodi (who reigned 1489-1517), say towards the end of the fifteenth century. He was a weaver by profession, and is said to have been born in the Muslim faith. He was perhaps the sincerest exponent of the desire for synthesis in religion, which was so prominent in the popular leaders of religion in his time. His attitude is summed up in his saying: "To that love am I a sacrifice, by which caste, colour, and family are set aside." He had great powers of satire, and freely attacked the abuses which he found among both the Hindu and the Muslim communities. But he was honoured by the commonalty of both persuasions, and it is said that his body was claimed by both at his death. Fragments of his hymns are to be found in every section of the Adi Granth, the original Sikh scripture.

Nanak.—Guru Nanak (1469-1539) was in every respect a spiritual brother of Kabir. He was brought up in a Muslim atmosphere in the Panjab, having been in the service of a Muslim Nawab. But he was more interested in religion than in worldly life, and wandered about in company with Muslim Shaikhs and Hindu Gurus (teachers). His inseparable companion was a Muslim musician called Mardāna, who played on the rebeck, a simple three-stringed instrument to which hymns were chanted in praise of the universal Lord. He performed a pilgrimage to Benares, but with no Hindu emblems—no rosary or mark on the forehead. He is supposed also to have performed a pilgrimage to Mecca, and defines a Muslim as one "who cleans his own self, who is sincere and patient, and pure in words," not one who clings to forms and creeds, against which he inveighs vehemently. His followers remained a simple Theistic sect for many generations. As we shall see in later history, some of them organized themselves into a community of armed warriors, and held the chief power in the Panjab in the first four decades of the nineteenth century.

Recapitulation.—All these spiritual movements to which we have referred were the chief contribution of the thirteenth, fourteenth, and fifteenth centuries to the making of India. They are seldom referred to in general histories, and yet they furnish the key to the larger movements which come to the surface under the Mughal Empire, and which led to remarkable transformations in the British period. As to the external history, we have seen how easily a small band of Muslims made themselves masters of Northern India. We saw the foundation of the Delhi sultanate and the extension of its influence over the whole continent of India. The means of communication then available could not maintain the authority of a centralized power at Delhi over so large an area and over a population neither harmonized socially, nor united in language or culture. Local dynasties, mainly Muslim, sprang up in all directions, and in the confusion resulting from constant conflicts, some of the remnants of the old Hindu powers reasserted themselves. In the fifteenth century Delhi held actual and effective power over a very small tract round the city and suburbs, although it still claimed a shadowy suzerainty over large areas in the country. The Mughal raids from the north-west helped in the process of disintegration—every blow aimed at the centre strengthened the centrifugal forces and the outlying dynasties. Timur's blow (1398) practically destroyed the central power. Although he withdrew personally, he looked upon India as an outlying province of his vast empire, and his descendants kept alive their dreams of the rich "ancestral" kingdom. The later Lodi Sultans of Delhi (1450-1526) kept large Mughal troops in their pay; Bahlol Lodi (1450-1489) had as many as 20,000. When, therefore, internal feuds and rebellions distracted the Delhi kingdom, and an invitation was sent by the disaffected Governor of the Panjab to the young and adventurous descendant of Timur, installed as King of Kabul, Babar seized it as a God-sent opportunity, and invaded Hindustan. He writes in his Memoirs: "In the space of these seven or eight years I entered it [India] five times at the head of an army. The fifth time, God most High, of His mercy and grace, casṭ down and defeated so powerful an enemy as Sultan Ibrahim [Lodi, of Delhi], and made me master and conqueror of the mighty empire of Hindustan." The decisive battle by which he won this empire was fought in the plains of Panipat, about fifty miles north of Delhi, and is known as the first battle of Panipat, 1526.

CHAPTER IX

THE MUGHAL EMPIRE IN THE MAKING

First Battle of Panipat, 1526.—Babar entered India with scarcely 12,000 men, including camp followers. He probably gained large accessions in the discontented Panjab, but in the battle of Panipat, April 1526, he mainly relied upon his Mughals, his own generalship perfected in the hard school of experience, and his artillery, an arm which figures prominently after this in Indian warfare. This was not, however, the first occasion of its use in India, for the Portuguese historians note its use against them by the vessels of the King of Gujarat in 1500. Ibrahim, the Lodi Sultan of Delhi, brought against Babar more than 100,000 men and the antiquated arm of elephants, which, after this, plays a very subordinate part in Indian battles. The larger host was weaker in cohesion, order, and discipline, as well as in equipment and generalship, and its rout was complete. The Delhi Sultan was slain in battle, and an energetic cavalry pursuit prevented his troops from forming again.

Fruits of the Victory.—Delhi was occupied immediately, and entered by Babar in person on the second day after the battle. Ten days later he was before the gates of Agra, having detached his son Humayun, immediately after the battle of Panipat, to invest the city. Agra capitulated after a feeble resistance on behalf of the Lodi dynasty by a son of the Raja of Gwalior, who had fallen at Panipat. The Lodi dynasty had evidently won the support and confidence of the Rajput feudatories, for the formidable Rajput confederacy, under the lead of Rana Sanga, which Babar had yet to meet, was formed with the avowed intention of supporting the cause of the fallen house. Babar's policy was statesmanlike and conciliatory. To friends he gave royal rewards. Nor did he forget his relatives or subjects in Kabul or Central Asia, nor the poor in the holy cities of Islam in Arabia and Iraq. To the family of the beaten enemy he was generous, though his generosity was only rewarded with treachery. To his new subjects he was statesmanlike.

He sought to heal the wounds which his conquest had inflicted. But on one point he had made up his mind: he had come to stay in India, and make his occupation effective. The Kabul territories were his, but he governed them by deputy. He sent for his family, including his aunts and dependants, to India. He freely offered to send back any of his officers or soldiers who wished to return, but as he stayed, no one took advantage of the offer except one, and he had to be invalided "home" as Governor of Kabul.

Contemporary World-Events: (*a*) *In Asia.*—The Mughal conquest of India was a world-event, and should be examined in relation to other contemporary events of world-wide importance. The epoch in which Babar's empire was established was notable for the evolution of strength and order in Islam. The anarchy of early days gave place to the integrating process, which resulted in the creation of three great empires, so that the Muslim world became practically the Ottoman Empire, the Persian Safavi Empire, and the Indian Mughal Empire. Thirty-nine years before the last of the Moors were expelled from Spain (1492) the Ottoman Turks had taken Constantinople in 1453. Under Sulaiman II., the Magnificent (1520-1566), they extended their conquests in Europe, made Hungary a Turkish province, and exacted tribute from Austria. Extending through Syria to Egypt they had already (1517) taken possession of the maritime trade routes that ran east through the Red Sea. The Turkish possession of Eastern Europe and Western Asia gave them also control of the overland routes between the Mediterranean and the East. In Persia the Safavi Empire was founded by Shah Ismail I. (1500-1524). His ancestors had been saints of great reputation, and one of them was visited in his cell by the great Timur when he overran Persia. He had got Timur to release some Turkoman prisoners, and the hereditary bond between his house and the house of Timur was continued when they became the imperial lords of Persia and of India. Babar's possession of India meant a strong government from Bengal to the Oxus, and his grandson extended the Mughal arms to the Deccan.

(*b*) *In Europe.*—A similar sorting-out process was at work in the Western world. Spain had been united; the discovery of America by Columbus had given her a footing in the Western world, which she consolidated between 1520 and 1540; in the person of Charles V. (1516-1556) she united for the time being the crown of Spain with the German Empire and Burgundy; while the Netherlands, the two Sicilies (*i.e.*, Sicily and Southern Italy), and Sardinia, were included among her possessions. Portugal, an older maritime kingdom than Spain, had already, under Prince Henry the Navigator (1394-1463), pioneered the European movement for navigation, discovery, oversea trade, and colonization; since the Papal bull (1493) of Alexander VI., as modified by agreement with Spain, assigned her the whole world east of longitude 50° W., she took Brazil (1500), and at the same time obtained naval supremacy in Eastern waters by the Cape route; in 1497 her ships reached Southern India, and in 1510 she established herself at Goa; throughout the sixteenth century she attempted to fight the Muslim powers in the East, including Turkey, Persia, the South Indian powers, and later the Grand Mughal. Meanwhile, a new movement had arisen in the West, fraught with momentous consequences to the world. The Reformation, which began in Germany with Luther's great public protest at Wittenberg in 1517, was not merely a religious movement; in its consequences it was also an international, political, and social movement of the first magnitude, and helped to transform the whole economic outlook of nations. Out of its conflicts emerged two powerful maritime nations, the Dutch and the English, whose struggles in the East we shall follow in greater detail later.

Significance and Duration of the Mughal Empire.—Babar's age was thus an age of great achievements all over the world. Babar's own work consisted in organization, and the formulation of a policy, rather than in concrete measures of administration. His four years in Agra were too short a time in which to do more than establish his dynasty in the face of the opposition both of the Afghans (or Pathāns*), whom he had displaced, and

* "Pathān" originally connoted a speaker of Pukhtu or Pushtu, the dominant language of Afghanistan. Racially, it may be synonymous with "Afghan." But it is convenient to distinguish and call Pathāns those members of the Afghan race who are settled in India, including the north-west frontier tribes that do not owe allegiance to Kabul, and Afghans those who are subjects of His Majesty the Amir of Afghanistan.

the local dynasties, Hindu and Muslim, who had profited by the weakness of the Lodi Empire at Delhi. The merits of the Mughal Empire founded by Babar were:

1. It became an Indian Empire, not only firmly based on India, but enlisting in its support the military, financial, and artistic talents of India, and rallying round its flag the Pathan, Turkish, Persian, and Arab elements in India, as well as the Rajputs (the aristocracy of Hinduism) and other Hindus.

2. Though it continued to be a Muslim Empire, and had relations of friendship and amity with the other great Muslim Empires—namely, that of Persia and that of the Ottoman Turks—it upheld its own dignity and equal status in the Muslim world.

3. Whereas the Delhi Sultanate before it had been very much under the influence of ecclesiastics, and ecclesiatic dignitaries came first in the order of court precedence, the Mughal Empire was frankly secular, and even Akbar's attempted combination of Church and State in his own person was more a political movement aiming at unification and the consolidation of an Indian nationality than a religious movement; in this respect it may be compared to Henry VIII.'s Reformation in England.

4. The learning, history, and traditions of the Hindus began to be studied as a part of a national movement, and not merely out of missionary or propagandist motives.

5. Architecture, the fine arts, the useful arts, gardening, dress, and court etiquette, all felt the inspiration of the new movements in thought and sentiment, and gave rise to definite schools whose influence endures to the present day.

6. The opening up of India to Europe made India a link in the larger movement towards the unification of the world; India's economic life began to be systematically affected by the economic conditions in Europe, further Asia, Africa, and America.

The seeds of all these movements were sown in Babar's time, although their widespread influence does not appear until the reigns of Babar's successors. The Mughal Empire remained a strong and living reality from 1526 to 1707, the date of Aurangzib's death. After Aurangzib the central power grew weaker and weaker, and local dynasties or States began to assert themselves more and more, until the European struggles left the British East India Company, and eventually the British Crown, as the supreme authority over the whole continent. The last remaining descendant of the Grand Mughal (Bahadur Shah II.) was exiled after the Mutiny in 1858.

Babar's Second Great Indian Victory.—The battle of Panipat in 1526 decided the fate of Northern India. But it was too easily won. Babar's masterly strategy gave no time to the defeated elements to recover themselves. His rapid movements and the prestige of his great military reputation, combined with the feebleness of the Lodis and the feuds among the minor Pathan powers that had defied Delhi, enabled him to sweep everything before him. By 1527 the discontented elements had formed a powerful confederacy headed by Rāna Sanga, the Rajput chief of Chitor, who put into the field an enormous army, ostensibly in the interests of a brother of the dispossessed Lodi. Some Muslim chiefs joined him, and the flower of Rajput chivalry came out to fight the Mughal near his own capital. Babar was conscious of the enormous danger involved in this movement, and met it with his usual decision and thoroughness. He gave the fight the colour of a holy war. In a dramatic scene which he has described in his diary, he took the vow to abstain for ever from intoxicating drink in order to set the example to his officers and army, and all stores of liquor were poured out on the ground, and drinking cups were broken in solemn ceremony. The battle was fought in March 1527, a short distance from Fatehpur Sikri, and about twenty-eight miles west of Agra. Babar again used the military formation of the Ottoman Turks, who were then, under Sulaiman the Magnificent, the foremost military power in the world. Babar won a complete victory.

Babar's Peace Work.—He now followed up the scattered Pathan chieftains who were taking counsel in the East. He had no difficulty in establishing his power as far east as Bengal, and as far south as the borders of Malwa and Gujarat. He felt so firmly established that he sent for the ladies of his family, including his daughter, Gul Badan Begam, who came from Kabul to Agra in June 1529. Gul Badan Begam has left us a valuable description of those early days of the Mughals in

India, and we get a vivid account of the domestic life of the great conqueror. He took a pride in showing the ladies the sights of his new empire. Agra as he had found it was ugly and repulsive; he made it beautiful. It was in a monotonous plain; he took the ladies to see the views from the hills in the neighbourhood. He had planted gardens and built works at Dholpur and (Fatehpur) Sikri, which the ladies no doubt admired as a romance planted in the heart of Hindustan. It was in a house in (Fatehpur) Sikri that Babar sat and nearly completed his Memoirs, a remarkable piece of self-revelation. Babar died in his garden-house in Agra in December 1530. His body was taken to his beloved Kabul, where he rests, remote from the scene of the greatest work of his life.

His Character.—Babar combined in himself the qualities of a rough soldier of fortune, a skilled commander and leader of men, a refined and elegant scholar, a frank and genial companion, and a devout and God-fearing man, good to his family and friends, and generous to his foes. He loved nature and manly sports. The vigour of his constitution was maintained to the last years of his life, in spite of the hardships which he had endured. Since the age of eleven he had not kept the annual festival of Id twice in the same place. As late as March 1529, he wrote in his diary: " I swam across the river Ganges for amusement. I counted my strokes, and found that I swam over in thirty-three strokes. I then took breath, and swam back to the other side. I had crossed by swimming every river I had met, except only the Ganges." But there was one fatal vice, which not only tainted his life, but the lives of many of his descendants. He was fond of the cup, and though he abjured liquor before the battle with Rana Sanga and kept his vow of abstinence faithfully, he never got clear of drugs, and the drug habit grew on him with age. He was only forty-seven when he died. In his last years in Agra we can already detect a decline in some of his great moral qualities. The Darbar which he held in Agra in December 1529, with its shows of elephants, jugglers, and dancing girls, breathes a very different atmosphere from that of the sturdy rider and the scorner of luxury of his strenuous days. And a Pathan enemy in his camp—Sher Shah Sur, who afterwards overthrew his son—had watched him and found him wanting; for he had begun, in the transaction of business, to rely less and less on himself, and more and more on his subordinates.

Capitals of India.—Agra, 120 miles south of Delhi, had now definitely become the capital of the empire. The later Lodi Sultans of Delhi had resided there, and Sikandar Lodi had died there in 1515. The earliest buildings of the city date from Lodi times. The chief danger to the Delhi Sultanate, the danger which the Lodi Sultans went out to meet in person, was from the east and south. From that point of view Agra was better situated than Delhi. Babar also, for the same reasons, made Agra his capital in Hindustan. His successor, Humayun, was a wanderer and an exile during the greater part of his reign, but on his restoration the political centre of gravity was more in the west, and he died and was buried in Delhi. Akbar built the magnificent dream city of Fatehpur Sikri, about twenty-three miles west of Agra, and lies buried near Agra. It was in the reigns of Jahangir and Shah Jahan that the chief architectural glories of Agra were added. But Shah Jahan also left great buildings in his new Delhi (called after him Shah-Jahanabad). His successor, Aurangzib, was proclaimed emperor at Delhi in 1658, and was always partial to that city, and treated it as his capital, although during the latter half of his reign of forty-nine years he was continually engaged in warfare in the Deccan. During the reigns of his feeble successors, Delhi remained the capital till the formal extinction of the Mughal Empire in 1858. Meanwhile, Calcutta had become the capital of British India from 1774, and it continued to enjoy that position till 1911, when the Government of India made Delhi its capital.

Babar's Son, Humayun, Emperor, 1530-1556.—Babar left four sons. The eldest was Kamran, and the second Humayun. It was Babar's wish that Humayun should succeed him. He had specially trained Humayun, and in spite of occasional lapses the boy was dear to his heart. Babar had contracted his last and fatal illness after an earnest prayer that he should die vicariously for his son. Humayun was actually at Agra, and succeeded naturally. Kamran took Kabul and Kandahar, and eventually the Panjab also, nominally under the suzerainty of the emperor. In fact, Kamran was a rival and a thorn in Humayun's side until he was finally captured in 1553. The younger brothers also gave Humayun trouble.

Humayun's Difficulties. — Humayun's difficulties were numerous. His brother Kamran not only held the ancestral seats beyond the Indus, and later the Panjab, but cut off Humayun from the Mughal recruiting grounds on which Babar had relied as the source of his chief fighting strength. Even the Mirzas (the Perso-Turkish chiefs) who were actually with Humayun were discontented, and rebelled in 1533. The Pathans were gathering strength in the eastern provinces of Bihar and Bengal. Rana Sanga, who might have held in check the southern provinces of Gujarat and Malwa, had been humbled by Babar, and Gujarat raised its head, and refused to acknowledge the empire. It further aggrandized itself at the expense of its neighbours. The Portuguese, who had obtained the complete mastery of the west coast of India, from Cape Comorin to the Indus, played off Gujarat against the new Mughal Empire, and intrigued with both.

His Defeat and Exile.—Humayun was not equal to the task. He was irresolute in character, and was in the grip of the opium habit. While he was in the south fighting with some success against Gujarat, in 1535, Sher Shah Sur was consolidating his position in Bihar. Humayun hastened to Upper India, and marched eastwards, through Bihar to Bengal. He seemed to have some success in Bengal, but Sher Shah raised his head again, and lay astride his communications with Agra. Humayun, returning to Agra, 1539, was defeated at Chausa on the Ganges, some twenty miles east of Ghazipur, and again when he mustered his forces for a final blow next year (1540), at Kanauj on the Ganges. On the second occasion he lost his whole army, and thousands of Turks were drowned in the river. Everything was now lost. Lahore was in the possession of his brother Kamran. Five months of irresolution on the part of Humayun gave Sher Shah time to pursue him into the Panjab and gain possession of that province. Humayun expected no kindness from his brother in Afghanistan, and no mercy from his enemies in the Panjab. He turned to the sandy deserts of Rajputana and Sindh. At Umarkot, ninety miles east of Haiderabad

(Sindh), his son Akbar was born, 1542. Akbar's mother afterwards remembered the place as "a beautiful oasis, where food was very cheap." Humayun then went as a fugitive, by way of Kandahar, to the Persian court at Ispahan, where the Safavi Shah Tahmasp received him hospitably, and promised him an army with which to reconquer his dominions. His infant son, Akbar, was sent to his uncle at Kabul.

Sher Shah Sur, *de facto* **Ruler, 1540-1545: Administrative Reforms.**—Meanwhile, Sher Shah Sur proclaimed himself sultan, and sat on the throne of the Mughal for five years. He was not only a good general, but a statesman, and the period of his rule was marked by many administrative reforms. He was also more in touch with the country. He reorganized the coinage, and fixed the standard of the silver coin (rupee) at 178 grains. This standard was maintained by the Mughals, and is still approximately maintained in British India, whose rupee weighs 180 grains, but is less fine. He carefully divided his territory into workable administrative units, and laid down fixed principles of land survey and land revenue administration, which were further elaborated by Akbar. He improved the judicial machinery, and devoted much attention to roads and public works. He was most assiduous in the transaction of public business personally. After his death in 1545 India relapsed into chaos. His two feeble successors were unable to exercise undisputed authority, and the way was cleared for Humayun's restoration in June 1555.

Humayun's Restoration, 1555, and Death, 1556.—The Shah of Persia was only too glad to have an opportunity of intervening in the affairs of his rival, the Great Mughal. He furnished Humayun with an army, with which he started to reconquer his empire. The greatest obstacles in his way were his own brothers in Afghanistan. In 1545 he took Kandahar and Kabul, and rejoined his son Akbar, now three years old. His brother Kamran fled to Turkestan, but kept up an intermittent fight with Humayun, until he surrendered finally in 1553. In 1554 Humayun invaded Hindustan, where different Pathan chiefs were in possession of fragments of the territory unified by Sher Shah. He entered Delhi in June 1555, but was killed by an accidental fall in January 1556. His court was visited by the famous Turkish admiral, Sidi Ali Rais, who was in Delhi at Humayun's death. The Turks, under Sulaiman the Magnificent, were fighting the Portuguese in Eastern waters. Sidi Ali travelled from Surat to Ahmadabad, where he completed a treatise on navigation in the Indian seas. After visiting Delhi and Lahore, he travelled overland to Constantinople, and wrote an account of his travels.

Akbar (1556-1605) : His Early Life.—Akbar's first command was in Afghanistan at the age of nine. He came with his father to India, and fought under the Turkoman Bairam Khan in the campaigns which re-established Humayun at Delhi. At Humayun's death Akbar was only thirteen years of age, and was proclaimed emperor under the tutelage of the tried friend of the family, Bairam Khan. The conquest, however, was not yet complete. It was the second battle of Panipat, November 1556, which destroyed the hopes of the Pathan pretenders to the Imperial throne. The work of conquest and military consolidation went on. The boy-emperor was served well by Bairam Khan, though the ladies of the family exerted much influence on public affairs. Akbar showed no inclination for studies. He was devoted to sports and hunting, but his gradual assertion of his personality in State administration leaves no doubt that he was gathering up the threads, forming a policy, and developing that character for far-sighted statesmanship and a comprehensive grasp of practical administrative problems, which has stamped his period as one of the most prosperous in Indian history.

Territorial Expansion and Moral Ideals.—From the first a generous treatment was accorded to fallen foes, and while conquest was pushed on with unceasing vigour, and discipline enforced with a firm hand, measures were taken to bind every interest to the throne and person of Akbar. In 1560 Akbar took the reins of power into his own hands, and dismissed Bairam Khan with honourable provision. In 1562 and 1564 he made an example of some of his own relatives, whose violence or contempt for State dignitaries called forth severe but just punishment from Akbar. Bairam Khan had seated Akbar firmly on the Imperial throne, undisputed master in the nucleus of his empire. But Akbar went on enlarging the boundaries of his effective occupation practically to the end of his life, for in 1602 he assumed the additional title of "King of the Deccan," and in 1603 he recaptured Kandahar. His wars were not merely wars of aggrandizement. In theory he claimed an overlordship over all India, as well as over his ancestral possessions beyond the Indus. He aimed at enlisting the co-operation of his beaten foes, and his interest in war was merely as a means towards unification, good government, law, and order. Side by side with territorial expansion he laboured constantly for the improvement of the administrative machinery, for the welding together of the different classes and creeds under his sway, and for the encouragement (according to his lights) of the practical arts, the useful sciences, and the moral and spiritual advancement of his subjects.

His Difficulties, and how he Surmounted them.—His difficulties were even greater than those of Humayun, but he met and surmounted them. He bore a reputation for great luck, and believed in his own good fortune. But for every one of his enterprises he brought the qualities that ensured success. He often failed in his first attempts, but his courage and self-confidence never flagged. In many cases he carried off a hopeless adventure by his personal dash and energy. In his first expedition to Gujarat (1572) he prevented the junction of two enemy forces by impetuously charging a force of 1,000 men with barely 156 trusty followers, and doggedly snatching victory after he had been hemmed in and nearly killed. In the following year he covered 450 miles in nine days, and at immense personal risk beat the enemy before he knew he was upon him. By swift movement, personal gallantry, the capacity of winning the hearts of those around him, and repeated generosity after victory and even after ill-requital, he built up the splendid fabric of the Mughal Empire.

Absorption of Diverse Interests.—His brother and relatives in Afghanistan were disloyal and rebellious; he left Afghanistan a peaceful appanage to India. The Mirzas, Timurid Mughals settled in India, rebelled and intrigued; by policy and show of strength he brought them to subjection. The Uzbegs, turbulent Turki warriors who had been rivals as well as contributories to Babar's power, were put down with a firm hand, and taught their place. The gallant Rajputs, who had made a brave fight for their honour, both against Babar and Akbar, were converted into Akbar's staunchest friends and allies. In the fights (1586-1587) against the Pathan tribe of Yusufzai round the Khaibar, Akbar's chief representatives were Raja Man Singh, of the Rajput house of Amber (now Jaipur), Todar Mal, the great Khatri financier, and Bir Bal, the Brahman (Bhat) poet and wit—representing the warrior, the mercantile, and the priestly castes of Hinduism. The Indian Pathans, representing families that had lost their power, were ever surly and discontented; but the grant of power and place absorbed them into Akbar's comprehensive system, especially after the pacification of Bihar and Bengal (1575-1576).

Direct European Contact.—The Portuguese had been supreme in the Eastern seas in the sixteenth century, especially before 1580, the date of their absorption into Spain; they had meddled in the politics of the southern kingdoms, Bijapur, Ahmadnagar, and Gujarat, and had systematically ravaged the western coasts of India. Akbar had no strong sea force with which to meet them. But his conquest of Gujarat (1572-1573) and of Ahmadnagar (1595-1600) brought him face to face with the Portuguese politically, while they are said to have furnished armed forces to assist unsuccessfully in the resistance of Sindh to the Mughal arms (1591). Three Jesuit missions went by invitation from Goa to Akbar's court between 1580 and 1595, while Akbar himself sent a mission to Goa in 1601. The English, too, were not unacquainted with his court. Ralph Fitch, the merchant adventurer, was in Fatehpur Sikri in 1585, and his companion, Leedes, entered Akbar's service. John Mildenhall arrived in Agra in 1603 by the overland route through Turkey, and actually brought a letter from Queen Elizabeth to the Mughal court, where he had to counteract the Portuguese intrigues. Akbar, whose mind was alert, and whose curiosity was insatiable, learned something of the Europeans by personal contact —of their naval power, their capacity for military and political organization, and their ideas and civilization. He was also interested in their religion, and learned about the distinction between Protestants and Catholics, and the different characters of the Protestant and Catholic nations. We need not take seriously all that the Jesuit Fathers said and wrote about him, nor did he take seriously what they said to him. But it is not extravagant to suppose that he appreciated the merits of the English nation, which was afterwards to inherit his power and policy in India, and to add a not inconsiderable wing to the edifice of a united India.

Extent and Organization of the Empire.—Apart from the pacification and consolidation of India, Akbar's chief title to fame rests upon his restless energy in administrative reform, his progressive social policy, and the breadth of his vision in the matter of education, the arts and sciences, and religion. The *Ain-i-Akbari*, that wonderful record which is at once the code and the gazetteer of the empire, presupposes a well-organized Civil Service, with a large staff at headquarters and in the provinces, accustomed to collect, tabulate, and handle statistics of a very complex character. Akbar's empire was built up step by step, and the military, fiscal, political, and administrative arrangements must have varied enormously in its different parts, as well as at different periods. In its final form its fifteen *Subahs* (provinces) comprised not less than a million square miles. Though Bijapur, Golkonda, and the territory further south was not directly included, there was an extensive territory beyond the Indus, now comprised in Afghanistan and Baluchistan. The population of Akbar's empire has been estimated at a very modest reckoning at 100,000,000. Its revenue figures have been estimated as low as the equivalent of £9,000,000, and as high as £19,000,000. Its system of communications, post, and news-reporting was probably better developed than in other contemporary kingdoms, while in religious and personal freedom it afforded a pleasing contrast to the state of contemporary Europe. Special attention was devoted to agriculture. Land was surveyed; advances were made to agriculturists; superior crops were encouraged; and the State's demand on land was carefully systematized on principles which still form the basis of land revenue administration in Northern India.

Education, Arts, and Sciences.—Though deeply interested in philosophy and learning—the learning of all times and all nations—Akbar favoured in education the practical and the useful—the "modern" as opposed to the "classical side." Music and painting he encouraged, as well as the exact sciences. To architecture he was passionately devoted. His mother built Humayun's tomb at Delhi, a monument in which can be traced the first outlines of the splendid conception of the Taj Mahal. In Akbar's own dream-city of Fatehpur Sikri, twenty-three miles west of Agra, we have a perfect model of royal town-planning. It has its gates and mosques, its saint's shrine, its inn and baths, its lake and water-works, its girls' school, and ladies' retreats, its treasury and mint, and its numerous palaces and reception halls, carefully designed to give Akbar his hours of meditation, State work, and State gatherings, as well as access to his intimate friends. Nor were the humble stables nor the shooting box forgotten, for Akbar was a lover of animals, and a votary of sports. But the most characteristic feature was the central *Ibādat Khāna* (House of Worship), not existing now, where Akbar held religious discussions with all schools of thought, as a preliminary to the promulgation of his new sect, the "Divine Faith," in 1580.

Religious Movements.—This period was remarkable for the stirring of religious thought all over the world. Doctrines and spiritual organizations were being questioned and re-examined, and great political movements became mixed up with religious movements. While the West was ringing with the doctrines associated with Luther, Calvin, and Knox, and Anglicanism and Puritanism were beginning to gather their forces in England, many parallel movements, spiritual and politico-spiritual, were taking shape in the East. In Akbar's empire Hinduism passed through a remarkable rejuvenating phase in the doctrine of personal adoration worked out with such beauty and spiritual insight by the poet Tulsi Das. He wrote in Hindi, the vernacular of Northern India. He commenced his *Ramayan* in 1574. Though the story is that of the great Sanskrit epic of the same name, the atmosphere is entirely different, and reflects the light won by Hindu and Sufi saints of a refashioned India. In the same year, 1574, the headship of the Sikh fraternity devolved upon Ram Das, to whom Akbar granted a site for the building of a Sikh temple, the nucleus of the sacred city of the Sikhs, Amritsar (1577). It was here that the Granth

Saheb—the Sikh scripture—was afterwards collected by Guru Arjun (1581-1606), and still later, a militant political system was founded, which dominated the Panjab. In Islam itself there were numerous schools of thought. The year 1592 of the Christian era was the thousandth (lunar) year of Islam, and as it approached, a whole crop of movements arose, as heralds of a new age. One such was the sect of the *Raushaniyas* (Illuminati), which was responsible for the revolt of the Yusufzais suppressed by Akbar (1586-1600).

Akbar's "Divine Faith."—Akbar's own mind seems to have been impressed by the popular expectations of a millennial age. His "Divine Faith" differed little in doctrine from the Sufi Orders, which had each its own mystic tokens and ceremonies. We know that he had a superstitious veneration for his Sufi Saint of Fatehpur Sikri. But Akbar engrafted on Sufi rites the new doctrine of the king's spiritual supremacy. We do not know whether he ever heard the name of Henry VIII., but he must have eagerly enquired into the meaning and political bearings of the Protestant Reformation. At any rate, he claimed no less a position for himself in his empire than Henry VIII. did in the Church of England. Indeed, Akbar's claim was far greater, for he claimed not only the headship of an organization, but a special position with regard to the interpretation of doctrine. Akbar's position was the less tenable, because (1) he had no unified nation behind him; (2) his claim was not acknowledged by more than a score of people in immediate touch with him; it originated and died as a personal whim rather than as a movement; and (3) he set against himself all that was most effective in his own people; his advisers, Abul Fazl and Faizi, had too much of the unquestioning spirit of worship of him to be wise or safe counsellors, or to bring out the real strength of his character. In this respect his failure was attended with mischievous consequences, and must be set against his splendid achievements in other fields.

Unfortunate in His Sons.—There were other disappointments of a more intimately personal nature. He had no family life. He lost two sons in their infancy, and two in vigorous manhood, from the effects of intemperance. Prince Salim, who succeeded him under the title of Jahangir, disgraced himself by rebellion, and even by worse disloyalties, of which his father knew nothing. A plot was formed, when Akbar was dying, to supersede Jahangir and set up on the throne Jahangir's son Khusru, a boy of gentle manners and high moral principles, beloved of the people. The plot was foiled, Akbar himself unmistakably designating Jahangir as his successor. But it earned much suffering for Khusru, and eventually a tragic death in 1622.

CHAPTER X

THE MUGHAL EMPIRE AT ITS ZENITH

Jahangir's Reign (1605-1627) : His Character.—It is eloquent testimony to the workmanlike character of Akbar's organization that it continued to function without marked deterioration in the twenty-two years' reign of his feeble successor. Jahangir reigned from October 1605 to October 1627. He was irresolute, dependent upon whoever held the ascendancy over him for the moment, a slave to alcohol (both wine and spirits), and in the later years of his reign unable to transact much business on account of asthma and his moral thraldom to an ambitious and imperious queen. Nur Jahan's family and she herself had passed through the most violent vicissitudes of fortune. After her marriage (as a widow) with the Emperor in 1611, her father and three brothers were advanced to the highest positions in the State; while she sought by matrimonial alliances between her family and the Royal house to strengthen her hold on the throne in any eventuality. Endowed with masculine energies, she was the centre of court intrigues, which made the last years of Jahangir's reign a tangled web of feuds, rebellions, negotiations, and reconciliations. But the feminine in her character loved power and splendour, and devised new fashions in elegance, dress, and perfumes, whose influence survives to the present day. The heir-apparent, Shah Jahan, who had acquired fame and experience, both in war and administration, had been the victim of her jealousies and intrigues. On Jahangir's death, October 1627, Shah Jahan was in the Deccan, almost a fugitive. But he had a strong party at court. He hurried to Agra, and was formally proclaimed Emperor in February 1628.

Portuguese and Dutch : English Visitors to Jahangir's Court.—It was in Jahangir's reign that the first English settlement was established in India—in Surat, 1612. The Dutch also got a footing in Southern India in 1609. The Portuguese were still strong, both in their own settlements and in their intrigues at the Mughal court, and in local politics all over India. But their power was on the wane. Both the Dutch and the English inflicted defeats on them at sea. Among the distinguished English visitors to Jahangir may be mentioned two who brought letters from James I. Captain William Hawkins, of the good ship *Hector,* landed at Surat in August 1608, and reached Agra in April 1609. His linguistic attainments enabled him to converse with Jahangir in Turki. He was appointed to a rank and dignity in the Mughal court, where he remained till 1611. Sir Thomas Roe came as a properly accredited diplomatic agent to negotiate a commercial treaty. He saw Jahangir at Ajmir in March 1616, travelled with the court in the Mughal dominions, and left in September 1618. Both he and his chaplain have left valuable accounts of what they saw in India.

Shah Jahan (1627-1658): Expansion in the Deccan.—Shah Jahan's reign (October 1627 to July 1658) was, on the whole, peaceful and prosperous internally, though there were constant wars on the frontiers. An attempt was made to extend direct rule in the Deccan, and to assert the hereditary claims of Babar's family in Central Asia. Akbar had destroyed the independence of the southern kingdom of Ahmadnagar in 1600. But the heirs of the Ahmadnagar sultans still ruled; they sometimes asserted themselves, and were sometimes used as tools in the hands of ambitious ministers or chieftains. In 1632 the kingdom was completely wiped out. Part of it was taken over under the direct administration of the Mughal Empire, and a part was added to the territory of Bijapur, which itself became a subordinate ally of the Mughal. The destruction of Ahmadnagar gave the opportunity for the rise of a new and vigorous nation in Southern India. The Marathas, whose homelands lie round the tract in the neighbourhood of Ahmadnagar, began to feel their power. Their great chieftain and national hero, Shivaji, was born in 1627. His father, as a dignitary of the Ahmadnagar Sultanate, made a gallant fight when he was transferred to Bijapur. Eventually he submitted to Bijapur, and even commanded expeditions further south on behalf of the Bijapur Sultanate, by which he was rewarded with further jagirs, or assignments of land. The southern kingdoms were, however, crumbling, and Shivaji grew up in dreams of sovereignty for himself and power for his nation. The remaining Deccan Sultanate, Golkonda, was also made tributary under Shah Jahan, and its politics and its ministers now began to be mixed up with the affairs of the apparently expanding Mughal Empire of the north, and the really increasing importance of the European nations from across the seas. It may be noted that Golkonda as a Shia kingdom had acknowledged before this the overlordship of Persia.

Fruitless Wars beyond the Hindu-Kush.—The prestige of the Mughal Empire had now become so great that Shah Jahan attempted to establish his grip in Afghanistan and Central Asia. Afghanistan was not then a self-contained nation. Kabul was fairly safe in the hands of the Mughals. But Kandahar had always been a bone of contention between the Mughal Empire and Persia, and it was finally severed from India in 1653. Balkh really lies in the Oxus region, beyond the Hindu-Kush mountains, and had to be abandoned to the Uzbegs of Central Asia in 1647. The policy of holding these mountain regions from a base in India was mistaken. The population is hardy and turbulent. The passes are difficult, and communications with India are cut off by the snows of winter. These fruitless expeditions squandered the resources of the empire. But they showed how staunchly the Rajputs could fight for the Mughals, even in losing causes, if only their heart was won. The disasters in Afghanistan also turned the rivalry of the two princes Dara and Aurangzib into a hatred which afterwards flamed forth into a civil war, costing Shah Jahan his throne, and Dara his life, and clearing the way for the assumption of the Imperial throne by Aurangzib. Shah Jahan, like his father Jahangir before him, had used Kashmir, and sometimes Kabul, as his summer residence. This practice forms the precedent for the establishment of the summer capitals of British India in the hills—viz., Simla for the Government of India, and other hill stations for provincial governments.

Shah Jahan's Consort, Taj Bibi: Their Four Sons.—Shah Jahan's famous consort, Mumtaz Mahal, affectionately known among the people as Taj Bibi (the Lady Taj), had been a salutary influence in his life. As a prince he had shown himself

8

endowed with vigour and capacity, and during the earlier part of his reign he commanded the devotion of his subjects, including the Rajputs, and the admiration of the numerous European travellers who visited India. Her death in 1631 deprived him of the key to a pure and happy private life, and he commemorated her in a monument—the Taj Mahal—the most splendid architectural tribute ever paid by a man to the memory of the woman he loved. Unfortunately Shah Jahan lost his moral balance after her death, and his strength was sapped and his character undermined by his subsequent excesses. She left four sons and two daughters. Pre-eminent in ability, judgment, and statecraft was the third son, Aurangzib, who held the viceroyalty of the Deccan for a long number of years. The eldest, Dara, the heir-apparent, remained with his father at headquarters, and as Shah Jahan grew older and less active he leaned more and more upon Dara. This did not make for more cordial relations between Aurangzib and Dara. Shah Jahan's second son, Shuja, was viceroy of Bengal, and his fourth son, Murad, was viceroy of Gujarat.

Scramble for Power among the Princes: Shah Jahan's Death.—When Shah Jahan fell seriously ill in September 1657, there was a scramble for power among the four sons. Dara had the support of his father, and he had no difficulty in checkmating Shuja. But Aurangzib acted in concert with Murad, and ostensibly in Murad's interests. Their joint forces moved cautiously from the south towards Agra. Dara was impetuous, and no match for Aurangzib's strategy. Confident in the superiority of his numbers and the backing of his father, he attacked his two younger brothers, and was totally defeated, June 1658. Aurangzib pushed on his advantage, and took possession of Agra. As Shah Jahan could not be weaned from Dara's cause, he was made a State prisoner, and Aurangzib, assuming the government, marched to Delhi in pursuit of Dara. At Delhi he proclaimed himself emperor, August 1658, though his formal coronation took place a year afterwards. Shah Jahan passed the remaining years of his feeble life in honourable captivity in Agra, and died in January 1666.

His Contributions to Artistic Monuments.—Shah Jahan's love of magnificence has endowed India with monuments of noble beauty. The modern city of Delhi, with its red sandstone walls, its palace-fort by the river, its broad Chandni Chauk, the centre of a busy and opulent commerce, and its spacious and dignified Jāmi Mosque, was his erection, and was ready in 1648. It was furnished with a canal by Ali Mardan Khan, which still exists. This was just one in a whole series of Delhis, the latest of which —that being built by the British at Raisina—has not yet (1925) been completed. Shah Jahan's Pearl Mosque at Agra (finished 1653) is small in size, but exquisite in design, and affords a subtle study in light and shade. Inside, it is built entirely of marble, white, blue, and grey veined; even the inscription consists of Arabic letters in black marble inlaid on white. But the most superb monument left by Shah Jahan is the Taj Mahal, the tomb of his beloved wife. Alike in design and construction, in embellishments and accessories, in natural situation and the grouping of contemporary buildings around it, it is unrivalled. It stands in a well-proportioned and well-laid-out Mughal garden, which is entered from the south. At its back to the north is the broad stream of the Jamna. Viewed either from the garden or from across the Jamna, its white marble domes, minarets, and gold finials stand out against the blue sky, while their reflections in the water have a different meaning if seen through the placid rectangular reservoirs in the garden, or through the broken current of the deep flowing Jamna in its rugged stony bed. Priceless gems of many colours form mosaics in the interior. The loving pens of Mughal historians have recorded the distant places from which the gems were imported, including the marts of Balkh or Baghdad, or the waters of the Nile (for cat's-eye), or the Indian Ocean (for coral or mother-of-pearl). Its " sanctified and exalted " atmosphere (to use the words on Taj Bibi's tomb) places it above any human calculations of cost and material. It was begun in 1632 and completed in 1653. In spite of Shah Jahan's magnificence, his finances were prudently managed (unlike Jahangir's), his subjects were lightly taxed, and he left a full treasury.

Aurangzib, the Last of the Strong Mughals.—Aurangzib's long reign of forty-nine years (1658-1707) was the last reign of an efficient Mughal Empire. His successors were weak, and the new elements that were rising to power gradually asserted themselves. There was a century of anarchy, and another half-century of a purely nominal Mughal Empire. It will be best, therefore, to review rapidly the salient points of Aurangzib's reign and the genesis of the new elements that appeared in that reign, and then transfer our main interest to the rise of the British power in India, which won after a struggle with the rival European nations and "country powers."

His Policy.—When Aurangzib assumed the government of the empire his father was still alive and his brothers at large. But Shah Jahan was content with his dignified captivity, and Aurangzib's brothers brought about their own destruction. He wisely did not pursue the wild adventures across the Hindu Kush, whose futility he had seen as a prince. His generals extended his empire in the East; played off the Dutch against the Portuguese, whose power and piracy were suppressed in the Bay of Bengal; and annexed Chittagong and Arakan to the empire. Except for the discontent of the Hindus and the wars in the Deccan there was general peace within his territory.

His Character.—Aurangzib was a Puritan and a man of very simple habits in private life, but he kept a splendid court, and was untiring in work and personal exertion to the last days of his life. The Neapolitan doctor Gemelli Careri had an audience with him in 1695. Aurangzib was then seventy-six years of age, but he transacted all his State business personally, and wrote his orders on petitions in public darbar with his own hand without spectacles. He was courteous, cheerful, and alert, and asked the Neapolitan, as he had travelled in Turkey, about the Turkish wars in Hungary. But his undoubted abilities, courage, and strength of character, and his puritanism and asceticism, had another side. He had no friend, and he could trust no one. He treated the Hindus with contempt, and alienated the Rajputs, who had fought with valour and devotion for his ancestors, and for himself in the early years of his reign. Even his conquests were in a sense the undoing of his empire.

Affairs in the Deccan: Shivaji the Maratha.—From 1681 to the day of his death at Ahmadnagar* in March 1707, he waged

* He lies buried in a very simple tomb near Aurangabad (Nizam's Dominions).

war personally in the Deccan. Aurangzib considered himself as an authority on the tangled affairs of the Deccan, as he had twice served there as viceroy when he was a prince. But the situation had changed there greatly, and none of the agents whom he sent out gave him satisfaction. A freebooter of genius had arisen in the person of the Maratha chief Shivaji, who was thirty-one years of age at the accession of Aurangzib, 1658. We saw how Shivaji's father, still alive, was in the service of the Bijapur Sultanate; he did not die till 1664. But the feelings of loyalty that animated his father did not restrain the unruly Shivaji from committing depredations on Bijapur territory. Beginning with 1646, Shivaji, then only nineteen years of age, took possession of remote fortresses in Maratha country. When the Government of Bijapur interned his father as a hostage for the good behaviour of Shivaji (1649-1653), Shivaji intrigued with the Mughals, and got a command in their service. Under Mughal influence his father was released. Shivaji, grown more powerful, began his depredations again. When the Mughals were embroiled with Bijapur, Shivaji took advantage of the war to plunder the territory of both.

Shivaji's Career and Death.—The civil war in the Mughal Empire, which ended in Aurangzib's enthronement at Delhi, gave further opportunities to Shivaji in the remote Deccan. By 1662 he had extended systematic depredations into Mughal territory. In January 1664, he plundered the rich city of Surat for six days. He even fitted out ships to plunder the Muslim pilgrim ships that went to and from Surat. He assumed, on his father's death, the title of Raja, and began to claim independent sovereignty. He established his capital in the remote crag fortress of Raigarh or Rajgarh, near the Konkan coast, some fifty miles south of Bombay. The possession of Bombay island was then being disputed between the English and the Portuguese. A strong punitive expedition compelled him to surrender to the Mughals. He even went to the Delhi court with his son in 1666, but was disgusted with the reception he received, and escaped back to the Deccan. For a time there was truce between him and the Mughal, and he plundered the territories of Bijapur and Golkonda. He had mobile mounted troops, with which he appeared and disappeared with lightning rapidity, levying the *Chauth*, or fourth part of the revenue. This became afterwards the regular object of Maratha attacks. He sometimes joined Bijapur against Golkonda, sometimes Golkonda against Bijapur, and sometimes the Mughals against both, or either of them against the Mughals. He thus continued fighting with varying success until his death in 1680. He left no worthy successor; his sons were feeble; but the Brahman ministers whom he had employed formed an oligarchy which directed the Maratha power, as we shall see later in our history.

Destruction of Southern Kingdoms : Birth of Nizam's Dynasty.—In Aurangzib's eyes the three sores in the Deccan were the two crumbling sultanates of Bijapur and Golkonda and the elusive power of the ever mobile Marathas. He spent the maturest years of his life (1681-1707) trying to realize his dream of a settlement of the Deccan. He had no difficulty in overthrowing the kingdoms of Bijapur (October 1686) and Golkonda (September 1687). One of the bravest deeds at the siege of Golkonda was performed by a distinguished officer, Ghaziuddin Firoz Jang, whom Aurangzib afterwards rewarded with the governorship of the Deccan. It was this Firoz Jang's son, Nizam-ul-Mulk, Asaf Jah, who was viceroy of the Deccan (1713-1748) when the Mughal Empire was crumbling to pieces under Aurangzib's successors. Asaf Jah consolidated his power and founded a dynasty, that of the Nizams of Hyderabad, which still remains. His Exalted Highness the Nizam is the premier Prince of the Indian Empire, and enjoys the title of the Faithful Ally of the British Government. From another point of view his State is the last surviving fragment of the Mughal Empire, and his court continues Mughal forms, ceremonies, and traditions.

Causes of Failure with the Marathas.—As regards the Marathas, Aurangzib failed the more signally, because (1) he destroyed the counterpoise to their power in the two southern kingdoms; (2) his policy alienated the Hindus, and rallied Hindu sentiment to the Maratha standards; and (3) the Mughal camps and armies were unwieldy, and their operations were costly, whereas the Marathas were fighting mainly in their own country, with practically no baggage, and in small bands under individual initiative. After Shivaji's death the Marathas had internal dissensions; their forts were taken, and their chiefs captured and executed. But their guerilla warfare continued, and local leaders arose, urged on by hope of conquest, and protected by that light and elusive warfare which could not be defeated as long as the spirit of the people was behind it. When Aurangzib died, March 1707, a broken and disappointed man, the Deccan tangle was further from a solution than ever before.

The New Forces from Europe.—But by that time new forces had gathered strength, which offered a wholly unexpected solution after the great turmoil and anarchy of the eighteenth century. The Portuguese power had already declined, in the world as well as in India. The Dutch held a few isolated stations, but they had found their main sphere of work in the Dutch East Indies—in the islands near Java and Sumatra. Colbert's French East India Company had been formed in 1664, and had purchased land and formed the French settlement at Pondicherry (Puducheri) in 1674. Two Danish East India Companies had been formed in Copenhagen in 1612 and 1670, but had done nothing worth recording, except the acquisition of Tranquebar, eighty miles south of Pondicherry, and the establishment of the first Protestant Mission there in 1707. But the greatest progress among the European nations in India had been made by the English, who had their own settlements at Madras, Bombay, and Calcutta, besides several factories all over Aurangzib's empire. They were destined to play a leading part in subsequent history. We must now shift the scene and examine how they came to be there, what were their transactions with the Portuguese, Dutch, and French, and in what way they built up the delicately poised machinery of the British Indian Empire.

CHAPTER XI

HOW ENGLAND WON AGAINST PORTUGAL AND HOLLAND

New Vortex of European Expansion.—The story of British establishment in India is so full of romance and adventure, of deeds of reckless courage and of challenges to seemingly impossible odds, that we are apt to forget the chain of inevitable causes that led up to it. In history we have to deal soberly with the steady march of events, and view in their proper perspective acts of individual heroism or deflections caused by exceptional events. These are like the crests of the waves. It is the mighty currents which we have to examine and explain. The previous chapters have told us how India became ready for the new order—what were the forces that made for chaos, and required a new co-ordination. The subsequent chapters will show how she was drawn into the new vortex of European expansion, and how England won her supremacy, and placed herself in a position to direct the further evolution of India.

European Supremacy in the World.—Previous to the fifteenth century the Eastern and Western worlds had remained separate on the whole. There had been attempts at inter-penetration. There had been cultural and economic intercourse in varying degrees at different periods. But the balance had been maintained between them. The discovery of America (1492) not only added a new world to the horizon of the old: it offered new conditions, economic and geographical, for the expansion of the old world. The religious Reformation of the sixteenth century gave a new direction to cultural movements, with incalculable results for the progress of the world. After this the Western portion of the old world began to encroach on the Eastern portion. Europe spread out to the vast waste lands of America, and acquired the resources and the maritime skill which made her culturally and politically supreme on this globe. From the end of the eighteenth century her offshoots in America have acquired an independent existence, whose vigour and freshness may shift the balance, and make Europe relatively less important again in the world, but that question does not concern us in this history.

Three Movements that Killed Feudalism.—In what are called the Dark Ages of Europe (from the fifth to the fifteenth centuries) Europe had played a comparatively minor part in the history of the world. Before that period the Eastern Mediterranean portion had taken the lead. After that period the lead passed definitely to the Western Atlantic portion. Towards the end of that period feudalism, which had become the bulwark of law and order in a scattered agricultural population, crumbled in face of three institutions which had been gradually gathering strength for centuries. These were: (1) strong centralized monarchies, with the political ideas of territorial nationalism; (2) the growth of cities, with the economic organization of commerce and commercialism; and (3) the growth of individualism, with the ethical ideas of personal freedom and responsibility. All these three movements were factors in the establishment of the great complex of movements called the Reformation.

Why Italy Fell Back in the Race.—Although Italy had taken the lead in the Renaissance and all its intellectual movements, she had no strong centralized monarchy, and she was unable to organize her efforts to practical ends and by means of national machinery. Her cities had developed political organizations and commerce and (in the case of maritime cities like Venice and Genoa) sea-power earlier than in other parts of Europe. Italians had also discovered the land routes to the furthest Asia, and established trading and mission posts in Tartary and China. But they had no cohesion among themselves. In this respect the Italian cities contrast very unfavourably with the German cities of the north, which formed the Hanseatic League, and which developed a commercial federation of great strength. The central position of Italy, in the heart of Europe, made it a prey to the conflicts of the Empire and the Papacy, and placed Genoa and Venice at a great disadvantage before the rising power of the Turks in the Eastern Mediterranean. When the maritime power of Genoa and Venice was broken, their men of maritime genius could only find an outlet through other nations more fortunately circumstanced. The Genoese Columbus started Spain on the path to become the mistress of America; John Cabot, the son of a Venetian pilot, discovered Newfoundland under letters patent from Henry VII. of England; and Italian navigators helped in the great movement for discovery in fifteenth-century Portugal.

Portugal's Early Discoveries.—The strongest centralized States of Europe were those of the western seaboard: Portugal, Spain, France, and England. In the fifteenth century the Iberian Peninsula had been the closest in touch with Italian navigators and Arab and Jewish mathematicians, and it took up navigation, discovery, and oversea colonization first. Compared with Spain, Portugal got her complete national independence first. It became the national passion with the Portuguese to follow up the Moors to their own country, by way of the sea. Their attempt to subjugate the Moors in Morocco failed, but they pushed on by sea towards equatorial Africa, the tract which the Arabs had long known as the "rich country," *Bilād Ghana*, which from its Arabic name came to be known as the *Guinea* coast. The "riches" were the alluvial gold dust and the African slaves, both of which Portugal was the first of modern European countries to exploit. On account of the dense forests of Central Africa the Arabs had not penetrated in historical times to South Africa, but they were well acquainted with large tracts of East Africa, and held the keys of the navigation of the Indian Ocean not only from the Red Sea, but from East African ports. It was the Portuguese ambition, ever since they rounded Cape Verde in 1445 and found the African coast turning eastwards, to get round by the south of Africa to India. That was why they refused to entertain Columbus's proposal to get round to India by sailing west, as he would have done had there been no continent of America. By 1488 they had doubled the Cape, since called the Cape of Good Hope, and though they had encountered storms which made navigation difficult, they continued to work for the south-eastern passage to India round Africa, and accomplished it in 1498.

Spain's Expansion in the West.—The Spanish king and queen adopted and financed Columbus's scheme for a westward passage to India. By doing so Spain missed India, but by the discovery of America in 1492, eventually became mistress of the riches of Mexico and Peru. In those days of European expansion the nation which discovered a land claimed not only sovereignty over it, but a monopoly of its trade. The Pope still claimed to be the arbiter between the nations, and in 1493 Alexander VI. issued a bull apportioning the world as between Spain and Portugal, the two Catholic countries in the van of exploration. A line of demarcation was drawn at a longitude 100 leagues west of the Azores and Cape Verde Islands, the first-fruits of Portuguese colonization. Spain was to have the monopoly west of this line, and Portugal to the east of this line. By treaty between Spain and Portugal this line was altered to one 370 leagues west of Cape Verde, which would be equivalent to 50 degrees west of Greenwich. This gave Brazil and all Africa and discoveries east of Africa to Portugal, and the greater part of America and discoveries west of America to Spain. When Magellan, in the service of Spain, rounded South America through the straits known after his name (1520) in pursuit of the original plan of a westward passage to the Indies, and actually reached the Philippines in the Indian Archipelago (1521), he was strictly poaching on Portuguese preserves, but his action explains how Spain got a footing so far east.

France and Holland on the Scene Later: First English Struggles with Spain and Portugal.—Beyond this the story of Spain does not concern Eastern history. French explorers and navigators had been busy quite early in the race of exploration, but France as a State was too deeply involved in wars at home and near home to turn her attention to maritime expansion. Moreover, her religion had not yet found national expression in the conflict between the Reformation and the Catholic Church. Her struggles for expansion came later. Holland was still, at the end of the sixteenth century, struggling for her independence against Spain. England had to fight her way, in the home waters and in the West, with Spain; and in the East with Portugal. The prize was the commerce and navigation of the East.

Trade Routes to the East: Their Importance.—In the fifteenth and sixteenth centuries the countries of Europe were more or less self-contained. The main streams of foreign commerce (taking no account of local currents) may be said to have run from East to West. Articles of luxury, such as silk and silk cloth, fine cottons (which as late as 1664 were classified for tariff purposes in England as "linen"), porcelain, pearls and precious stones, dyes (such as indigo), perfumes, incense, and gums, and above all spices (such as pepper, cloves, nutmegs, ginger, cinnamon, etc.), were imported from the East. With the growth of population in northern latitudes, where vegetables could not be grown all the year round, to temper a meat diet, spices ceased to be a luxury and became a necessity. There was nothing much that the East desired which could be exported from the West except woollen cloth of various sorts, leather, tin, and lead (these were the famous staples of England), but the greater part of the balance was made up with the precious metals, which the East absorbed in enormous quantities. The main trade route was through Constantinople or ports in the Eastern Mediterranean; it bifurcated (going eastwards) into a sea-route from the Persian Gulf to the coast of India and beyond, and a land route across Persia and Central Asia to China. A secondary route, which in certain political conditions became the main trade route between East and West, was through Egypt to Suez, and then by the Red Sea to the ports of Southern India and beyond. As the Ottoman Empire grew, it deprived Venice and Genoa, its rivals in the Eastern Mediterranean, of their lucrative Eastern trade as fed by the main route. As it spread to Egypt (1517) it blocked the Red Sea route. The problem for Christendom was to turn the flank of the Turks, and discover some other route by sea.

Quest for the North-Western and the North-Eastern Passage to India.—The search for such a route led Spain westwards to America, and Portugal south-eastwards round the continent of Africa. Both these nations grew powerful by sea, and, having parcelled out their spheres of maritime influence, sought to establish monopolies, and keep out other nations. The English (as well as other nations) tried to discover a north-west passage to India through the polar regions as early as the end of the fifteenth century. Norwegian mariners had, from their geographical position, for many centuries explored these regions.

Many of them were settled in Bristol, where English capital and enterprise, backed by the national monarchy under the Tudors, used their experience and the science of Italian navigators to provide an outlet for English energy. No north-west passage to India was discovered, but the fisheries of Newfoundland and Labrador were added to England's source of wealth, and eventually led to the expansion of the British Empire in that direction. An alternative passage tried was the north-eastern passage "to Cathay," round the northern coasts of Norway. This search, too, failed in its main object, but it opened up communication between the English and the Tsar of "Muscovy." The Russia or Muscovy Company was formed in 1554; through Russia it traded with Persia, and through Persia an attempt was made to open up the Indian trade, but the route was too circuitous, and altogether impracticable. What was wanted was a through route to the spice-producing countries by sea.

Significance of Discovery of Cape Route.—The discovery of such a route—that round the Cape of Good Hope, in 1498, by Vasco da Gama—forms the story of the *Lusiads*, the national epic of Portugal. That discovery was not merely a national event in the history of Portugal. It was a world event. It completely altered the relations of the East and the West, not only commercially, but culturally and politically. It was the realization of a dream of which another and earlier consequence was the discovery of America, with its gold and its boundless lands for the absorption of the energies and the populations of an awakening Europe. After the discovery of the Cape route to India all the transport services passed into the hands of Europe—not only those between Europe and Asia or Europe and Africa, but also between the ports of Africa and Asia themselves, and side by side, and connected with the movement, there was a corresponding growth in the American direction. The tremendous sea-power developed in consequence made Europe—and an America colonized from Europe—supreme in the world. New discoveries in tools and appliances were stimulated, and the supply of manufactured articles became the privilege of the West, while the East was gradually reduced to the position of a supplier of raw materials. The country which eventually reaped the greatest benefits from this movement was England, and the discovery of the Cape route by Portugal may well be considered an event in the British history of India.

Vasco da Gama's Voyage: (*a*) *From Lisbon to Mozambique.*—We have seen how and why Portugal was the first of the European nations to take up navigation, and her motives for pushing on her discoveries and conquests—for she considered them synonymous—in Africa. She was the first European nation to use the mariner's compass. Prince Henry the Navigator, of Portugal, who died in 1460, devoted his life to the study of charts and navigation. His mother was an English princess, a daughter of John of Gaunt. In his day the Portuguese caravels (fast sailing ships) excelled those of any other nation. The science and art of navigation became the care of the State. A State policy—sustained for three generations—led to the dispatch of an expedition, in July 1497, consisting of three ships under Vasco da Gama. By November 20th he had doubled the Cape of Good Hope. After this his real exploration began. The course now was northwards. The coast was green and wooded, unlike the desert coast of West Africa. But there was a dreadful current between here and Madagascar, which combined with storms to render further progress extremely hazardous. Vasco overcame all difficulties with his skill, daring, and resolution. After arrival off the coast of Mozambique on March 1, 1498, he was practically in the region of Arab ports and Arab seas.

(*b*) *From Mozambique to Calicut: Arab Organization of Trade, Shipping, and Navigation.*—The Arabs were not at that time an organized nation. Some centuries before, they had spread themselves over Western Asia, Northern Africa, and Southern Europe, and the Arabic language had become the language of the arts and sciences, including that of navigation. The standard work on the navigation of the seas of India, China, and Indonesia was written in Arabic between the years 1462 and 1490 by Shihab-ud-din Ahmad bin Mājid. It summed up the theory and the experience of a community which had dominated the Eastern seas for some centuries. Nearly all the ports, commerce, shipping, and navigation of the Indian Ocean, the Red Sea, and the Asiatic coasts of the Pacific were in their hands. Their power was even more real than that of the Hanseatic League in the Baltic and the European coasts of the Atlantic. But they had no organized State behind them and no political policy, nor had the rule of force yet been introduced into commerce east of Suez. Into such a world came the three ships of Vasco da Gama, the first scouts of the crusading and filibustering warriors whose aim was to "destroy the Arab and Oriental Turk, and Gentoo" (Hindu), "and drink the water of the sacred Ganges" (*Lusiads*, i., 8). Their fury was to be particularly directed against the Muslims. The flank of the conquering western Turk was to be turned in the East, and even Mecca and Medina were to be overthrown if possible. Port Melinda, about fifty miles north of Mombasa, was reached in April 1498. There they saw gardens, flowers, and orange groves; a flourishing city, with stone-built houses; dresses of silk and embroidery; and merchants from the west coast of India. They lingered for some weeks, and were provided with an experienced Muslim pilot, who considered Gama's astrolabe "very imperfect." Under his guidance they recrossed the Equator, and picked up one by one the familiar northern constellations. About 10° N. they struck due east, and arrived off Calicut (Southern India) about May, June, or August, 1498.

What Gama Saw and Did in Calicut.—This was not the first time that the Portuguese had been seen in India. Many years before this John II., King of Portugal, had sent two of his equerries overland, and they had visited Malabar to reconnoitre. Gama's adventure was also a preliminary reconnaissance, but it established the sea link round the Cape. At Calicut Gama found a Tunisian Muslim who spoke Spanish as well as the Indian languages, and acted as his interpreter. Later he met a Polish Jew who came to him as a minister from the "King of Goa," but whom Gama put to the torture as a spy, and took with him to Portugal. The Zamorin (king) of Calicut was at first inclined to be friendly to Gama, but according to the Portuguese accounts, the Arab traders saw their trade monopoly threatened by the new arrivals, and set the Zamorin against them. This is probable, but it is equally probable that the high-handed action of the Portuguese was a factor in turning the Hindus of Calicut as well as the Arabs against him. For the present he had no sufficient force behind him, and he seems to have sailed on the return journey to Portugal early in 1499, arriving at Lisbon by the month of September. He did not fail, however, to take a few captive noblemen from Calicut, on the plea of treachery to him, and with the promise that they "should be returned to India when they were enabled from experience to give an account of Portugal." History is silent as to the fate of these miserable men.

Subsequent Portuguese Expeditions.—But the Portuguese returned. They had spied out the riches and the weakness of India, and the divisions that made India an easy prey from the sea. They were rewarded handsomely by their King Emmanuel, who assumed the high-sounding title of "Lord of the Conquest, Navigation, and Commerce of Ethiopia, Arabia, Persia, and India." A more powerful fleet—of thirteen ships—was fitted out and dispatched in March 1500, under the command of Cabral. In sailing a little too far west of the western bulge of Africa Cabral incidentally reached Brazil, and took possession of its enormous territory for Portugal. Brazil still remains the strongest bulwark of Portuguese civilization, although long since (from 1822) separated from Portugal. Cabral duly reached Calicut, and established a factory, but there was conflict and bloodshed. Some Portuguese were killed, and in revenge they burned some Calicut ships in harbour, and returned to Lisbon in July 1501. The Portuguese were now launched in their career of revenge, hatred, and destruction. In February 1502, an armada of twenty ships, including some fighting vessels which were to be left in Indian waters to protect Portuguese interests, sailed from Lisbon, under the command once again of Vasco da Gama. He bombarded Calicut, committed horrible atrocities on unarmed Indians, and behaved like a pirate of the worst sort, though under the flag of Portugal. Such conduct was not likely to advance the commerce of Portugal. Show of force had to be supplemented with diplomacy. Negotiations were opened with Cochin (about 100 miles south of Calicut), Quilon (about eighty miles south of Cochin), and Cannanore (about fifty miles north of Calicut)—a sort of Hindu coalition against the Hindu Zamorin of Calicut who had dared to protest against the high-handedness of the Portuguese. Trade rivalry and political jealousy also helped to throw these ports into the arms of the Portuguese, who were able, on this occasion, to carry much wealth and booty to Portugal.

Policy of Building Forts and Perpetual Warfare against Muslims.—Hereafter the Portuguese sent ships and soldiers in much greater force, and began to build forts, not only on the Indian coast, but also on the African coast on the way to India. They began also to maintain permanent sea and land forces in the East. Almeida in 1505 brought 1,500 Portuguese soldiers, and was given the title of Viceroy of Cochin, Cannanore, and Quilon. Hindu Rajas were set one against another as occasion demanded. But against the Muslims a policy of constant warfare was adopted. In pursuance of this policy Muslim ships were attacked wherever they were met with, whether they were merchant ships or pilgrim ships, and whatever nationality they belonged to. In this way the southern Muslim kingdom of Bijapur, the Muslim kingdom of Gujarat, which was afterwards incorporated into the Mughal Empire, the Mughal Empire, the King of Persia, the Sultan of Egypt, who commanded the Red Sea before his power was absorbed in that of the Ottoman Turks, as well as numerous petty Arab powers which were also absorbed in the Turkish Empire, were attacked in turn. The Ottoman Turks had been an increasing sea-power in the Mediterranean, and after they conquered Egypt in 1517 they spread out into the Red Sea and the Arabian waters. The Turkish navy in the days of its power tried to grapple with the Portuguese in Eastern waters with varying success. They tried to help such naval forces as Gujarat possessed on the western coast of India, but there was not much solidarity between Gujarat and Turkey. Nor were the Turks able to find any timber for shipbuilding on the arid coasts of the Red Sea or of Eastern Arabia. There was then no canal between Suez and the Mediterranean. The Portuguese had little difficulty in establishing their naval supremacy in the Eastern seas long before the complete destruction of Turkish naval power in the Mediterranean by the combined attack of Europe at Lepanto in 1571.

Albuquerque, 1509-1515: Portuguese become Masters of Goa and the Eastern Seas.—By 1507-1509 the Portuguese had visited Ceylon (which they conquered later), and penetrated to the Malay Peninsula and the coasts of China, which had not yet been identified with the "Cathay" of the overland travellers of mediæval Europe. The greatest statesman, conqueror, and administrator whom the Portuguese sent out to the East was Affonso d'Albuquerque. From 1509 to 1515 he was the Governor of the Portuguese possessions in the East, which he both extended and consolidated. In 1510 he captured Goa, and made it the capital of Portuguese Asia. The Bijapur kingdom, to which it had previously belonged, made two temporarily successful and several unsuccessful attacks on it, but it has belonged to the Portuguese ever since. It was the chief port of Western India, through which horses were imported from the Persian Gulf. In 1511 he took the important city of Malacca, in the Straits of that name, between Sumatra and the Malay Peninsula. It was estimated to have a population of 100,000, and was the headquarters of the four principal Muslim sea-faring communities, from Gujarat, Bengal, Java, and China. It commanded the whole westward trade of the Spice Islands (otherwise called the Moluccas), in the Eastern Archipelago, just east of Celebes. The most important of them, for our purposes, was Amboyna (latitude 3·36° S), the island *par excellence* of cloves, as the Banda Islands (latitude 4·35° S) were *par excellence* the nutmeg islands. Albuquerque sent out an exploring expedition to the Spice Islands from Malacca in 1511, though a Portuguese factory was not founded there till ten years later.

Arabia and the Red Sea: Albuquerque's Disgrace and Death.—Albuquerque then turned his attention to the Arabian Sea and the Red Sea. His object was to exclude Indian traders from these regions, and take possession of the whole commerce for Portugal. In 1513-1514 he made a strong attempt on the Red Sea and its gateway, the harbour of Aden. In this he failed. But his attack upon Ormuz, at the entrance to the Persian Gulf, succeeded in 1515, the last year of his governorship. Before his death at sea, off Goa, December 16, 1515, he had made Portugal mistress of the principal trading ports of the

East, covering over 12,000 miles of coast, and supreme at sea. But he had made many enemies, who played upon the King of Portugal's jealousy of his power. He just received the orders about his supersession before he died. Among his last words were: "In bad repute with men because of the King, and in bad repute with the King because of the men, it were well that I were gone."

Causes of Portuguese Decline.—Albuquerque was a strong man; but his policy, though immediately successful, carried with it the seeds of decay. He tried to incite the Hindus against the Muslims, and later, Hindus against Hindus, and Muslims against Muslims. In religious fanaticism, though he was less extreme than some of his successors, he was not free from the mental attitude which ended in the establishment of the Inquisition at Goa in 1560 and won for the Portuguese the implacable hatred of all nations in the East. Goa was a magnificent city in the sixteenth century, and many great Portuguese (individuals and families) lived and died there, but it never became the centre of a new culture, and the Portuguese never attempted to understand the East. Though Camoens' epic, the *Lusiads*, is the very embodiment of Portuguese patriotism, it does not fail to lament the failure of the Portuguese to appreciate the refinements of culture. Even in trade, commerce, and material civilization, the Portuguese were unable to introduce any permanent new factors into the East. Goa soon became luxurious and corrupt, from the Governor downwards, and its poison spread to all the Portuguese settlements in the East. The cynical saying about governors was based on truth: that they were installed the first year; they robbed the second; and then packed up in the third to sail away. In these circumstances no large or fruitful policy could be developed. The strict State monopoly of trade allowed no chance to private enterprise. Added to all was the undoubted fact that the population of Portugal was too small for the enormous area over which Portugal tried to spread. Within a century of their first expansion their decline began. King Sebastian's disastrous expedition into Morocco ended with the battle of Alkazar Kabir, 1578, in which the flower of his army and the manhood of his country were utterly destroyed, and from which he himself never returned. In 1580 Philip II. of Spain absorbed Portugal, and thus began the sixty years' captivity for Portugal (1580-1640) which irrevocably destroyed her power in the East. Portugal's greatness in world history spans but three generations. Vasco da Gama, the discoverer, was born (1460) in the year in which Prince Henry the Navigator died; and Gama died (1524) in the year in which Camoens the poet was born.

Rise of Holland.—The decline of Portugal was connected with the same series of events which brought up Holland and England to the front in world politics and in sea-power. Holland had been a part of the Spanish Netherlands in the empire of Charles V. (1516-1556). By the middle of the sixteenth century Protestantism had definitely won its place as a political power in North Germany, Scandinavia, Holland, and England. Spain under Philip II. (1556-1598), who married Mary Tudor, Queen of England, attempted to crush Protestantism both in Holland and in England. In Holland it led to revolt (1572) and the proclamation of the Dutch Republic in 1581. The Dutch had for some time been the carriers of Western Europe, and had distributed the merchandise of the East from the port of Lisbon, thus forming the last link in the chain of Portuguese commerce. In 1580 Philip, having seized Portugal, closed Lisbon to his rebel "subjects," the Dutch. But the effect was the very opposite to that intended. It forced the Dutch, who had hitherto, like the English, attempted the north-eastern and north-western passages, to defy Spain and her Portuguese shipping, and force the Cape route for their own ships and commerce. But Dutch commerce was not a State monopoly. Indeed, their State was younger than their commerce. The Dutch formed numerous trading companies after the destruction of the Spanish Armada by England in 1588. They were amalgamated by their States-General into the Dutch East India Company in 1602.

Dutch Enterprise and Supremacy in the East.—The first Dutch fleet to double the Cape of Good Hope and visit what has since become the Dutch East Indies (in the Malay Archipelago) sailed from Holland in April 1595, and returned in 1597. They had (as was inevitable) a conflict with the Portuguese at Bantam, on the north-west extremity of the island of

Java. Bantam, though now unimportant, figures prominently in the history of both Dutch and English expansion in the East Indian Archipelago, and was the capital of a powerful and imperial sultanate before the Dutch conquest. It is situated close to Serang, the little European settlement usually shown on ordinary maps. A British factory was located at Bantam from 1601-1603 to 1682, and in the early days of Madras (1639-1654) Bantam was given control over Madras. The Dutch were not slow in profiting by the weakness of the Portuguese in the East. In 1601 they attacked the Portuguese in Ceylon, of which they became masters in 1658. By 1602 they had defeated a powerful Portuguese fleet in the Banda seas south of the Molucca Islands, after which their naval supremacy was speedily established. They founded the new city of Batavia, in Java, a few miles east of Bantam, on the site of an older Malay city, in 1519, and have held it as the headquarters of their East Indies ever since. Between 1616 and 1628 they explored the west coast of Australia, which they called New Holland. Both New Zealand (from Zeeland, a province of Holland) and Tasmania (from the Dutch navigator Tasman) bear evidence in their names of early Dutch work in exploration. Cape Town was built by the Dutch in 1652, and the colony they established there was not formally incorporated in the British Empire until 1814.

Two Points in Dutch Policy: How Holland Dropped out of India Proper.—Dutch policy was actuated by two main motives. One was revenge on Spain and Portugal, which were under one Crown when the Dutch entered the East, for the injustice which they had suffered under Spain in their own country. The difference of religion was a subordinate motive which was mixed up with the political motive. This resistance of Protestant to Catholic powers also coloured the English attitude against Spain and Portugal in the last days of the sixteenth century. But when Holland became all-powerful in the Eastern seas early in the seventeenth century, and economic and political jealousies asserted themselves, England was more in conflict with the Dutch in the East than with the Portuguese in the days of Portuguese decline. The other motive governing Holland's policy in the East was that of colonization and settlement. She not only sought the monopoly of commerce and the carrying trade, but she entered the field of production in the Spice Islands, and sought to establish a monopoly in such production. From this point of view India proper was not a promising field for her. On the other hand, the Jews who had been persecuted out of the Iberian Peninsula settled in Holland, and became a valuable asset under the Dutch flag for the development of new financial and colonial enterprises connected with the East. Thus it came about that although Holland possessed early in the seventeenth century an enormous number of factories all over the Eastern seas previously dominated by Portugal, she began to restrict her activities more and more to the Malay Archipelago, and England, especially after 1623, to concentrate more and more on India.

Different Outlook of England.—In the East England's outlook was different. There she sought only economic and naval and subsequently political expansion (until Australasia and the Cape fell to her lot). In the matter of colonization and new fields and methods of production her activities were directed to the boundless lands of the New Hemisphere. But these Western activities in their early stages must be studied side by side with her Eastern activities, for the latter became a big factor in her economic life at home and in her expansion all over the world.

Her Enterprise as a United Nation under a National Monarchy.—England was neither the first nor the last European nation to join in the race for European expansion. When once her strong Tudor monarchy had been established over a re-united nation she asserted her right to Imperial dignity in her Crown. Her sea-dogs were as bold and as intrepid as any. In support of the anti-Spanish policy of the Tudors England's sea-captains roved the seas all round the world. Drake, in 1587, in anticipation of the conflict with the Spanish Armada, burnt 10,000 tons of Spanish shipping in Cadiz itself—a daring feat described with the lightness of Elizabethan humour as "singeing the King of Spain's beard." The destruction of the Spanish Armada in 1588 broke up the Spanish and Portuguese monopoly at sea (Portugal being then under Spanish "captivity"). In bringing about this result Holland and England co-operated, and the defeat was practically the defeat of the Counter-Reformation as against the Reformation. But it had, nevertheless, an intensely national significance for England. English Catholics and Protestants—and in English Protestantism there were various shades which afterwards appeared in the conflict of the Puritans and Independents against the Established Church—all united with an intensity of English national life. And their sovereign, Queen Elizabeth—whose boast was that she was "mere English"—knew the heart of the nation, and became the very embodiment of the national aspirations.

Her Resolve to Seek the Riches of the East by the Cape Route.—Englishmen now refused to be contented with the search for the north-eastern and north-western passage, and resolved to seek riches and power by attempting the Cape route. The Dutch, as we have seen, had been a little before them. In 1599 they raised the price of pepper against England from 3s. to 6s. and 8s. per pound, and the London merchants resolved, under their Lord Mayor, to establish direct connection with the East Indies. That was how England (Scotland still held aloof) came to India, with momentous consequences to both countries and to the world. We have already seen how and why other nations of Europe, who took up the adventure first, dropped out in the struggle. We must now consider in detail the growth of English commerce, the foundation of the East India Company, its work in the making of India, and the legacy it left to the British Crown and the British and Indian peoples.

CHAPTER XII

THE GROWTH OF ENGLISH COMMERCE AND OF THE EAST INDIA COMPANY

A Romance of Commerce.—An extraordinary romance of commerce is to be found in the history of the East India Company. We must briefly review the growth of English commerce in order to understand the inception of the Company. Its constitution, laws, and privileges, and its position in relation to the English State and the States in India, are grounded in precedents. And yet the history which it pursued is unique, as are also the problems which it has left behind for the British Empire and for the Eastern and Western worlds.

Foreign Merchants and their Privileges in England.—Under the Great Charter (1215) trade was to be free (chapters 41 and 42), and the ancient liberties and free customs of London were specially safeguarded (chapter 13). It was with reference to foreign trading companies that State charters were first used in England. The Hanseatic League, an association of German traders of the Baltic, spread themselves north and east. They established "Counters" (Komtors) in outlying trading posts and factories, in Russia, Scandinavia, Flanders, and England. Their object was to secure trading privileges for German towns, with the right to administer justice among themselves according to their recognized legal customs, and to make financial provision for their common interests. Cologne was the first of these towns to have a guildhall in London and to form a "hansa." Other German towns established similar hansas in London. In a parliamentary petition of 1422 the London "counter" is mentioned as the Steelyard; it claimed jurisdiction over the other factories in England. These privileges granted to foreign merchants were confirmed by various charters of English kings.

English Export Trade and Manufactures.—The earliest foreign commerce of England had been mainly in raw commodities. The earliest trading companies were the merchants of the Staple. The "Staples" were five in number: wool, woolfels (sheepskins with the wool on), leather, tin, and lead. The merchants of the Staple had the monopoly for the purchase and export of these staple commodities. Staple towns were appointed as centres of trade, and their customs and privileges confirmed by a statute of 1353. With the decay of feudalism and the growth of towns, English manufactures grew. The eastern counties led off with the woollen manufactures in the fourteenth century. These manufactures spread rapidly in Yorkshire and the Midlands, and increased the prosperity of the eastern ports, and in Somersetshire, for which the port of Bristol provided an outlet already noted for other staples. By the fifteenth and sixteenth centuries the export wool was already manufactured woollen cloth rather than raw wool. Side by side with the growth of English industry went the growth of English shipping. The best English kings had always put English commerce at the forefront of their policy. But there was always a conflict of interests between the foreign merchants and English merchants with regard to the foreign trade.

Tudor Policy of Extending Foreign Trade.—The Tudors were the first to solve this conflict in the interests of English merchants. Henry VII. negotiated commercial treaties which advanced the interests of English commerce and shipping both in the Netherlands and in Scandinavia. In Antwerp and Holland he obtained for English merchants freedom from local tolls, and the permission to sell cloth retail as well as wholesale. By an alliance with Denmark he obtained privileges for English merchants and shipping, which broke the monopoly enjoyed by the Hanseatic League in that country. The Mediterranean trade was similarly opened up to English goods and shipping by a treaty with Florence, which broke the Venetian monopoly of the carrying trade. His charter and financial assistance to John Cabot on his westward voyages of discovery (1496-1498) led to the acquisition of Newfoundland, which Cabot mistook for the land of the Great Khan of Tartary in Asia.

Chartered Companies under Elizabeth.—As English manufactures grew and began to predominate among the exports, the merchants of the Staple fell into the background, and the

Merchant Adventurers began to develop their influence. They were an offshoot of the Mercers' Company, the premier company among the twelve great Livery Companies of London, with a charter dating from the end of the fourteenth century. In those days "mercery" was simply merchandise, such as could be sold by the small balance, and included spices and drugs. Under Elizabeth the Merchant Adventurers not only got the Hanseatic privileges curtailed in England, but they were able to establish a factory in Hamburg. English chartered companies for different foreign countries began to be formed. The Russian Company was formed in 1554. The Turkey and Levant Company was formed in 1581, and sent merchants through the Mediterranean to Aleppo and Baghdad, and thence through the Persian Gulf and the Arabian Sea to India, to purchase goods at Lahore and Agra, and some of these merchants penetrated as far as Malacca. Shakespeare mentions Aleppo more than once. Where the witch exclaims, in *Macbeth* (I. iii. 10): "Her husband's to Aleppo gone, Master o' th' *Tiger*"; the allusion seems to be to Fitch's voyage in the *Tiger* begun in 1583 and ended in 1591. This Master Ralph Fitch and his two companions were the first English merchants to visit India, and they carried a letter from Queen Elizabeth to Akbar. It commends their "curteous and honest boldnesse" to Akbar, who took one of Fitch's companions (Leades) as a jeweller into his service at Fatehpur Sikri.

Fitch the First English Merchant in India.—Fitch on his return wrote an account which seems to have stirred much public interest about India. He crossed Asia Minor and got to Ormuz (or Hormuz), which he describes as "the driest island in the world; for there is nothing growing in it but only salt." But it was the emporium of the trade between East and West in spices, drugs, silks, tapestries, and pearls (which mainly went westward), and horses, which were the chief article of import into India from the Persian Gulf. Both on account of its commercial and strategic importance the Portuguese had occupied it in 1514. The Englishmen were treated very roughly by the Portuguese; they were imprisoned and robbed, and sent to Goa. They were in prison, and afterwards under detention on charges of espionage for four and a half months, after which they made good their escape. An impartial Dutch observer, Linschoten, who saw them in Goa, gives them a very good character, praising their great courtesy and commercial manners, "whereby they won much credit, and were beloved of all men." Fitch seems to have made a roundabout journey, through Bijapur, Golkonda, and Malwa to the court of Akbar at Agra and Fatehpur Sikri. "Agra and Fatehpur," he says, "are two very great cities, either of them much greater than London, and very populous. Between Agra and Fatehpur are twelve miles [actually about twenty-three], and all the way is a market of victuals and other things, as full as though a man were still in a town, and so many people as if a man were in a market." From Agra to Bengal he travelled down the rivers Jamna and Ganges in a caravan of 180 boats laden with salt, opium, asafœtida, lead, carpets, and "divers other commodities." He has many shrewd observations on cities, men, and manners. Of a Fakir in a market-place he writes: "They took him for a great man, but sure he was a lazy lubber." He passed on to Burma and Malacca, and returned via Ceylon, the west coast of India, the Persian Gulf, and overland through Aleppo.

Lancaster the First English Sailor to Use the Cape Route.—It was obvious that the overland route to India was not only hazardous, but gave no scope to the expansion of British shipping. The Portuguese were astride the route in their fort at Ormuz. They must be beaten at sea by British ships. The thirst for riches and discovery was coupled with the thirst for maritime adventure. Captain James Lancaster was the first British seaman to go by the Cape route and appear in Indian waters. He carried out a series of privateering exploits in the Bay of Bengal and the Indian Ocean against the Portuguese in 1591-1592. But English ships were not yet well equipped, and this was merely a piece of reconnoitring by sea, as the Turkey Company's efforts through Fitch and others had reconnoitred India by land.

Elaborate Preparations and Foundation of East India Company, 1600.—In 1592 some English privateers captured a great Portuguese carrack (heavy merchant-ship) returning from Goa to Lisbon, and richly laden with Eastern merchandise—jewels, spices, drugs, and textiles. With it they captured an important document, "The Notable Register or Matricola of the whole Government and Trade of the Portuguese in the East Indies." The merchants of London now (1599) drew up a memorial to Queen Elizabeth for the incorporation of the East India Company, and obtained their charter on December 31, 1600. The foundations were well and carefully laid. The merchants had armed themselves with every kind of information and furnished detailed memoranda, and the Queen's officers had, by way of precaution, demanded and obtained "the names of such kings as are absolute, and either have war or traffic with the King of Spain" (who was also then King of Portugal), right round the coasts of Africa, and in India, Further India, China, Japan ("the manifold and populous silver islands of the Japones"), and the newly discovered country of Korea. The people who had contributed information included navigators, travellers, ambassadors, merchants, and that great collector of voyages, Richard Hakluyt, Archdeacon of Westminster. Charts, maps, lists, and notes about political and economic geography, were carefully prepared or translated for the Company, including one on the commodities of the East, and another on the chief places where "sundry sort of spices do grow in the East," together with their political conditions. The venture was thus launched under the best auspices, and after the most elaborate preparations.

Constitution of the Company.—The East India Company's official name in the charter of 1600 was: The Governor and Company of Merchants of London, trading to the East Indies. To them was assigned the monopoly of trading to the East Indies—that is, to all places between the Cape of Good Hope and the Straits of Magellan, except such as might be already occupied by the subjects of States in amity with the Queen of England. They were allowed to export in each voyage £30,000 in gold and silver, also English goods for the first four voyages exempt from duties, and to re-export Indian goods in English ships to the end of the charter. The period was fifteen years, subject to earlier cancellation on two years' notice if not found advantageous to the country. The coat-of-arms granted to the Company in 1601 was a purely English coat-of-arms, without any of the local colour introduced by the Emperor Charles V. to the first circumnavigator* of the globe in 1522; for he gave branches of clove, cinnamon, and nutmeg as armorial bearings. The East India Company, on its reconstitution in 1708-1709, received a new coat-of-arms and motto, "Auspicio Regis et Senatus Angliæ." These are the ones so familiar in India, and were really the arms of the "New" Company which absorbed the Old Company in 1708. But the history of the Company was continuous (from 1600 to 1858), though chequered, as we shall see.

"Separate" Voyages, 1601-1612: Profits 200 per Cent.—The first operations of the Company were not those of a joint-stock company. From 1601 to 1612 a series of "separate" voyages were arranged. For any given voyage a separate capital fund was subscribed by such members of the Company as chose to do so; they managed that particular voyage, and took the whole of its profit or loss; and at the end of the voyage they wound up its accounts. The original capital subscribed for membership must have been of a small amount, and merely entitled the member to use the monopoly conferred by charter. The first expedition sailed in May 1601, under the command of Captain Lancaster, who had already been to the Eastern seas. It ended in 1603. In round figures the subscription was £68,000, of which the greater part was expended in the purchase and equipment of ships, and the provision of bullion to carry abroad for trade purposes, and a very small proportion was invested in goods. Queen Elizabeth struck some special coins for the Indian trade.† But the English payments abroad must mainly have been in bullion. The small quantity of goods taken was more for presents than for stock in trade, as there was then very little demand in the East for Western goods. Thus both British commodities and foreign goods were taken, as advised by experts. The first voyage was directed entirely to the Spice Islands, and succeeded

* To Magellan must be ascribed the first circumnavigation of the globe, but he died in the Philippines and never returned to Spain. The honours were awarded by Charles V. to Sebastian del Cano, the commander of the sole surviving ship of Magellan's squadron.

† The "portcullis" crowns, and half-crowns, which were meant to displace the Spanish dollars, or "reals of eight," then used widely in European commerce in the East (also called "piastres" or "pesos"= about 4s.).

in establishing a "House of Trade" (factory) in Bantam, 1603. The profits of the voyage were derived from the capture of a Portuguese ship, with its cargo of calico and spices, the sale of the spices purchased in the East, both at home and the surplus to other European countries, and the realization on the fleet. Speaking generally, the profits on the spice trade were enormous. In the Third Voyage (1606-1607) a small quantity of cloves of Amboyna, purchased for £2,949, were sold in London for £36,287 (being over twelve times the cost price). The net profits on this voyage were 234 per cent. Taking all the "separate" voyages together, and allowing for the loss of ships and other misadventures, the net profits were hardly ever below 100 per cent., and were usually over 200 per cent.

Company's Transactions in India.—The Third Voyage was remarkable in that one of its three ships visited India proper. The commander was Captain William Hawkins. He had had previous experience in Turkey. On August 24, 1608, this dashing young English sailor anchored off Surat, a Mughal port, then called the Gate of India. He sent off his ship to join her consorts at Bantam, and proceeded to Agra to the court of the Great Mughal. Jahangir was on the throne, and though the Portuguese used every art to prejudice the Englishman's chances, his winning manners and ability to converse in Turkish made him a favourite with the Emperor. He won recognition and privileges for his Company and his nation, and was given an estate and position in the Mughal Court. By 1611-1612 the Company was trading in the western Mughal ports, Cambay and Surat, notwithstanding the hostility of the Portuguese at sea. Captain Best successfully engaged a superior force of the Portuguese in a river fight near Surat in 1612, and much enhanced the prestige of the English. They were now able to establish factories at Surat, Ahmadabad, Cambay, and other places in Mughal territory, with an agreement to pay no more than a 3½ per cent. duty on their goods. This arrangement was confirmed by a decree of the emperor in 1613. In 1611 a factory had also been established on the east coast of India, at Masulipatam, in territory belonging to the southern kingdom of Golkonda, not yet brought under Mughal sway. The trade of the east coast ports was mainly in fine cottons; that of the western ports of Gujarat consisted of cotton and silk textiles, indigo (" the blues," used for dyes; bought in Agra at 1s. 2d. per pound, and sold in London at 5s.); raw silk (mainly received from Persia), and other miscellaneous goods. The lower western coast (Malabar), producing pepper, was still closed to the English.

Renewal of Company's Charter in Perpetuity, 1609.—The Company was not only exposed abroad to the hostility of the Portuguese and the competition of the Dutch. At home it had to meet the jealousy excited by its profits and its monopoly. The Stuarts, who now occupied the throne of England, had not the same understanding of the national life as Elizabeth, and in 1604 James I. granted a licence to Sir Edward Michelborne in violation of the Company's charter. This was the court favourite whom the Treasury had suggested for employment by the Company in 1600, but whom the Company had refused on the ground that they did not want any " gentleman " in any place of charge, but men of their own quality (*i.e.*, merchants and adventurers). The Company was powerful, and got redress for the Michelborne licence by a further strengthening of their position, for their charter was renewed in 1609 (long before its expiration) *in perpetuity*, with all their previous rights and privileges, subject only, as before, to a notice of termination (now three years'), if found injurious to the nation.

Ship-Building and "Joint-Stock" Operations.—The Company began to build large ships, and was the most powerful agency for the growth of British sea-power. The good ship the *Trades Increase*, 1,110 tons, was by far the biggest merchant ship yet built in England, and was launched with great ceremony before the King himself in the Company's dockyard at Deptford, for her maiden voyage in 1610. The Company abandoned the system of " separate " voyages after 1612. In future they resolved to carry on trade by a joint-stock only. The profits had been sufficiently large to enable them to raise £429,000 for the trade of four annual voyages in the years 1613-1616. In 1617-1618 a second joint-stock was raised, and in 1631-1632 a third. A fourth joint-stock was attempted to be issued in 1638-1642, but it failed. The Company's affairs had by this time fallen into very low waters, partly on account of the selfish policy of the Stuarts, and partly on account of the new Puritan spirit in the nation, which brought on the Civil War (1642-1649), followed by the Commonwealth (1649-1660). These joint-stocks were not, however, like the capital of modern joint-stock companies. They were separate funds, with separate sets of proprietors, sometimes intercrossing; each also with a separate committee or directors. Each joint-stock was supposed to be wound up before a new joint-stock was called for. But this was not done in actual practice, and there was much confusion in accounts.

Transformation of Company's Trade: Withdrawal from the Archipelago.—But both the nature of the Company's commerce and its credit and status in the country were undergoing transformation. As regards the nature of its commerce, we saw how it started with the idea of capturing the spice trade. This was mainly to be had in the Archipelago, where the Dutch had established themselves before. The Dutch had also, then, superior shipping (three to one in 1609), more capital, and better organization, both in the East and in their home country, where their young republic aspired to a leading position in the politics of Europe. In their "East Indies," as we saw, they were colonizing and producing. They were also building cities and developing political power. The English had befriended the Dutch in establishing their independence, but their first two Stuart kings followed a Spanish policy, and almost brought their nation into international contempt. The various attempts made by the British Company to work jointly with the Dutch in the Spice Islands were a failure. Gradually the feelings grew more and more bitter, and ended in the catastrophe of Amboyna, 1623. The Dutch were in a blind panic about the English. They believed a story of a conspiracy against them at Amboyna, and executed the English Resident, Towerson, together with nine Englishmen, a Portuguese, and nine Japanese as conspirators. The story of Amboyna stirred very deep feeling in England, which was reflected in sermons, plays, pictures, and the Press. The East India Company demanded a "real reparation." But James I. was not the king to bring the Dutch to book. It was left to Cromwell, after teaching the Dutch some lessons at sea, to exact some compensation for

Amboyna, by the Treaty of Westminster, 1654. But the English gradually withdrew from the trade of the Archipelago.

Openings for England's Exports and for a Permanent and Healthy Circulation of Capital and Energy, with Development of Shipping and the Carrying Trade.—As early as 1608 the English factors at Bantam had pointed out that cloths and calicoes from India held the markets of the Archipelago. The Company, by buying these in India and selling them in the Archipelago for spices, made a triple profit; first on the trade in cotton textiles, secondly, on the spice trade (spices could be sold both in Europe and India), and thirdly, though this was not shown separately in the accounts, on the carrying trade. India was also a good and established market for China goods; here was a fourth source of profit, to which was added later the export of Chinese tea to Europe. The Surat trade opened up the Persian trade. Persia, having a colder climate, could take English woollens and supply raw silk, so much in demand for the brocades and silk manufactures of India. With the failure of the Portuguese, the Perso-Indian trade could be captured; here was a fifth source of profit, besides the opening for English cloths, which opened up a sixth. Then there was the import of indigo into England, a valuable addition to her dye-stuff resources, which were auxiliary to her textile manufactures. The Siam and Japan trades were also held in view. The development of all these, and many other lines of trade, pointed to magnificent openings for British manufactures, commerce, shipping, and the carrying trade, and promised to keep a healthy flow and circulation of British commerce and energy, beyond any trade that the Dutch were monopolizing in the Archipelago. This was clearly seen and pressed home by the English factors in India, and their superb vision was more than realized in actual practice.

Conditions Favouring Company's Profits in India.—India enjoyed a more organized and (as it then appeared) stable government that could be found in the island principalities of the Archipelago. In the banking caste of the Hindus (the "Banyans," who early attracted English attention) there was a ready-made agency for financial and mercantile transactions, of many centuries' standing, and in no way inferior to anything then known in England. Deposit banking only began in England under James I. This mercantile community, moreover, was in no way identified with, and was sometimes secretly hostile to, the power of the Muslims, the ruling class in India. The economic weakness of the Muslim governments, when once the Arab network of shipping, commerce, and carrying trade was destroyed, must have at once been apparent to the English merchants, and contrasted strongly with the economic strength of the Hindu merchants. Add the entire absence of national feeling among the Hindus of that age, and of prejudice against foreigners, and it will be understood how favourable were the conditions under which the East India Company started in India, and how the transformation of the nature of its commerce was almost rendered inevitable by a whole chain of circumstances. Later in the seventeenth century (about 1675) Indian calicoes and fine cottons and printed cloths began to invade the English market, and caused a good deal of alarm to the British linen trade; Indian saltpetre was brought to Europe for manufacture into gunpowder for its wars, which alarmed Aurangzib, who thus saw his country's resources being used in wars against the Turks, his co-religionists; and, later still, Indian opium began to be imported in enormous quantities into China, the opium monopoly (not counting shipping profits) yielding the Company over 2½ millions sterling per year on an average of ten years, 1845-1855.

Footing Established on West Coast and in Arabian Sea.—The Company therefore took every step to secure and develop its position in India. The agency at Masulipatam, 1611, and the settlement at Surat, 1612, with its agencies in the interior, have already been mentioned. In 1615-1618 was the embassy of Sir Thomas Roe, accredited in due form by James I. to Jahangir, and charged with the mission of negotiating a commercial treaty, which was only partially successful. But he gave good advice to the Company, one item of which was to prohibit private trade to their servants, and give them good salaries. "Make good choice of your servants, and use fewer," he said. Private trade was prohibited in the reorganization of 1659, but it survived and even flourished under Clive as late as 1765-1768, and was not really abolished till much later. In pursuit of the Persian trade the Company lent their naval forces to co-operate with the Persian military forces, and took Ormuz from the Portuguese in April 1622. Thereafter the Portuguese ceased to contend against the English at sea, and in 1634-1635 a treaty of amity between the two nations gave free access to each other's ports. The Anglo-Portuguese amity then established has never since been broken, and was further cemented by the marriage of Charles II. with Catherine of Braganza, 1661, which brought the island of Bombay and its dependencies to the British Crown. Charles II. handed it over to the Company in 1668-1669.

Footing on the East Coast and in Bengal: Dreams of Dominion.—Meanwhile, the Company had not been idle on the east coast and in Bengal. From Masulipatam they had extended their trade to two or three factories in the Bay of Bengal. In 1639 they obtained the chance of leasing a strip of land which had no natural advantages, and which would, on that very account, excite neither the jealousy nor the cupidity of the Government officials. On this site was built the town of Madras and the fort which they called Fort St. George, from the patron saint of England. The position of Madras was useful for the trade with Further India and China. The province of Bengal, the most fertile and most populous in the Mughal Empire, also attracted early attention. A factory was attempted in Patna in 1620, but the Mughal order permitting trade with Bengal was not obtained till 1624, and it then gave entry to a single port. But the misdeeds of the Portuguese helped the English with the Mughals as a contrast and a counterpoise. The Portuguese in the days of their power had settled at Hugli, a town on a river of the same name, on the left bank of which stands modern Calcutta. Hugli is about twenty-seven miles north of Calcutta. The Portuguese not only set up a customs house of their own, but started capturing Mughal subjects for their slave trade, and kidnapping orphan children to be turned into Roman Catholics. Even the easy-going Shah Jahan was stirred into action. He captured Hugli after a three months' siege in 1632, and turned out the Portuguese. But the foreign commerce of Bengal was of considerable value. This consideration, coupled with bribes, presents, and services, soon obtained for the Company special privileges, and the right of trading duty free in Bengal (1651-1652). In 1690 the town of Calcutta was founded. By that time the Company was already working consciously towards the acquisition of political power in imitation of the Dutch in the Archipelago. "The foundation of a large, well-grounded, sure English dominion in India for all time to come" is put forward in a letter of the Company in 1687.

Company's Difficulties at Home: Change in Public Opinion and Taste.—While the Company was making a brave show in the East, their position at home was transformed in a remarkable manner. Soon after the abolition of "separate" voyages the Company's agents in the East made more gains than its stock-holders at home; and in London itself the Directors had an inner ring which profited at the expense of the shareholders. Interest in the Company began to flag, and open hostility was manifested towards their monopoly and even their trade. The growth of Puritanism to power in England meant a slump in the luxury trades. The religious motive, which maintained and accentuated the interest in the American colonies, had no bearing on India. Both the American and Eastern adventures had been started in the City under the Elizabethan wave of adventure and quest of gain. For over a century the energies which fed the one also fed the other. But in the course of the seventeenth century the English nation generally got divorced from the East India Company's interests.

Company's Relations with James I. and Charles I.—The behaviour of the first two Stuart kings to the Company was on a par with their behaviour to the nation. When Ormuz was captured, the prize money was estimated at £100,000. A claim for shares was put forward against the East India Company by the King (James I.) for droits of the Crown, and by the Duke of Buckingham, as Lord High Admiral, for droits of the Admiralty. The Company settled with the Duke for £10,000. In 1624 the King granted the Company, without reference to Parliament, the power of punishing its servants abroad by martial law. But the Company's credit had by that time fallen to a low ebb. Its stock had fallen to a discount of 20 per cent., and it was in debt. In 1635, by means of a court intrigue, Sir

William Courten obtained a licence from Charles I. to trade in the East, in violation of the Company's monopoly. The King himself had a share in the trade. From this time the Company's appeals to the King and the nation are in a minor key. In 1642 the King, being sore pressed for money to carry on his civil war, seized the pepper of the Company. Nominally it was a trade bargain. The Company received a bond for the price, which the Company took care should cover its risks. On sale by the King in the open market it realized 3d. per pound less. But as Charles never paid the price to the Company, he made a clear profit of the sale money which he got, amounting to over £50,600.

Under the Commonwealth.—Like the Company's first profits, the profits of Courten's Association were in the nature of windfalls. There was no element of permanency in their trade. Under the Commonwealth both the monopoly of the Company and the trade of Courten's Association were an object of suspicion. And their mutual jealousies injured both in the East. Courten's had meanwhile projected a settlement on the island of Assada, near Madagascar, from which they got the name of the Assada Merchants. They agreed, after negotiations, to unite with the East India Company (1650). Cromwell, as we saw, following a strong national policy, obtained some compensation for the Company from the Dutch. But the principle of its monopoly was strongly subjected to attack under the Commonwealth, particularly by the Merchant Adventurers, who were for open trade—*i.e.*, trade without a monopoly, as in the case of the Turkey or the Russia Company. After some controversy Cromwell and the Council of State decided that the East India Company's trade on the joint-stock principle, and under a monopoly, was, on the whole, not contrary to the national interests, and renewed the Company's charter (1657-1658). The Merchant Adventurers now amalgamated with the Company.

After the Restoration.—After the Restoration (1660) there was a tremendous fillip to the Company's trade. A brisk demand set in for silks, taffetas, jewels, and luxuries generally. The diarists of the period, both Pepys and Evelyn, have many references to the East India Company and its trade. Says

Pepys, September 25, 1660: "I did send for a cup of tea (a China drink), of which I had never drank before." This must have been from Dutch imports, for the East India Company ordered its first imports in 1668. Says Evelyn, December 10, 1682: "I sold my East India adventure of £250 principal for £750 to the Royal Society, after I had been in that company twenty-five years, being extraordinary advantageous by the blessing of God." Charles II., in confirming their privileges, had given them authority to make peace and war with any prince or people, not being Christians, and to seize unlicensed persons (English) within their limits, and send them to England. Most of the vested interests were drawn into the Company's orbit. But its monopoly still rankled in the heart of the nation, the more so that it rested exclusively on a royal charter not sanctioned by Parliament. The decision of Judge Jeffreys in support of the royal prerogative (case of Thomas Sandys, 1683) was not likely to convince the nation. "Interlopers" (those who tried to invade the Company's monopoly in India) received more and more support from the Commons.

The Glorious "Revolution" of 1688: Fight Between the Commons and the King's Prerogative.—Matters came to a head after the Glorious Revolution of 1688. A Commons Committee in 1690 recommended the establishment of a new Company *under the authority of Parliament* to supersede the Company established by charter, and the House petitioned the King accordingly, 1691. But the King and his advisers granted a new charter to the East India Company by Letters Patent in 1693, augmenting its capital. Among the subscribers for 1693 Their Majesties King William and Queen Mary are down for £7,000. The Company, however, was not content with merely winning the interest of the highest authorities in the State by legitimate means. It resorted to underhand means of corruption, and £90,000 was traced from the Company's books to the account of bribes to the Privy Council. The Commons impeached the Duke of Leeds, Lord President of the Council, and these lively transactions were ended by a prorogation (May 1695).

Commons Decide to Bring Eastern Trade under their Control.—The Commons were, however, determined to pursue their advantage, and to bring the rich trade of the East and its machinery under parliamentary control. Finance then played a large part in public affairs. The foundation of the Bank of England in 1694 was itself connected with the necessity of a loan to Government. Money was required to finance the large wars of policy waged by William. But they were also national wars, and Parliament, while controlling policy, tightened its hands on finance. The Bank had been formed to provide a loan of £1,200,000. In 1698 Parliament passed a Bill to form a new Company for the loan of £2,000,000 at 8 per cent., with the monopoly of trade to India, the old Company being given the required three years' notice of extinction. In accordance with the Act the King incorporated the new Company as the "*English* Company trading to the East Indies."

New Company Created by the Commons: Fight between the Old and the New Company.—From 1698 there were thus two rival companies: the old Company or the London Company, doomed to extinction after three years, and the new Company, or the English Company, which could be determined after 1711 on three years' notice and the repayment of their loan. Illogical as it sounds, they both had the monopoly of the Eastern trade till 1701. The old Company were equal to the occasion. They subscribed heavily, as a Corporation, to the new Company, in order to maintain their footing should the new Company succeed. At the same time they instructed their servants in the East, as "veterans," to thwart and kill the new Company. Meanwhile they had never ceased to court the King and the authorities. In delicate flattery to William III. they named their new fort in Calcutta Fort William, commenced in 1696, but never entirely completed. Among the great names in their subscriptions appear: Marlborough, 1694; the King's Majesty (William III.), 1699; and the Queen's Most Excellent Majesty (Queen Anne), 1702. King William used his good offices to bring about the amalgamation of the two Companies, and they were actually amalgamated under Queen Anne in 1702, as the "United Company of Merchants trading to the East Indies." All outstanding questions between the two bodies were settled under the arbitration of the Earl of Godolphin, who had had Treasury experience in no fewer than four reigns, in 1708.

Their Amalgamation: New Position of the Reconstituted East India Company.—It may be noted that the United Company was to advance to the Government a fresh loan of £1,200,000, in addition to the old loan of £2,000,000, which was taken over. It thus became a national institution, holding a national loan of a little short of three times the amount held by the Bank of England. Its existence was now expressly based on an Act of Parliament. Its trade rested on a permanent basis, admitting of unlimited expansion. It had forts, possessions, and settlements in India. The old Company's sudden activity in Bengal soon after 1687 may partly be explained by their desire to present the nation with the *fait accompli.* But more important than all, the established political order in India was undergoing a complete transformation, and its inner weakness was known to no one better and more comprehensively than to the English merchants and factors who haggled in the bazaars, and were in touch with the bed-rock opinion of the vast and silent masses of India.

CHAPTER XIII

THE THREE PRESIDENCIES: THE COMPANY'S ORGANIZATION IN INDIA IN THE COMMERCIAL PERIOD

Company's Organization in the East.—The Company, in their organization and in the nomenclature of their officials in the East, imitated the Dutch. Where they settled they had a house of trade, or factory. It was not a place for manufacture. It consisted merely of warehouses and yards for their goods, counting-houses and offices, and residences for their officials. The latter had four principal grades or ranks, which they filled successively. "Writers" learned their business by taking charge of clerical work. "Factors," with a little more responsible work, remained in that grade for three years. Then they had a service of three years in the grades of junior merchants and senior merchants respectively. Some Blue Coat boys (from Christ's Hospital, London) were sent out as apprentices for seven years, after which they had to find security for employment. The chief factory had a President and Council, selected by the directors at home, but usually by right of seniority, from among the Senior Merchants. The curious title of "Commodore," as borne by officials in charge of warehouses (*e.g.*, "Commodore of the Peppers," "Commodore of the Blues," or indigo), had nothing to do with the sea; it was from the Dutch term "Kommandoor," or commander. The salaries paid were low, but private trade was allowed, and yielded big emoluments. The salary of a "writer" in 1674 was only £10 a year.

Mode of Doing Business.—The sale of commodities brought out from Europe was usually by auction. The sale of the goods they imported into England was also by auction in London. The majority of goods imported by the Company from the East, especially in the earlier stages of its history, consisted, as far as India was concerned, of textiles. An elaborate machinery for obtaining these goods was maintained. The English agent of the Company had his " banyan," a Hindu of the trading caste, to assist him in his transactions. The Englishman and the banyan went into the centres of the weaving trade, and through intermediary brokers made contracts with the weavers. These artisans were generally an ignorant and indigent lot. In order to get the goods as cheap as possible, advances of cash were made to the weavers for the purchase of their raw materials and for their maintenance until the full prices were paid off. When the goods were ready, they were inspected and passed, and that particular transaction closed.

Armed Retinues and Guards.—It became the policy of the Company, wherever they could get a lease or grant of land, or of a village, to encourage the weavers or artisans to settle under their very eyes. It lessened the cost of obtaining their goods, and it improved their hold on those to whom advances were made. In any circumstances, the Company handled large sums of money, and had to make efficient arrangements for the protection of their servants and agents, and of their goods and buildings, and for securing proper facilities for the lading and unlading of their ships. They kept quite a large armed retinue and guard, and this was in accordance with the custom of the country. But the building of forts was not allowed by the Indian Governments, and this constituted the most fruitful source of conflicts when the Company began to entertain dreams of sovereignty.

The Three Historic Presidencies.—The place where a President and his Council had their headquarters was called a Presidency. The term was afterwards applied to the whole area for whose operations a President (with his Council) was responsible. The first Presidency, that at Bantam in Java, does not concern us much in this history. But it is desirable to review the growth of the three historic Presidencies of India—viz., Bombay (which grew out of Surat), Madras (Fort St. George), and Bengal (Fort William). When the Company became a political body, with its commercial transactions in the background, the word acquired a new meaning. As its territory grew it was organized round one or other of the Presidencies. Bombay was mainly the sea-board on the western coast of India, with accessions from time to time from the Marathas and, later, the Amirs of Sindh.

Madras was mainly the eastern sea-board of Southern India, the old province of the Carnatic, to which additions were made from time to time with territory taken from the Nizam or the new Mysore power. These two became definite provinces, each with a certain number of States attached, in subsidiary alliance. The territory of the Presidency of Bengal accrued in large bits: first the site of Calcutta, with villages around it; then the provinces of Bengal, Bihar, and Orissa, and later other provinces. This was the residuary Presidency. Any further additions in India that could not be grouped with Bombay or Madras were in the Presidency of Bengal. With the gradual creation of separate provincial administrations, the Bengal Presidency was strictly confined (for general administration purposes) to the area of Bengal, of which the definition, however, varied from time to time. In the latest statute of Parliament relating to India (the Government of India Act, 1919) the three Presidencies are named and contrasted with the other provinces. But the term " Presidency " has lost all practical significance.

Relics of Presidency Organization.—And yet its history is important. Even now the three cities of Bombay, Madras, and Calcutta are called Presidency towns. Certain magistrates in them, called Presidency magistrates, have different powers from ordinary magistrates. The governors of the provinces known as the Presidencies are usually statesmen appointed from England, while the governors of the other provinces are appointed from among members of the Indian Civil Service. Until January 1921, there were three Presidency banks, which were semi-Government institutions; the Bank of Bengal operated in all provinces outside Bombay and Madras. These banks have now been amalgamated, and the name changed into " The Imperial Bank of India." But it was in army administration that the Presidency system left its deepest and most abiding mark. The three Presidential armies of India had each an interesting and separate history, and each had its own commander-in-chief. It was not till 1891-1895 that the army was unified into one Indian army, with a single Commander-in-chief.

Bombay Presidency Grew out of Surat.—The Bombay Presidency grew out of the Presidency of Surat. But while Bombay, from the moment the British connection began, was under the sovereignty of the Crown of Britain, Surat, to the last moment it enjoyed the dignity of a Presidency, was a mere trade factory. As such it started its career in 1612, but it was under the Presidency of Bantam until 1629. From 1629 to 1633, and again from 1657 to 1662, it was a Presidency controlling all the Company's posts in the East, from Persia to Java. Except for those years of pre-eminence, it was the western Presidency until 1687, after which that honour was transferred to Bombay.

Surat in about 1638.—We have many word pictures, drawn by European travellers, of the life in the factories in those early days. In Surat the Dutch and English Presidents lived side by side, in palatial houses, and kept much state. The Portuguese factory did little business. When the English President, usually in a coach drawn by two oxen, came out of the factory, a banner was carried before him, and he was followed by his merchants on horseback, with "native attendants, armed with swords, and bucklers, and bows and arrows." The Holstein traveller Mandelslo was in Surat in 1638, and has left a vivid account of the open hospitality and the pleasing kindness of the good English merchants to all visitors from Europe. The dinner consisted of fifteen or sixteen dishes of meat, besides the dessert. Everything was arranged in the most orderly manner, and there was collegiate discipline. On weekdays there was divine service at six in the morning and eight at night, and on Sundays thrice. On convivial occasions some of the merchants took more drink "than they could well carry away." There was a plentiful variety of drinks, including tea and coffee. The name of one locally devised drink has found an abiding place in the English language. "Punch" or "bowl o' Punch," was a sort of mixed liquor; the five ingredients drunk by the Surat merchants were brandy, sugar, lemons, spice, and rose-water. Even at that date the river Tapti (on which Surat is situated, about fifteen miles from its mouth) showed signs of silting up, admitting with difficulty ships of 80 tons and over.

Acquisition of Bombay.—Bombay island was ceded to the English by the Portuguese in 1661, as part of the dowry of the King of Portugal's sister, whom Charles II. married. The English and Dutch had already taken the island from the

Portuguese in 1626 and abandoned it. It was inhabited mostly by fishermen. Its climate was feverish and unhealthy. It had only one spring of fresh water. Its wealth consisted in its coco-nut groves and its saltpans. Its splendid harbour had not yet been developed. As an island it had no communications with the interior, and the mainland, which it adjoined, was cut off both from Northern and Southern India by the mountain chain of the Western Ghats. There was nothing specially promising in the island. But it took the local Portuguese authorities four years to obey their king's orders and deliver it up to King Charles's officers. To the King himself it was of no use; it did not pay the expenses of maintenance. In 1668 he handed it over to the Company, "to be held of the King in free and common soccage, as of the manor of East Greenwich, on the payment of the annual rent of £10 in gold."

English Standards Contrasted with Portuguese.—Bombay was the first piece of land in India under British sovereignty, and here began the first impact of English ideas and institutions on Indian soil. A remarkable petition addressed by 225 inhabitants of Bombay to Charles II. complains of the previous Portuguese régime as consisting of "men powerful, arrogant, and exorbitant violators, Ecclesiastiques as well as Civil; whose manner of government was absolute, and bringing the inferior sort of us so much under, and made so small account of them as comparatively we may say the elephant doth of the ant." In another picturesque phrase they complain that those men "had sucked from the veins of the people"; that the magistrates had taken bribes; that none but Catholics had been allowed to exercise their religion; that orphan children used to be converted by force, the oppressors "stopping their ears to the cries of the mothers"; and so on. The English régime was characterized by two parallel movements. One had to do with law and revenue administration, and the other with economic reforms.

Legal, Administrative, and Economic Reforms.—With regard to law, courts were established, under the Company's power, to enforce ordinances "not repugnant to English law." In domestic matters Indians were governed by their own personal law, which was mainly the religious and customary law. Perfect liberty was granted for the exercise of religion. With regard to revenue administration, Aungier's Convention of 1672 established the principle that the landholders and 120 of the "eminents of the povo" (= people) were to be called into council, to help in establishing a reasonable, as opposed to an arbitrary, assessment. As regards economic reforms, the Bombay Mint was established in 1676, and authorized to coin the rupee, the standard currency of India, and subsidiary coins. These coins, however, bore the English arms, and were for local trade. They obtained no currency in the Mughal Empire, as did the "Mughal" coins issued by the Company under authority in the eighteenth century. Ships had hitherto been built by the Company at Surat, but two brigantines were ordered to be built in Bombay in 1671. Later a very skilled Parsi foreman was brought over from Surat, and the famous Bombay Dockyard was established. The Parsis took readily to artisan trades and to commerce on modern lines, and have played a notable and honourable part in the development of Bombay. The Post Office was established in Bombay in 1688.

Armed Forces at Company's Disposal.—Bombay being British territory, the beginnings of the armed forces which the Company employed so largely afterwards can best be traced here. Ships of the Royal Navy visited here frequently, with the King's commission. In the latter part of the seventeenth century piracy was rife. The Marathas in 1679 made an attack on Bombay by sea, but were unsuccessful. There was no sea-power left in the Arabian Sea to compete with British sea-power, slight as it was in these regions in those days, once the Dutch became a friendly power on the accession of William III. to the throne of England. Besides ships of the Royal Navy, the Company had armed merchantmen of its own to police the seas. And yet piracy was not finally suppressed till 1820. Among the land forces the English soldiers whom the King had sent to garrison Bombay took service with the Company when the island was handed over to the Company, and became the Company's first European regiment, afterwards the 103rd Foot. The "Topases," or mixed Indo-Portuguese population of Bombay, were also put into uniform and disciplined, and later the Indians themselves were drilled on the

European model. Thus, when the Company started its political and military career, it could count, at sea, on the King's Navy and its own armed merchantmen; and on land, on the assistance of the King's soldiers, besides its own "European" army (which included deserters or recruits from other European nations in the East) and its "native" army, the precursor of the modern Indian Army. There was much jealousy between the King's forces and the Company's forces, but in the face of external danger Englishmen always stood true to each other.

Presidency Headquarters in Bombay.—The Presidency headquarters were removed from Surat to Bombay in 1687. Surat was still the most important city in India in point of trade and manufactures, and its communications with the interior, unlike those of Bombay, were good. But the Marathas pillaged Surat in 1664, and again in 1670, and on both occasions the English factory put up a brave defence, and won the admiration of the Mughal authorities. The Company continued to trade in Surat, but for shipping purposes and as headquarters Bombay was more convenient, as well as more secure, being British territory. The President was also the Governor of Bombay. Dr. Fryer, who visited Bombay in 1674, calls the Governor of Bombay also *Vice-regis* (=Viceroy). The Governor had his staff of chaplains, physician, surgeons, interpreter, and mint-master, besides his Council. From 1686 to 1715 (but not without a break) he was given supervising power, with the title of "General," over the rest of the Company's settlements. In the hands of a masterful man like Sir John Child, with his namesake,* Sir Josiah Child, among the Company's Directors in London, it led to a forward policy and a war with Aurangzib. This forward policy may, however, have been adopted to impress public opinion in England, and save the Company's charter from the threats to which it was seriously exposed, as we have already seen.

Madras Settlement: Its Title-Deeds.—The history of the Madras Presidency followed different lines. In 1639 the Dutch were still in a state of hostility, both to the English and

* It was supposed that the two Childs were brothers, but apparently no relationship can be established between them, or between either of them and the famous proprietor of Childs' Bank, Sir Francis Child. The Governor, Sir John Child, died in Bombay in 1690.

the Portuguese, and the Portuguese were friendly to the English. The Portuguese had a settlement at St. Thomé (about five miles south-west of where Fort St. George was afterwards built), the reputed site of the martyrdom of St. Thomas the Apostle. In the neighbourhood there was a great population of weavers, the artisans whose cottons and prints the Company exported from India, and the Company could buy their stuffs here cheaper by 20 per cent. than elsewhere. This part of the country was still in an unsettled state, and was likely to welcome the newcomers in its own interests better than the Muslim sultanate of Golkonda, in whose jurisdiction the English factory of Masulipatam was situated. For this very reason the Dutch had settled at Pulicat, about twenty-five miles north, which was also then nominally in Hindu territory. They had built themselves a square fort in Pulicat, but their relations with the Hindus were getting unfriendly. The local Hindu Naik (=chief) offered very tempting terms to the English, represented by Francis Day, who accepted them. The English were to build a fort at Madraspatam (now Madras), and were to be allowed to mint coin, and their imports and exports were to be duty free, and to pay only half duty on the mainland outside Madraspatam. The lease was to be only for two years, but the Naik who granted it was soon in disgrace. In November 1645, the Company got a grant from the fugitive Raja of the Vijayanagar family, the sovereign of the Naik. But the Raja was himself being pressed back by Golkonda, which was in complete possession of the territory by July 1647. The Company got a confirmation of the grant from Golkonda, as well as much succour in the famine of that year, in return for two brass guns and other presents made to the Sultan's general.*

Fort Built and Artisans Attracted.—The surf round the coast was heavy and dangerous, and there was not even the making of a harbour, as in Bombay, acquired in sovereignty twenty-two years later. But the lease (whatever the value of its first title might have been) gave the Company its first lodgment in India—not a mere trading post, but space in which to make

* This story of the foundation of Madras differs from the usual version in the textbooks, but is based on the latest researches. See [Sir] William Foster's *Founding of Fort St. George* (London, 1902).

a settlement and attract weavers, dyers, and artisans. A fort was immediately constructed (1640), and called Fort St. George, after the patron saint of England; the unwilling directors at home were confronted with a *fait accompli*. The disturbed state of the country around made the artisans all the more anxious to flock to Madras. Under the security of the Fort and the orderly discipline of the English merchants the settlement grew. In 1661 it assumed control over all the English stations in Bengal. In 1684 Fort St. George was raised to the rank of a Presidency. The Madras Mint was established soon after the settlement at Madras, by the Company's authority, and a royal charter was obtained from James II. in 1686. Its first issues were pagodas of the Hindu type. The pagoda was a gold coin current in Southern India, and valued at about 7s. to 10s. Later it imitated Muslim coins of Southern India. The pagodas of Madras did more than local duty. Some were sent to Java and Sumatra for the purchase of pepper and spices, and some to Bengal for the purchase of silks and muslins. As gold they were sought after everywhere, and the saying "shaking the pagoda tree" was applied to the Company's servants seeking private fortunes in the East.

English Life in Madras.—Life in Madras in the seventeenth and the early eighteenth centuries was much what it was in other settlements. For the Company's servants there was a common mess and common prayers. There was a chaplain on £100 a year, and a schoolmaster on £50. There were regular prayers, and penalties for swearing, drinking more than half a pint of brandy at a sitting, or getting over the Fort wall. Full judicial powers were exercised over Englishmen by the President and Council as judges, sitting with twelve jurymen, but no Englishman could be condemned to death, except for piracy. In 1688 a Mayor and Corporation were established, with twelve aldermen and sixty burgesses. In 1726-1727 the Mayor's Court was remodelled by Royal Charter for the European population; in this respect the other two Presidency towns were treated like Madras. There were alarums and excursions at various times: now from the Marathas, now from Golkonda, and after 1688 from the Mughal. It may be noted that in the wars between Golkonda and Aurangzib (1685-1688) the Company definitely asserted their sovereign rights in Madras.

Indian Life in Madras.—We get interesting glimpses of Indian life in Madras. There was a considerable Portuguese or semi-Portuguese population, but their Catholic religion excluded them from the municipal privileges of the English. In and after the Golkonda wars some Muslims from the conquered State took refuge in Madras, and engaged in trade. But the majority of the population was Hindu, and mainly of the artisan and agricultural castes. These two classes formed cliques, and faction fights sometimes occurred between them. These were the fights of the Right-hand and Left-hand castes, which lived in separate streets. Before the end of the seventeenth century Madras had become quite a big town. The seeds of representative government were sown in the consultations with the caste headmen about local taxation; these headmen also levied taxation for sanitation. The taxes were unpopular, and led to riots and strikes, but the city prospered and progressed. The slave trade was maintained by the Portuguese, and connived at by the Company. Aurangzib took a strong line on the subject when his forces prevailed in the south, and the Company abolished it in 1688.

Yale University Endowed by a Governor of Madras.—One or two features may be noted before we take leave of Madras. Among those who "shook the pagoda tree" in the southern Presidency were men with other titles to fame. From 1687 to 1692 the governor was Elihu Yale, who established the factory at Cuddalore (1690), where Fort St. David was built, barely twenty miles south of the French settlement of Pondicherry. This enterprising governor was a son of one of the original settlers of the Puritan colony of New Haven, Connecticut, in America. He had amassed a fortune in India, some of which went to the endowment of Yale University after his return to America. There were other instances in which the fortunes of the East served to feed the needs of the West. Sir Thomas Smith, or Smythe, who died in 1625, was one of the most notable governors of the East India Company. He was also the treasurer of the struggling Virginia Company. His profits from India made up to him for his losses from Virginia. Out of the surplus he endowed the famous public school, founded by his grandfather Sir Andrew Judd—Tonbridge School, which has maintained, and still maintains, direct contact with the higher public services in India.

Another Governor, Pitt, of the Diamond Fame.—The most interesting of the Company's governors of Madras was Thomas Pitt, grandfather of the Earl of Chatham. His term of office was from 1698 to 1709, and he was succeeded in the governorship by a brother of Joseph Addison the writer and Secretary of State. Pitt was a masterful spirit, and steered Madras through difficult times. Aurangzib was then in the Deccan, and he had appointed a Nawab, or deputy, to the province of the Carnatic, which figures prominently in later history. Madras fell within this Nawab's territory, and Pitt knew how to manage him, both by show of strength, by hospitality, and by playing upon his vices. Drunkenness was one of these, and he got a plentiful supply of cordial waters and brandy from Madras. Pitt's name is also associated with the famous diamond, weighing originally 410 carats, which he bought from a Golkonda jeweller. It was subsequently (in 1717) sold to the Duke of Orleans, regent of France, for £135,000. It is one of the notable diamonds of the world, and is called the Pitt Diamond or the Regent Diamond.

Presidency of Fort William in Bengal.—The Presidency of Fort William in Bengal was the youngest of the Presidencies, though ultimately it became the largest and most important, and its governor, becoming the Governor-General, was invested (1774) with supreme power in India. Bengal also rose very rapidly in importance in the Company's affairs. From the beginning of the life of the Company in India the highest political power had resided in the neighbourhood of Agra and Delhi, and such trading stations as the Company originally established in Upper India were subordinate to Surat. With the rise of Madras the Company found it more convenient to direct its affairs in Bengal and the Bay of Bengal from Madras (1661-1681). In 1681 the agent at Hugli (Mr. William Hedges) was given the title of governor, but two years later he was dismissed for misconduct, and the governor of Madras again took over the control of Bengal until 1698-1699. By that time

Fort William (in Calcutta) had made progress; the three villages around it had been acquired, and the Bengal Presidency had been organized. But the Company itself, as we saw, was threatened with extinction in England, and the "New Company" were sending out agents to India. It was after the union of the two Companies that the Presidency was formally constituted in 1707.

Why Bengal Rose to Pre-Eminence.—Bengal had many attractions for the East India Company. It was the richest province of the Mughal Empire. Its Mughal governor was usually a prince of the blood royal, often the eldest prince, who hoped to succeed to the throne. Concessions gained from him were therefore of more permanent validity than those obtained from minor governors, and he could always bring the Company into touch with the emperor. Above all, the province had, in its long water-ways, fine communications with its interior, and this was of special importance to a maritime nation seeking trade with the great towns in Northern India. The fine muslins of Dacca, the cheap silk stuffs of Kasimbazar, and the opium and saltpetre from Patna (the latter for the manufacture of gunpowder), and jute (then used for mixing with coarse cotton or silk stuffs) from the populous villages of Bengal, were in much demand for export to Europe; while rice and sugar and cottons and silks were also much sought after for the Company's coasting and Asiatic trade.

Company's War with the Mughal, 1686-1690.—We have already noted the early attempts of the Company to obtain the trade of Bengal, until about 1690. We must now consider in more detail the foundation of Calcutta, and the events leading up to it. Its founder, Job Charnock, apparently went out to India about 1655-1656, not in the Company's service. But he soon joined their service in Bengal, and rose to be (1686) their Chief of the Council of the Bay, with headquarters in Hugli. There was then a good deal of friction between the Nawab, who was the governor of Bengal, and the English. This friction was not confined to Bengal. There was a general war between the East India Company and the Mughal Empire, and Surat and Bombay were equally involved. Charnock in 1686 prudently collected the Company's goods and servants, and dropped twenty-seven miles down the river Hugli (on which the town of Hugli is situated) to a site now included in Calcutta. The Company persuaded James II. to send out a fleet of ten ships under Captain Nicholson, which bombarded the town of Hugli, and the Mughals made reprisals at Patna and elsewhere. Charnock and his men had to retreat further down the river, and eventually reached Madras.

Advantages of the Site of Calcutta.—After some desultory fighting and the dynastic revolution in England, peace was concluded in 1690. The Company lost much credit by the war, both in England and India. By that time a new Nawab had been appointed to Bengal, who was more favourable to the English. He invited them back to Bengal, and they returned, but not to the port of Hugli. They preferred the site lower down the Hugli. True it was marshy, but they could settle down here in peace and security, and yet be within twenty-seven miles of the great emporium of trade at Hugli. There were other European settlements higher up. Chinsura, the Dutch settlement, was two miles below Hugli, and Chandernagore, the French settlement, recently founded (1688), was five miles. The English at the new site were nearer to the sea, although ninety miles of intricate and dangerous navigation still separated them from the mouth of the tidal river. But the country gets more and more marshy lower down, and all the historic ports were higher up. The Hugli is just one—the westernmost—of the numerous intersecting mouths of the Ganges. The Gangetic delta has a sea-face of 200 miles, and an upward depth of a similar extent. This huge tract of marsh, fertile country, and interlacing and ever-shifting sluggish streams, has almost every hamlet approachable by water. But the Hugli is the most suitable for navigation, and when the higher reaches above Calcutta were dredged and kept in use, it afforded the best practical inlet to the Ganges and the Jamna, on which most of the famous cities of Northern India were situated. Besides commanding a navigable highway of over 600 miles, through the most important provinces of India, the new site gave the Company the power to bottle up French and Dutch commerce in Bengal, as well as the Mughal outlet from Northern India to the sea. Its situation on the eastern bank of the Hugli afforded the protection of the river from the Maratha incursions from the west. Charnock was therefore wise in selecting the site of Calcutta for the new settlement in Bengal. He died in 1693, and lies buried in the city whose site he chose with such sagacity.

Fort William Built: Villages Acquired.—A fort was necessary for protection, but the Mughal policy was against allowing fortifications in their territory. In 1696 some Hindu zamindars (landholders) rebelled against the authority of the Mughal governor. He allowed the English, as well as the Dutch and French, to protect themselves by constructing walls and bastions round their settlements. This was the beginning of Fort William, the original fort of Calcutta, about a mile to the north of the present fort, which was built by Clive after the battle of Plassey (1757). In 1698 the Company purchased the zamindari of three villages, one of which was called Kolikotta, from which Calcutta derives its name. The purchase was afterwards formally sanctioned by the Mughal emperor. The Company now had the definite rank and position of a zamindar in the Mughal Empire. As such, they paid a certain amount of annual revenue to the empire; but, on the other hand, they collected the rents of the tenantry, could hold courts, and had certain rights like those of lords of the manor in England.

Exemption from Duties Questioned.—Some of these collateral rights did not remain unquestioned by the local governors, but the settlement continued to grow, especially after the amalgamation of the old Company with the rival English Company. From its creation as an independent Presidency (1707) Bengal marched forward rapidly and with energy. The Armenians were accorded special privileges for their help as intermediaries both in Bengal and Madras, and they became a favoured community in Calcutta, and were much used in negotiations with the Mughals. The usual difficulties arose again under a new Mughal governor of Bengal. The Company claimed the right of trading free of duty, under the emperor's orders, especially as they paid a commutation tax of Rs. 30,000 a year. But like other provinces of the empire, Bengal was now practically becoming independent of Delhi, and was trying a vigorous policy in many directions, including that of curtailing the special trade privileges of foreigners.

Embassy to Delhi: Its Results.—In 1715 the Company sent two of their ablest Bengal factors, with an Armenian merchant well versed in both Persian and Arabic, as an embassy to the Delhi court, to seek the redress of all their grievances. Presents to the value of £30,000, which was exaggerated by the Armenian to £100,000, were taken, including a map of the world. But the Mughal was by now a shadow of his former self, both personally and politically. The English embassy were confronted with a scene of corruption, intrigue, and ineptitude, which laid bare to them the rottenness of the empire. They were put off from time to time. But the embassy surgeon, Mr. William Hamilton, cured the emperor of a malady, and obtained such high favour that through him the Company got practically all they wanted. The embassy returned to Calcutta in 1717. A few months afterwards Surgeon Hamilton died in Calcutta, where he lies buried, with a grandiloquent Persian inscription, evidently sent from Delhi. The result of the embassy was satisfactory as far as it went, but exemption from duties now depended more upon the Company's own power than upon the orders from Delhi. The most valuable concession for giving the Company a footing in the land was the permission to extend the Company's zamindari limits by the purchase of thirty-seven more villages round Calcutta. This placed the Company in a strong territorial position at the gate of Bengal. The right to coin Mughal money from the Bombay mint was an extraordinary privilege.

Internal Affairs Leading up to the Company's Political Struggles.—We have now traced the foundation of the three Presidency towns and seen how they grew. The Company's history from 1707 to 1744 was one of peaceful trade. But the Mughal Empire was on its death-bed. We must review the internal state of India between 1707 and 1773 before we deal with the political struggles of the East India Company.

CHAPTER XIV

THE MUGHAL EMPIRE IN ITS DECLINE

Prestige of Mughal Empire even in its Decline.—Aurangzib, who died in 1707, was the last of the great Mughal emperors. His successors were either weak or incompetent, or had to contend with so many rebellions, intrigues, and combinations at court and among the new political forces that were arising in India, that they soon became merely phantom rulers. Their name, however, continued to be invoked by the powers that contended for supremacy—even in those cases where they openly fought against the emperor's own authority. The reason was twofold. In the first place, the rising powers that sought supremacy were not necessarily rebels in intention. They sought some centre of authority; when Delhi broke down they attempted to substitute themselves as representing the Padishah better than any other power. In the second place, the sentiment and prestige of the Padishah of Delhi were so universally diffused among the people that an appeal to it was more effective as a rallying cry than a show of force, or at least helped to salve wounded susceptibilities.

The New Growing Powers Purported to Act in its Name.—The East India Company, although they knew that the emperor's authority was becoming weaker and weaker, and did not neglect to court the real repositories of power, treated the emperor's farmans (decrees) with ostentatious respect, when they conferred privileges on themselves. We have on record how the farman obtained by Surgeon Hamilton's cure of the Mughal emperor was received by the President and Governor of Bombay in January 1718 with public and military honours. An imposing procession was organized, salutes were fired, and banquets were held to celebrate the occasion. Mughal coinage, according to the privilege given to them by the Mughal and the authority they had already received from England, was issued by the Company, and continued to be issued till 1835—*i.e.*, long after the Company had become a territorial power. The Marathas, who were committing daily inroads on the territory of the empire, imitated its institutions, were proud of any titles received (sometimes extorted) from the emperor, and frequently acted in his name. The governors of the Mughal Empire, who practically set up independent dynasties of their own, continued to keep up a semblance of respect for the emperor even when they flouted the orders from Delhi, and ceased to remit the revenue of the provinces to its treasury. Their excuse always was that the emperor was in the hands of some faction hostile to themselves, and they were acting in the best interests of the emperor.

Only Two Long Reigns in a Century.—From 1707 to 1806 there were only two Mughal emperors with reigns of over six years. One was Muhammad Shah (1719-1748), whose death marks an epoch in Indian history, not because of anything in himself, but because it synchronized with a number of other events which unchained the forces of disorder all over India. The second was Shah Alam II. (1759-1806), who practically lived as a prisoner or pensioner in the hands of one or other of the contending parties seeking supremacy in India. His name occurs familiarly on the "Mughal" coins struck by the East India Company. It was in his name that the Company took up the practical administration of Bengal, even though the British Parliament regulated the conduct of the Company's servants, and public opinion in England made careful enquiries and laid down numerous regulations for the government of the Company's new territories in India. Muhammad Shah was a contemptible creature. He lived in an atmosphere of low pleasures, and gathered round him favourites of the same character. He disgusted able ministers like Asaf Jah, and the fashion set in among ambitious noblemen to consolidate their power in outlying provinces rather than seek advancement in the tangled intrigues and unsalutary atmosphere of Delhi. Shah Alam had some virtues in private life, but he was quite unfit to be a king, and his person was treated merely as a pawn in the game by the various competitors for dominion in India.

Extinction of the Dynasty.—After his death there were two more phantoms, even more unsubstantial than before. The Mutiny of the Bengal Army (1857-1858) was enacted in the name of the Mughal emperor, that tragic figure, Bahadur Shah II., with whom the line was formally extinguished. The dynasty ended, as it had begun, with a literary flash. Bahadur Shah's Urdu poetry is the supreme expression of pathos, the wail of helpless incompetence, as his ancestor Babar's Turki autobiography is a vigorous record of heroic deeds, breathless adventures, and brilliant successes.

State of the Country: (*a*) *Deterioration in the Panjab, near Delhi, and in Central India.*—The state of the country deteriorated generally. But there were wide local differences, according to whether there was any strong local authority to keep order. In a province like the Panjab, open to incursions from the Afghan frontier, as well as suffering from the uprising of the Sikhs, who now aspired to be a militant community, much of the country was laid waste. Cultivation was in a wretched state, and hardly any commerce was possible. In Central India and the northern parts of the Deccan the Maratha ravages were becoming more and more widespread. But wherever a Maratha chief got his authority fully established and was able to maintain order, that tract quickly recovered in cultivation. Some of the Maratha ladies to whose lot it fell to rule in those troublous times, followed a mild and benevolent policy, to which the country immediately responded. They built public works, which in these cases meant irrigation works, either newly constructed or repaired, or rescued from the neglect consequent on civil disorder. They restored production, raised the standard of comfort, and produced a feeling of contentment and security which are like pleasing oases in a desert of anarchy. But the Maratha chiefs had their own internal quarrels, and when they invaded each other's territory the usual results of war and insecurity followed. In the latter part of the eighteenth century the region round Delhi and the Doab (the country between the Ganges and the Jamna) suffered more than any other, as being the centre of the vortex of anarchy, and the scene of the most sanguinary feuds and adventures.

(*b*) *The Deccan: Comparative Security of Civil Population.*—The Deccan fell into the hands of a strong governor, the ancestor of the present Nizam of Hyderabad. Except when he had to maintain his ground against the Marathas, he kept peace and order by his organization until the middle of the century, when dynastic disputes and the war between the English and the French produced a new kind of unsettlement. These wars in their first stages were maritime. But we shall see how they developed into a game in which each side put forward rival claimants in disputed successions. There were, however, two points in which the Deccan wars differed from those round Delhi. The armies disciplined on the European model fought as between combatants, and left the civil population comparatively undisturbed. Moreover, these well-organized European powers fought with a backbone; though the warring individuals might change from time to time, the cause behind them stood like a firm rock, and did not shift its character like the ever-changing combinations of individual adventurers who were friends one day and enemies another.

(*c*) *Bengal Remained Prosperous.*—Bengal was a province that was more fortunate than any other. Although there were isolated incursions, the province on the whole maintained its prosperity. The wars between the Bengal Nawabs and the English were sharp and swift, and their results were decisive. There was (except between 1765 and 1774) very little harrying of the general population. When the English got the mastery they immediately began to organize trade and commerce, revenue administration, law and justice, currency and coinage, and roads and communications on a basis that gave some promise of a progressive policy. The early mistakes of the English authorities certainly cost the province dear, but they were mistakes that did not lead to a blind alley, but pointed to a constant endeavour to bring the standard of administration more and more into touch with the standards that prevailed in England, at that time probably the best-governed country in Europe. Bengal, before the East India Company took over its administration, also illustrates what might have become a salutary feature of Mughal provincial administration. If the large powers vested in local administrations had been intelligently used, they would have enabled them to make experiments to suit their systems to local conditions. In the eighteenth century Bengal was the province with the largest amount of foreign commerce. The Bengal governors understood the value of that commerce. They resisted the demand of the Company for exemptions from all Customs duties, and in this they were right, because on no reasonable principle could they allow a single foreign corporation a more privileged position than their own subjects or the subjects of other nations. In 1701-1702 a grandson of Aurangzib, then governor of Bengal, attempted a scheme of a State monopoly of commerce, in order to obviate the many difficulties which the East India Company's demands were creating. His proposal was disallowed by Aurangzib with many caustic and sarcastic comments. But it deserves note, as showing that the Mughal provincial administrations often gauged the local needs of the people better than the central administration.

News-Writers and Spies.—The Mughal Empire in its days of strength had maintained a service of news-writers to report all events of importance to headquarters. They touched not only on political subjects and the conduct of local officials, but on social and economic events, and on everything that a correspondent considered might interest his imperial master. When the Mughal Empire became a mere empty shell, these news-writers became spies pure and simple, as well as fomentors of quarrels, feuds, and factions.

Moral, Social, and Political Disruption.—Perhaps a short appraisement of the causes of the disruption of the Mughal Empire may be attempted. In the state of communications then existing, the empire was too large and unwieldy. Aurangzib, in one of his wills, seems to have contemplated its division into a northern and a southern empire. There would have been some hope if local autonomy had been developed and defined. But the large powers of the governors were often abused, and the central direction, where exercised fitfully, was neither intelligent nor helpful, and latterly got completely out of touch with actual facts. The rules of succession were not fixed, and there was civil war at the end of nearly every reign. There was no pure and united family life at the centre, and the poison of family jars spread outwards with alarming rapidity, and threatened to dissolve society. Luxury sapped morals. Suspicion took the place of trust. There was not much loyalty among the servants of the State. As one of Aurangzib's sons put it, even those "who eat salt destroy the salt cellar." When loyalty was not to be found in the royal family and in the select precincts of the court and the higher officials of the State, it could scarcely be expected from the subjects, in a vast and heterogeneous population like that of India. The early attempts made to weld them together were reversed, instead of being developed, and the Rajputs with their chivalrous and manly traditions were alienated. Economically, the proportion of parasites increased in the population, and production was checked. It was the eclipse of the moral qualities that brought about the collapse of the economic, financial, and military organization.

Internal Disputes among Marathas.—The Marathas rose to power as a young nation, with a leader of the genius of Shivaji. After Shivaji's death in 1680 their leadership was in weak hands. Shivaji's son and grandson were both prisoners in Mughal hands, and the latter was released in one of the Mughal succession disputes, with the effect of embroiling the Marathas among themselves. Their endless internal disputes are now of small consequence in the evolution of Indian history. But there were a few features of their policy which were permanent, and which demand attention.

Maratha Movement not Anti-Muslim.—The Maratha movement was not in its inception either anti-dynastic or anti-Muslim. Shivaji himself and many of his successors and generals respected the Muslim religion, and accepted titles and dignities from the Mughal Empire, or from the Muslim powers in the Deccan. The Maratha armies generally included an element of Muslim soldiers of fortune, and were sometimes led by Muslim generals. Shivaji himself was in the hands of Brahmans, but he showed great respect to the Muslim religion and to Muslim institutions. His Brahman minister was called by a Persian title, the Peshwa. Many of the administrative and revenue terms used by the Marathas were Muslim terms. In the great Maratha ceremonies Muslim as well as Maratha guests were invited, and joined in the feasts. It is not clear whether they all sat down together and were served out of the same pots, though a high Maratha authority considers that "this does not seem altogether unlikely."* To the present day Muslims enjoy consideration, power, and influence in the Maratha States.

Democratic and Against Caste.—The Marathas were not a high caste in the Hindu social system, although after they attained power, their chiefs were dignified with a sort of Kshatriya (warrior) rank. They were just rude, sturdy peasants, probably with some foreign blood in their veins, like the Rajputs. Their poets and prophets had prepared them, in a national literature of great merit, for a movement against the basic principles of caste, the characteristic symbol of Brahmanical Hinduism. Their centre of popular worship at Pandharpur (now in the Nizam's dominions), preached ideals of a religious democracy, very different from the graded hierarchy of orthodox Hinduism. In Namdeo we find such sentiments as the following: "There are none high or low with God; all are alike to him; the Ganges is not polluted, nor is the wind tainted, nor the earth rendered untouchable, because the low-born and high-born bathe in the one or breathe the other, or move on the back of the third." To the present day, in the Bombay Presidency, there is political and social opposition between the Marathas and the Brahmans, and this finds expression not only in British India, but in the Kolhapur State, a small State held by the direct descendants of Shivaji.

Brahman Power Centred in the Peshwas at Poona.—And yet the Marathas could not do without the Brahmans, and while the fighting was left to the Maratha chieftains, the organization, diplomacy, correspondence, accounting and finance —in fact, the major part of the work of government—was in Brahman hands. The Chitpāvan Brahmans (of the Konkan, the maritime strip south of Bombay) early established themselves in the chief strategic positions in Maratha polity. The Peshwa or Minister, in fact, became the head of the Maratha State, and moved the chiefs and generals about as if they were

* M. G. Ranade's *Rise of the Maratha Power*, Bombay, 1900, p. 303.

under him. The chiefs themselves did not brook his guidance and direction without a protest. Many complications occurred in consequence, not only between the Peshwa and the Maratha commanders, but also between the commanders themselves, who were played off against each other by the Peshwa, with his capital at Poona. When the East India Company definitely fought for political supremacy in India, they had first to curtail the power of the Peshwa at Poona, and finally extinguish it altogether. They also attempted to tackle the Maratha commanders in detail, three of whom (apart from Shivaji's descendant at Kolhapur) founded what are now among the most progressive of the Indian States, while one (the Bhonslê of Nagpur) was not extinguished till 1853.

The Dynasty of Seven Peshwas.—The first Peshwa was Balaji Vishwanath (1714-1720), who in 1718 sent up Maratha levies to take part in the disputes in the Mughal court at Delhi. He did a great deal to organize the Maratha power, and to win recognition from the Mughal Empire of the two characteristic institutions of the Marathas, the Sardeshmukhi and the Chauth. These will be described presently. The second Peshwa, Baji Rao I. (1721-1740), made large accessions to Maratha dominion, especially in Malwa and Central India. The third Peshwa, Balaji Baji Rao (1740-1761) got the Maratha power firmly consolidated. In his time the Marathas invaded Bengal (1742-1750) and the Panjab. The Maratha confederacy had hitherto worked together, but they suffered a crushing defeat at Panipat in 1761, when the Afghan invasion from the north-west again redressed the balance of power in favour of the Muslims. After this the Peshwa's attention was directed mainly towards the Deccan, where the Nizam and Haidar Ali were contending for supremacy. The Maratha confederacy was gradually dissolved, but its five component factors, the Peshwa and the four commanders, continued to act in varying combinations, but usually each one for his own hand. The Peshwa was himself overshadowed by an ambitious minister like Nana Farnavis (1774-1800). The last Peshwa, Baji Rao II. (1795-1818), was the seventh of his line, but his power was broken in fighting against the British. His territories were annexed in 1818, and formed the greater portion of the Bombay Presidency. He received a pension, and took up his residence in Northern India, where his adopted son, Nana Sahib, at Cawnpore, became one of the factors in the Mutiny of 1857.

Sardeshmukhi and Chauth.—The nature of Sardeshmukhi and Chauth has now to be explained. They illustrate the growth of Maratha power. The Deshmukh was from the earliest times a local official in the Deccan. Like the Shire-reef, or Sheriff, in early English polity, he was responsible to the Central Government for administration and the collection of revenue. He also represented before the Central Government the village officials, and the mass of the revenue payers. There were many village officials in the area under the Deshmukh's jurisdiction. He received, as remuneration for the collection of revenue, one-tenth of the revenue collected, and this tithe was called the Deshmukhi, the right of the Deshmukh. Over a number of Deshmukhs there might be a superior or chief Deshmukh. He was the Sardeshmukh, and his right was known as the Sardeshmukhi. The first claim of Shivaji was a claim of this nature, founded on old hereditary rights asserted to belong to his family. When Shivaji began to make incursions into territories beyond what he claimed as jagirs (estates in land given by Government in lieu of service), he claimed a fourth of the revenue (in Hindustani or Marathi, Chauth). If any territory met the Maratha demands the Maratha forces were withdrawn from further molestation. In later periods the two came to be levied on the same area. But their levy implied that the Marathas claimed certain rights in virtue of grants or assignments, in territory which they did not claim as their own jagirs. When they organized States of their own, they claimed not a share in the Government revenue, but the whole of the Government revenue.

These Concessions were Originally in the Form of Grants in Lieu of Service.—Aurangzib had been willing to concede certain dignities and emoluments to Shivaji, but he had ignored the latter's demands about Sardeshmukhi and Chauth. Aurangzib's successors were less cautious about recognizing and granting these rights to Shivaji's successors, especially as the successive Delhi court factions who held the real power wanted to use the Marathas, each against his opponents. Accordingly, in 1720, a formal grant was made out to Shahu (Shivaji's grandson), in the name of the Mughal emperor, of all the three items which were demanded by the Marathas. For his hereditary jagir—the old territory, also called Swarajya (a term now used in India for "self-government")—the Maratha was to pay a tribute of ten lakhs (1,000,000) of rupees. For the Sardeshmukhi he was to pay the usual premium of 651 per cent. of the annual income, and to take as his remuneration 10 per cent. of the revenue, but he bound himself to police duties (the suppression of every kind of depredation, and the punishment of thieves or restoration of stolen property). For the grant of Chauth, 25 per cent. of the revenue, he was to pay no initial fees, but he was to maintain a body of 15,000 horse in the emperor's service, to be placed at the disposal of the Subahdars and subordinate officers of the empire. This referred to the Subah of the Deccan, but later on grants were made for other Subahs. As the central power weakened and the Maratha power grew, these delegated powers were gradually converted into family or territorial rights, as in the case of the viceroys of the Mughal Empire.

The Three Great Surviving Maratha States.—The three Maratha commanders who carved out States for themselves from the ruins of the Mughal Empire and of the central Maratha power (in addition to the Bhonslê who has already been mentioned) were: Sindhia, Holkar, and the Gaikwar. The Sindhias eventually established themselves in Northern India, and made their capital at Gwalior, where they still rule over an extensive territory. They took, and still possess, the greater part of Northern Malwa. The Holkars established their capital at Indore, and are masters of Southern Malwa. The Gaikwars remained nearest to the Peshwa's power at Poona, and eventually established themselves in Gujarat and Kathiawar, where they possess scattered territory interlacing with what is now British territory. We shall have more to say about the Sindhia when we come to speak about a famous commander and statesman of his line, the great Mahadaji Sindhia, whose later career (1784-1794) runs through the mid-stream of that period of Indian history. All these Maratha States are outside the real Maratha country.

Sikhs Become a Militant Community.—We have already seen how the Sikh religion was founded by Guru Nanak as an eclectic sect, and how Akbar granted land to the Sikhs in Amritsar (1577), where the Golden Temple was built. The office of Guru became hereditary after the fourth Guru. In the reign of Jahangir the Sikhs mixed themselves up with politics. Guru Arjun helped the rebel prince Khusru, and incurred the wrath of the emperor. The conflict was not religious, but purely political, but it made what was a religious sect into a fighting community. Guru Arjun, who died in 1616, bequeathed to his successor the doctrine of armed resistance, as well as of worldly power and possessions. His successor, Har Govind (1606-1645), enlisted an army. After this the Sikhs were frequently in collision with the civil power. The ninth Guru, Teg Bahadur (1664-1675), was imprisoned and executed under Aurangzib. The tenth Guru, Govind Singh (1675-1708), finally established the Sikhs as a fighting community, with an initiation ritual and various symbolic military rites. He also added a new scripture to suit his militant mood (1696). A policy of aggression was now deliberately undertaken, to which the Mughal Government replied by retaliation. No spiritual Gurus were appointed after Govind Singh, but the Sikhs chose their leaders and commanders for military purposes, and perfected the Khalsa (or Sikh) army and organization. They were suppressed in 1714-1716, and do not appear in general history again until the rise of Ranjit Singh at the end of the eighteenth century.

Rajput States.—The Rajput houses, which had been among the best supporters of the Delhi throne, retired to their centres in Rajputana, where the three leading States of Jaipur, Jodhpur, and Udaipur (among others) still exist. Their organization is by clans, and they never developed a fighting confederacy like that of the Marathas. When the Marathas invaded Malwa they carried their depredations on to Rajputana, but there was not much plunder to be got from that desert country. Eventually, early in the nineteenth century, the British entered into relations with the Rajput States, and promised them protection against the Marathas and other neighbouring military powers. The treaties then signed are the basis on which the Rajput princes hold their States in the British Indian Empire.

Three Governors of the Empire's Provinces.—We thus see how new races claimed power on the break-up of the Mughal Empire and formed new States. Some of them were not new in the sense of having been first heard of in history. But in the case of all of them their aspiration to succeed to all or some portion of the heritage of the Mughals was new. The French and the English, who came up from Europe, also mingled in the fray with similar aspirations, which we shall consider presently. We must now notice the three great satraps of the Mughal Empire itself, who tried (in the case of two) to make themselves supreme in the Mughal Empire, and (in the case of all) to save for themselves and their families some fragments of the Mughal Empire. These three were the Subahdars (governors) of the Deccan, of Oudh, and of Bengal.

Extended Size of Provinces.—The three provinces which were associated with the names of these three governors were not single provinces like those into which the empire was divided in the time of Akbar, but rather bundles of provinces, for each ambitious satrap tried to extend his jurisdiction, and managed to get authority for the extension from the Delhi Court. The Deccan Subah (province) comprised not only the latest provinces of the Mughal Empire constituted out of the conquered sultanates of the Deccan, but also Berar, Khandesh, Malwa, and, for a time, Gujarat—practically the whole of Central and Southern India. Central India soon fell to the Marathas. The Oudh jurisdiction extended not only to the province of Oudh as now known, but the territory to the east of it (which may be roughly described as the province of Benares), a good deal of the territory to the west of Oudh, and some of the districts in the neighbourhood of Allahabad and Cawnpore. The province of Bengal in the eighteenth century included the three provinces of Bengal, Bihar and Orissa.

The Deccan: How Hyderabad State was Founded.—The Subahdars of the Deccan and of Oudh kept up for a long time a rivalry in the Delhi court for the office of Wazir, or prime minister, which gave them the supreme position in the empire. They were firmly established in their own respective Subahs, and their office of Subahdar had become hereditary, as was the tendency with so many offices in the later Mughal Empire. But when they were at court they left deputies in their outlying Subahs, and when they were in their Subahs they left deputies at Delhi, to counter the intrigues of their opponents, and keep them informed of any opportunities which made it safe or profitable for them to come up to court. In this respect the State of Hyderabad may claim a continuous history linking it with the Mughal Empire. Its founder was descended from a talented Turki general of Aurangzib, who had distinguished himself at the taking of Hyderabad and Golkonda. He was prime minister of the empire in Delhi in 1722, with the title of Asaf Jah. When he found that the intrigues in Delhi made his position hopeless there, he threw up the ministership and went back to his province in the Deccan, where he devoted himself to the consolidation of his power. But he left sons and grandsons in Delhi, who also became Wazirs. The higher title, Nizam-ul-Mulk, became the title of the dynasty in the Deccan, which is still borne by the ruler of Hyderabad. Ordinarily it is used in its short form, the Nizam.

Its Importance in the Indian Empire.—The Nizam, when he returned to the Deccan in 1723, found that he had to save his charge from the incursions of the Marathas. Several successive Nizams had to fight the Maratha armies with varying success. Their boundaries, where they touched the boundaries of the Peshwa, were constantly shifting. In the south and towards the east coast they had no rivals until the French and the English came on the scene. The Nizam's governor of the Karnatik, the east-coast strip of territory in Southern India, was more directly in touch with the maritime settlements of the French and the English, and succession disputes in his family were the first occasion for conflict between those two European nations in India. Later, the Nizam had also to meet the growing power of Haidar Ali, who founded the new kingdom of Mysore. Haidar Ali and his son, Tippu Sultan, played a very important part in Deccan politics. But their kingdom of Mysore was eventually extinguished by British arms. The Nizams, by a policy of alliance and friendship with the British power, maintained their State through all the difficulties of the eighteenth century. His Exalted Highness the Nizam of Hyderabad continues to rule a State which ranks as the premier Indian State in the Indian Empire, and which justly claims to be the last remaining fragment of the Mughal Empire.

Oudh and its "Nawab Vizier."—The other Wazir of the empire who established a State and eventually a kingdom, was Saadat Khan, who came of a Persian family from Khorāsān. He was appointed governor of Oudh in 1724, and rapidly advanced in power and dignities. He was called up to Delhi at the invasion of Nadir Shah (1739), and died the same year. His nephew and son-in-law, Safdar Jang, succeeded to the government of Oudh, and became Wazir (prime minister of the empire) in 1748. Though opposed by Asaf Jah's son and grandson, he retained the Wazirship till shortly before his death in 1754. His son, Shuja-ud-daula (1754-1775), succeeded to the government of Oudh, and was an important figure in the third battle of Panipat (1761), to be described presently. He became Wazir, and is the "Nawab-Vizier" of the early English records, whom we shall meet again in describing the growth of English power in Bengal and Upper India.

Growth and Extinction of the Oudh Kingdom.—The Nawab of Oudh made his province of Oudh a nucleus for the addition of a great part of the territory now included in the United Provinces of Agra and Oudh. As he was nearer to Delhi, he kept longer in touch with the politics of the capital city and the person of the emperor. On the other hand, he was early brought into touch with the English, advancing from Bengal. On his western frontier were the Rohillas. They were an Afghan community settled in the country round Ramput and Bareilly, the modern Rohilkhand. Their territory was conquered and annexed by Oudh with the aid of British troops (1773-1774). In 1819 Nawab Ghazi-ud-din Haidar assumed the title of King of Oudh, and his successors ruled as kings in Lucknow till 1856. Their administration, however, deteriorated rapidly, and their kingdom was annexed in 1856 under Lord Dalhousie's policy of annexations, which was one of the contributory causes of the Indian Mutiny.

Bengal and its Revolution.—The Bengal viceroyalty had been held by several of the princes who afterwards succeeded to the throne of the Mughal at Delhi. We have already seen how the advantages of Bengal attracted the English as well as other European nations, and what a large part foreign commerce played in its economic life. A similar attraction was exerted on the nobles of the Delhi court by the riches and fame of Bengal. The last governor appointed to the province by Aurangzib was Murshid Quli Khan (1704-1726), who founded the city of Murshidabad, and made it the capital of Bengal. His two successors did not possess his ability, and his family was overthrown by a usurper of Turki origin of the name of Ali Wirdi Khan (or Ilah Wirdi Khan) in 1740. It is not clear whether (after this revolution) any revenue was remitted from Bengal to Delhi beyond one or two instalments. The Marathas, though repeatedly repulsed, returned and exacted their chauth, and the English, under the concessions which they had received from Delhi, carried on their trade without paying any duties to the Bengal treasury. Not only did the Company claim exemption for its own trade, but the servants of the Company, who carried on an extensive private trade on their own account, claimed a similar exemption. Moreover, the exemptions were claimed on the coasting and internal trade, as well as the foreign trade. This threw the finances of Bengal into much confusion, and there was much friction between the Company and Ali Wirdi Khan's adopted son, Siraj-ud-daula, who succeeded in 1756. The story of that friction, and of the important events which led up to the assumption of the revenue administration of the province by the Company, will be told in its place later. But the previous financial history of the province furnishes the key both to the acrimony with which Siraj-ud-daula (Sir Roger Dowla, as he is playfully called by contemporary English writers) resisted the English and the ease with which the Mughal emperor signed away the revenue administration of the province from which he had practically received no revenue for some years.

Two Invasions from the North-West.—There were two external events which affected the dying Mughal Empire, and must be noticed before we pass to a review of British political progress in India. One was the invasion of Nadir Shah in 1739, and the other the invasion of Ahmad Shah Abdali in 1761. At critical stages in Indian history events happening beyond the borderland of India have turned the scale decisively in India. We have to see why it was that the age-long story of further conquests and settlements from the north-west was not repeated at this stage of her history.

Afghan Conquest of Persia.—We saw how the Safavi Empire was founded in Persia about the same time as the Mughal Empire in India, and how the Ottoman Turks were at the height of their conquests about the same time. It is a curious circumstance that the decline of the Mughal Empire also coincided with the fall of the Safavi Empire in Persia and the first check to the conquests of the Ottoman Empire in the west. The Safavi Empire (1499-1736) had kept up close relations with the Mughal Empire in India. The intervening mountain country of Afghanistan had been more or less partitioned between these two empires. Ethnologically and linguistically Afghanistan consists, like Switzerland, of three distinct factors. The western portion, with the towns of Kandahar and Herat, falls within the Persian region. The eastern portion, including Kabul and the tract of the Hindu-Kush, falls within the Indian region. And the north and north-western portion, watered by the Oxus and its tributaries, falls within the Turkish region. For centuries Afghanistan was not a political unit, but was the sport of the powers on its three frontiers. Early in the eighteenth century it began to show signs of national unity. Its social organization was, and is, tribal. The two important tribes of the Ghilzais and the Abdalis (later called Durranis) were gathering power, and contending for supremacy. The first honours rested with the Ghilzais, who not only obtained the upper hand in their tract of Afghanistan, but took advantage of the weakness of Persia to conquer it in 1722.

Afghans Driven Back by Nadir Shah, who Invades India.—A Turki adventurer named Nadir Shah helped to stem the Ghilzai irruption into Persia, and for a time restored the Safavi Shah. Soon afterwards, however, he set aside the Safavis altogether, and established himself as the Shah. The Afghans were now scattered, and some of them took refuge in India. Delhi in its weakened state was a favourable soil for fresh intrigues. Nadir Shah asked for some of his enemies to be delivered up to him. The Mughal emperor was either unwilling or unable to comply, and Nadir Shah decided upon an invasion of India. Delhi could offer but a feeble resistance, although the Subahdars of the Deccan, of Oudh, and other outlying provinces were summoned to its assistance. There was no unity, and the emperor is said to have treated the invasion with very little seriousness. Some of his own supporters were lukewarm in his cause, and intrigued with the virile invader. When the Delhi army was routed with immense slaughter near Karnal, the Mughal emperor, Muhammad Shah, visited Nadir Shah's camp, and made a weak surrender. He brought Nadir Shah to Delhi. An insurrection of the inhabitants against the Persians drove Nadir Shah into a furious rage, and he ordered a general massacre and loot. He returned to Persia with immense booty, including the famous Koh-i-nur diamond. The territory west of the Indus was ceded to Nadir Shah, and the Indian frontier was once more pushed back to the Panjab.

Nadir's Fall: Afghans United into a Nation under Ahmad Shah, 1747.—Nadir Shah ruled Persia with a rod of iron. He was never in sympathy with the Persians; their national religion was Shia, and his attempts to introduce uniformity of worship between the Shia and Sunni sects were resented. There were many risings against him, and he began to rely more and more upon the Afghans. He was assassinated in 1747, and the confusion in which Persia was plunged until she was reunited under the Kajar dynasty in 1795 made her a negligible factor in the politics of Asia. She lost her foothold in Afghanistan. On the other hand, the Abdali tribe of the Afghans had a born leader in Ahmad Shah, who united Afghanistan under himself (1747) as an independent nation, and founded the Durrani dynasty, which still rules Afghanistan. Before his death in 1772-1773 he had extended his conquests to the Oxus on the north, and to near the shores of the Caspian on the west. On the east lay India, which he stripped of Kashmir, the Panjab, Sindh, and Baluchistan.

Ahmad Shah's Invasions of India.—He invaded India seven times. His fourth invasion, and the great victory which he won at the third battle of Panipat, 1761, is connected with the whole tangled web of Delhi politics. When Ahmad Shah left Delhi for Afghanistan about June 1757 (while Clive was winning the battle of Plassey in Bengal), he and his son allied themselves with the Mughal emperor by marriages; he left an Afghan (Rohilla) nominee of his as commander-in-chief in Delhi, by name Najib-ud-daula, as a counterpoise to the Wazir Ghazi-ud-din, the grandson of Asaf Jah; and he left his own son as governor of the Panjab. As soon as his back was turned the Wazir superseded the commander-in-chief, and in order to effect a revolution in the Imperial line, called in the aid of the Marathas. The Marathas came again to Delhi (1758). Their ambitions now increased. They entered the Panjab at the invitation of another official who had been superseded by Ahmad Shah, and expelled Ahmad Shah's son. Ahmad Shah Durrani returned in September 1759, and had no difficulty in dispersing the Maratha forces from Northern India. Meanwhile, Ghazi-ud-din had effected his revolution by bloodshed, and raised a puppet emperor to the throne of Delhi. Ghazi-ud-din fled on the approach of Ahmad Shah. As the heir-apparent, whose title was subsequently recognized under the name of Shah Alam II. (1759-1806), was then in Bengal, Delhi was garrisoned by the Durranis, while Ahmad Shah proceeded to organize a government.

Third Battle of Panipat, 1761.—The Marathas did not take their reverses in Upper India lying down. The Peshwa at Poona called up all his available forces to meet Ahmad Shah, who, on the other hand, tried to get together all the available fragments of Mughal forces to resist the Marathas. But he had mainly to rely on his own Afghans, aided by the Rohillas. The family of Asaf Jah was against him. The Oudh Subahdar nominally joined him, but was lukewarm. On the other hand, the Maratha army, both in point of numbers and efficiency, was now a formidable fighting weapon. They had good artillery; they had a strong force of regular and irregular cavalry; and their infantry had been drilled after the European models introduced by the French and the English in the Deccan. Their chief executive command was given to a Muslim general, Ibrahim Khan Gardi, who had already seen service under the French and under the Nizam in the Deccan. He was an experienced artillery officer, and brought a good train of the light and mobile field pieces which the French had introduced into the Nizam's army. The various Maratha commanders brought their own contingents, including Sindhia, Holkar, the Gaikwar, and Shamsher Bahadur, the progenitor of the Nawabs of Banda. The political command was taken by a member of the Peshwa's own family. The Maratha host has been estimated at nearly 100,000 fighting men, with 200 guns, and, including camp followers, it had about 300,000 men. The Afghan fighting force was estimated at about 40,000, with another 51,000 miscellaneous Indian troops of little fighting value. The Afghans were particularly weak in artillery, but mainly relied on hand-to-hand charges, superior morale, and superior generalship. The Maratha armies at first gained ground, but Ahmad Shah brought up his reserves, and a flanking movement turned the fortunes of the fight. The Marathas broke and fled, and were hotly pursued. The whole Maratha army was broken, and their leaders were nearly all killed.

Why the Afghan Invasion was not Turned into a Conquest.— The Maratha Confederacy was now practically at an end. Until 1795 the commanders continued to be called in for consultations, but they did not obey the Peshwa's authority. The Maratha fights after 1761 (and there were many) were those of individual chiefs, not those of a united Maratha nation. There was no emperor or government at Delhi, as Shah Alam did not return till 1771, and both before and after he was practically a captive. Ahmad Shah left Najib-ud-daula as the chief noble in authority at Delhi, and Najib remained at his post till his death in 1770. But the nominal Wazir of the empire was the Subahdar of Oudh. He lived in his own capital at Faizabad.* Ahmad Shah might have made himself master of India. But his hardy mountaineer soldiers had had enough of the heat of the plains during the fourteen months they had already spent in India, and would have mutinied if he had not returned to Kabul. His own kingdom in Afghanistan had not yet been consolidated, and his absence was dangerous at home. And the beginnings of the terrible disease (said to have been cancer in the face) which killed him in 1772-1773 were perhaps already giving him warning. He left the Delhi territory in confusion,

* Lucknow was not made the capital of Oudh till 1775.

but the heirs of the Mughal Empire were already creeping up from Bengal. During the Durrani's lifetime Clive had won Plassey, the Company had acquired the Diwani of Bengal and control of the emperor's person, and the British House of Commons had already appointed a Select Committee whose labours resulted in the famous Regulating Act of 1773.

CHAPTER XV

FRENCH BID FOR SUPREMACY

Extension of Company's Trade.—Before proceeding to the subject of the French bid for supremacy in India let us take a general view of the Company's affairs between Godolphin's award (1708) and the declaration of war between England and France about the Austrian succession in Europe (1744), and the consequent Indian hostilities in 1746. It was a period of quiet extension of trade in the Presidencies, and of the strengthening of the Company's position at home, in spite of the growing opposition to the import of Indian textiles into England.

Strength as a Financial Corporation.—The legislation of the British Parliament during the period shows the very important position the Company occupied as a financial corporation in the city of London. The Company was looked upon as a rival to the Bank of England. It was expressly forbidden to do banking business. It was not allowed to discount bills, keep current accounts, or receive deposits, or borrow for shorter periods than six months, or for other purposes than its trade or loans to Government. After the South Sea Bubble in England and the Mississippi speculations in France (1720), when financial credit was shaken, the East India Company's stock rose to 445 per cent., although their dividend was only 10 per cent. When Parliament in 1721 attempted some relief from the financial distress, they authorized the South Sea Company to place their stock with the Bank of England and the East India Company, although the latter did not actually take up any. The charter of the East India Company was renewed in 1730 and 1744, but on each occasion the Government took further loans from the Company.

Progress of Inventions and Manufactures in England.—Meanwhile, general manufacturing and commercial activity had increased enormously in England. The union with Scotland had put an end to the tariff wars within the island. The Treaty of Utrecht (1713-1714), had greatly strengthened the position of England as against both France and Spain. England got a footing in the Mediterranean, and important concessions in North and South America, including a thirty years' monopoly of the lucrative slave trade with South America, previously in French hands. The size of London increased rapidly, and villages like Liverpool, Manchester, and Birmingham became important towns and centres of industry. Inventive skill began to be applied to textile machinery. John Kay's fly-shuttle (1738) started the big-scale cotton industry of Lancashire, which received a further impetus from the inventions of Hargreaves (1764) and Arkwright (1769), and by the use of steam-power in place of water-power (about 1790). Sir Thomas Lombe's patent (1719) for a silk-throwing machine was worked by water-power, and was directed not only to manufacturing processes, but to the warming, by heated air, of the extensive premises in which workers were now congregated. These inventions were added to from time to time all through the eighteenth century, until they ushered in the era of steam and factory and great capitalistic industrial enterprises.

Their Effect on India.—It was these inventions and the brains behind them, combined with the economy, capital, and organization which they introduced into the working of manufactures, which reversed the position between India and England as regards textiles. But England's victory was also seconded by protective legislation. In 1700 the import of silks, calicoes, and prints into England was prohibited. The East India Company's custom had greatly stimulated these manufactures in India; the Company merely diverted them to the China and Continental trade. By 1740 England not only supplied her own manufactures of cotton, but also exported them to the colonies. It was not till the end of the eighteenth century that the Indian textile manufactures felt the competition of England in the Far Eastern markets and in her own markets.

Anglo-French Conflicts in India; Phases of World Conflicts; Influence of Sea-Power.—But British supremacy, economic or political, was not won without more than one world contest with her neighbour and age-long rival, France. Two such contests occurred in the middle of the eighteenth century. Their Indian phases alone interest us here, but they should be studied in their more general bearings before we can understand their full significance in the building up of the British Empire. The war of 1744-1748 was indecisive, but the Seven Years' War (1756-1763) sealed the fate of France in the Western and Eastern worlds, and established the supremacy of British sea-power, which has never been lost since. It was threatened by France in the war of American Independence, whose echoes we shall find in Admiral de Suffren's vigorous demonstrations in the Indian seas in 1782-1783. But its overwhelming strength in the wars of the French Revolution saved Britain from a dangerous situation, out of which she emerged the acknowledged mistress of all India.

Colbert's East India Company Founded, 1664.—As we have seen, France was not yet ready for Eastern adventures in the sixteenth century. In the seventeenth century, when England was torn by civil dissensions, or weakened by the nerveless policy of the last two Stuarts, France turned towards the East. Her early efforts were confined to Madagascar. Cardinal Richelieu, that masterful statesman who prepared the way for the strength of France at home and abroad, formed an Eastern Company with exclusive privileges, just before his death in 1642. But that Company did very little. It was Colbert who, in 1664, founded the really active East India Company, with a State loan and a State guarantee. At that very time the French philosopher, doctor, and traveller, François Bernier, was at the Mughal court in India, and writing letters home describing the political, social, and economic conditions in that country. Colbert's Company took root, and by 1667 had extended its operations from the islands round Madagascar to the continent of India.

French at Surat: Foundation of Pondicherry, 1674.—The French have a happy knack, both by their manners and their temperament, of appealing to the Oriental mind. But their efforts in history have been more brilliant than sustained. And they have shone more as soldiers, statesmen, and men of letters than as merchants. An English traveller (Dr. Fryer), visiting

Surat in 1674, thus sums up his impressions of the French factory there: "Better stored with Monsieurs than with cash; they live well, borrow money, and make a show." On the other hand, the French agent, Martin, had that year acquired by purchase, with the permission of one of the Deccan sultanates, a tract of land on the east coast comprising 113 square miles, about 86 miles south of Madras. The principal village was Puducheri, now known as Pondicherry. It was sheltered against the monsoons, and had good communications with the interior. The Dutch did not leave it unmolested. But the French secured the confidence of the people, built up a good trade in textiles, and constructed a fort and a handsome town with regular streets after French models. They also drilled native troops, and by the beginning of the eighteenth century had a fine settlement, well planned and well organized, with a great deal of influence in the local politics of the country around.

Governor of Pondicherry as a High Dignitary of the Court of the Grand Mughal.—But economically it was not prosperous. In 1717-1720 came the grandiose schemes of John Law, the Scotch speculator and financier, who had complete hold of the Regency and Government of France. His system absorbed the Company. When the crash came the system disappeared, but the Company remained, with a perpetual charter and reconstituted finances (1723). Thereafter Pondicherry prospered materially, and gathered power by mixing itself up in local politics. By 1741 its governor was director-general of French India, comprising, besides Pondicherry, Chandernagore on the Hugli (eighteen miles north of Calcutta, acquired in 1688), Karikal (eighty miles south of Pondicherry, and acquired in 1739), and Mahé on the west coast (about thirty miles north of Calicut, and acquired in 1722), besides scattered factories in other places. But he was also a high dignitary of the court of the Grand Mughal, with a definite rank and status, which passed on to each holder of the office of governor. Dupleix held this office from 1742 to 1754.

Contrast between Pondicherry and Madras.—The English settlement at Madras was quite eclipsed, but only for a time. If it had no "Monsieurs," it had cash. If it had no brilliant leaders dreaming of glory, it had hard-headed men of the counter, who, despite all their own petty feuds, trusted and upheld each other in a crisis. Above all, it had a country behind it at home that recognized services, honoured its agents who won renown for it abroad, and steadily supported, without abdicating its right to pass judgment, all efforts in its cause, irrespective of success or failure. Dupleix, with incompetent subordinates, jealous colleagues, and ignorant and suspicious superiors, withholding resources and rewarding failure with disgrace and infamy, was no match against Clive and Stringer Lawrence, active and resourceful, well supported with colleagues piecing together slender means with a unanimous purpose, and a directorate at home well informed in all details, and responding to all local calls with energy and promptitude.

Four Stages of Anglo-French Conflict in India.—Between 1746 and 1763 there was almost constant conflict between the English and the French in Southern India. It may be divided into three stages. From 1746 to 1748 it was a part of the European war between France and England, about the Austrian succession. The Indian powers, though they watched the struggle, and drew their own conclusions, were not much involved in it. Between 1749 and 1754 the English and French authorities in Southern India took opposite sides in various fights and disputes between Indian powers. There was a local war, although their nations were at peace in Europe. From 1758 to 1761 the Indian conflict was a part of the world-wide Seven Years' War (1756-1763), in which England, by virtue of her sea-power, wrested Canada from France in America, and practically eliminated French competition from India. There was an interval of fifteen years in which France was quiet in India. In 1778-1782 the French made a naval demonstration in India in connection with the War of American Independence. It will be convenient to discuss these four stages of the conflict together in this chapter. But before doing so let us review the political state of the Deccan during the few years before and after 1746.

The Deccan.—In this connection the Deccan may be taken to mean roughly the whole of the country south of the Narbada and the Mahanadi, from sea to sea. All this enormous territory was claimed in theory by the Nizam as his Subah. At that time his capital was in Aurangabad. The English had their settlement in the island of Bombay. At this time Bombay was detached from general Indian politics, except in so far as its fine harbour made it the British naval base in the East. The Marathas were firmly established in the territory round Poona and Satara, and in the strip of western sea-coast called the Konkan, but as we have seen, they made wide incursions north and south and, indeed, to all parts of India, except where the Nizam's authority was effectively exercised. One of the largest provinces of the Nizam's dominions was the Karnatik, ruled by a Nawab (or deputy) under the Nizam. Subject to the reservations to be mentioned presently, the Karnatik may be taken to be the country, from sea to sea, south of the river Krishna. The strip of sea-coast running north-eastwards from the mouth of the Krishna to Ganjam was the Northern Sarkars (or Circars—*i.e.*, districts).

The Karnatik.—The term "Karnatik," or "Karnata," is in origin the same as "Kanara," and formerly denoted the tract of country in the western half of the Deccan plateau, in which the Kanarese language is spoken. It included the south-western corner of the present Hyderabad State, with the British territory adjoining, and the greater part of what is now Mysore State and Coorg. The extension of Muslim rule in the south made political boundaries different from linguistic boundaries. The absorption of the Deccan sultanates in the Mughal Empire made the southern or Deccan Subah an enormous Subah, with ill-defined boundaries to the south. The southern portion of this Subah was made into a sub-province, whose northern boundary was the Krishna, and the eastern and western boundaries the Bay of Bengal and the Arabian Sea. The southern boundary of effective occupation was marked by the Kaveri river, but the Nawabs of the Karnatik were expected to extend and exercise their sway right down to Cape Comorin. There were many Hindu Polygars (or zamindars) in the far south, who only acknowledged the overlordship of the Nawab when it suited their purpose. Practically Mysore and the west coast territory was not in effective occupation. Tanjore was a little Maratha Jagir, which in its family quarrels sought the aid of the English (1741-1749). Trichinopoly was another Hindu rajaship which had troubles with its overlords, the Nawabs of the Karnatik, as early as 1736, when its limited autonomy was extinguished by the Nawab. But the Marathas were constantly interfering with the Karnatik, especially in the affairs of Tanjore and Trichinopoly. The French, whose settlement at Pondicherry had acquired great local influence, took every opportunity of interfering in local disputes. About the middle of the eighteenth century we may distinguish between three tracts of the Karnatik: (1) the east coast territory between the mouths of the Krishna and Kaveri, in which was situated Arcot, the capital of the Karnatik; this was in effective occupation; (2) the east coast territory, south of the Kaveri, in which Trichinopoly was the storm centre, as the seat of a newly established sub-governor appointed by the Nawab of Arcot; (3) the part of the Karnatik on the Deccan plateau—*i.e.*, above the Eastern Ghats—which was subject to incursions from the Marathas, and soon afterwards from Mysore. Travancore was practically independent.

Variety of Political Forces.—If we take a place like Trichinopoly, and consider the many political interests that claimed some sort of authority there, we shall understand the extreme sub-infeudation that had taken place in theory in the Deccan in this period of Indian anarchy. Supreme was the vague authority of the Mughal emperor at Delhi. Nominally the Nizam was his viceroy—his Subahdar of the Deccan. The Nawab of the Karnatik was the Nizam's deputy, and a local governor held Trichinopoly as the Nawab's deputy. But his authority was not exercised without question, for the family of the old displaced Raja were always intriguing to regain some measure of power, and called in the aid of outsiders. Among these the Marathas were the most enterprising. But the English and the French, whose settlements were in the Karnatik, had well-drilled armies, superior artillery, and an organization based on their home countries, with a sea-power that made their forces mobile and their supplies secure against land forces. The petty zamindars or rajas around, like that of Tanjore, or their ministers, sometimes took a hand in the scramble. Mysore, especially after it became aggressive under Haidar Ali in 1760,

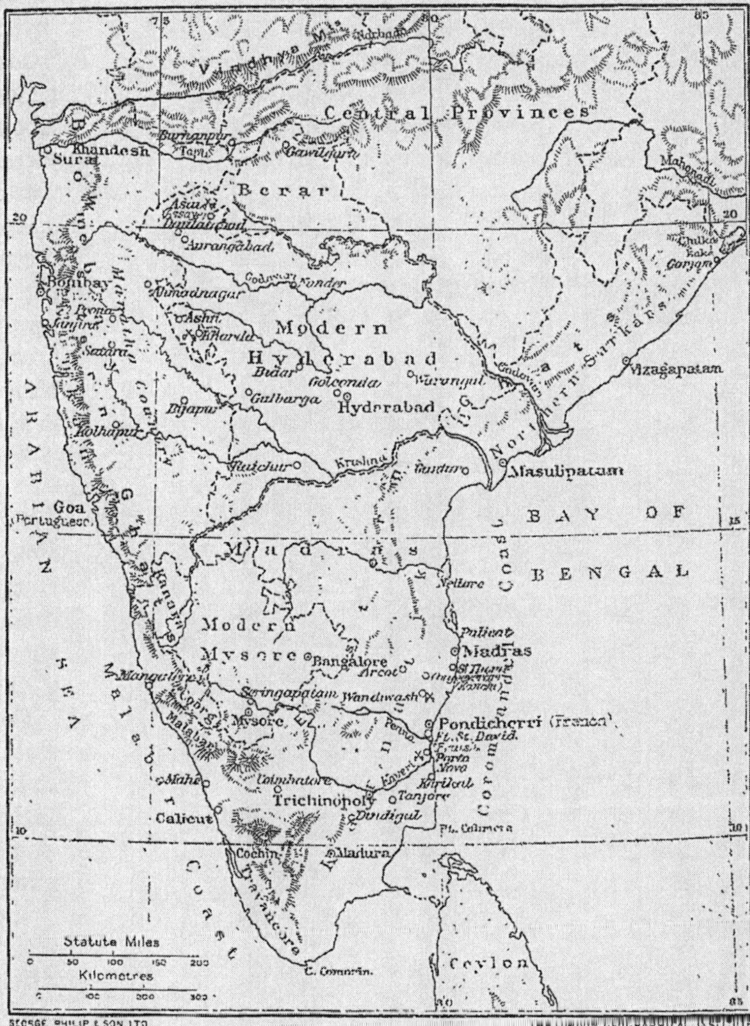

MAP OF SOUTHERN INDIA

To accompany "THE MAKING OF INDIA," BY A. YUSUF ALI (A. & C. BLACK, LTD., LONDON)

was a strong factor in Karnatik politics. When there was a disputed succession at any of the stages of power, there might be two or three claimants for a single office or seat of authority. And there was no real or effective subordination as between one stage and another. Thus there could be, and were, innumerable permutations and combinations in which the political forces could be grouped.

First Anglo-French Conflict in India.—The possession of sea-power, superior artillery, and superior military organization and drill gave the European powers an advantage over the warring "country powers," which was bound to prevail in the end. But in the rivalry between France and England it was not purely local causes that gave England the final victory. Their local conflicts must always be studied in relation to their world history. Their first conflict came in the War of the Austrian Succession, whose effects were felt in India in 1746. As far as South India was concerned, the French were entirely successful. By one swift stroke their admiral, La Bourdonnais, took Madras (September 1746), and the English Presidency was removed to Fort St. David. The English siege of Pondicherry, 1748, was a failure. But the French had no sea-power as against England in Europe, and they were compelled to restore Madras by the Peace of Aix-la-Chapelle (1748), which they did in 1749. The French had greatly improved the fortifications of Madras, for they had meant to keep it if they had won the European war.

French Prestige Enhanced.—This first contest between the French and the English in India is notable for the unseemly jealousy between the French admiral (La Bourdonnais) and the French governor on land (Dupleix), and for its effect on Indian opinion. The English sea operations were badly conducted in India, but the French had the advantage in their base at Réunion (Bourbon) and the Isle of France (Mauritius), islands more productive and better situated as a half-way house to India than the rocky island of St. Helena, the English half-way house. La Bourdonnais was a man of great energy and capacity. In the islands he had practically made his own navy, and created his own sailors and soldiers out of the rough material, French and African, that he had at hand. In spite of all his successes in India, he incurred the bitter hostility of Dupleix, whose charges of corruption and treason against him brought him to the Bastille, from which he was only released to die. As regards Indian opinion, this little war added greatly to the prestige of the French. The Mughal Subahdar of Bengal had forbidden the belligerents from waging war in his jurisdiction. In the south Dupleix, himself a Mughal Nawab, had prevailed upon the Nawab of the Karnatik to declare Pondicherry under Mughal protection, and to ask that the belligerents should confine their hostilities to the sea. He had promised Madras to the Nawab. When the French took Madras, and failed to deliver it to the Nawab, the Nawab's son tried to take it by force, but was signally beaten by the French disciplined forces and the rapid fire of their artillery.

Second Anglo-French Conflict: Disputes about Succession to Asaf Jah.—The second Anglo-French conflict (1748-1754) was nominally a scramble between the "country powers" of the Deccan, for France and Britain were at peace at home. But the real protagonists in the contests were the French and the British. An ambitious man like Dupleix was not content to rest with his first successes, especially as their fruit was taken away from him by the action of the home authorities. A nation like the British, after its successes in the world contest, was not likely to sit still in the humiliating position to which it had been reduced in India. Both sides had very powerful armed forces, collected before the Peace of Aix-la-Chapelle, which required employment. The opportunities for their use came in unexpected abundance. In June 1748, the Nizam, Asaf Jah I., died at the advanced age of a hundred and four. For over three-quarters of a century he had kept the peace of the Deccan—such peace as was possible in those troublous days. There was a dispute about his succession. His eldest son was at Delhi, engaged in the high game of retaining the supreme power round the person of the emperor. His second son, Nāsir Jang, was on the spot at Aurangabad, and seized the reins of power. But Muzaffar Jang, a grandson of Asaf Jah I. by a daughter, got some authority from Delhi to carry on the government of the Deccan. In order to translate his pretensions into power he began to look around for powerful allies. These allies he found in the French.

Disputes about Nawabship of the Karnatic.—There was another source of disturbance in the Deccan, which gave Dupleix a double opportunity. Asaf Jah I. had always insisted on the subordination of the Nawab of the Karnatik to himself, and on treating the nawabship as an office to which he made appointments at will, and not as a hereditary right to which sons or adopted sons could succeed as a matter of course. During one of his absences in Delhi such a succession had occurred. In 1743, on his return to the Deccan, he had visited Arcot and cancelled such a succession. When he died he left Anwar-ud-din Nawab of the Karnatik, the man whose forces were defeated by the French before Madras. But a connection of the superseded family of Nawabs, by name Chanda Saheb, was a ready tool in the hands of Dupleix, to contest the unpopular rule of Anwar-ud-din in the Karnatik. Chanda Saheb made common cause with Muzaffar Jang, the claimant to the Subahdarship of the Deccan. With the aid of French troops they defeated the aged Anwar-ud-din, who was slain in battle at the age of a hundred and seven, and took Anwar-ud-din's eldest son prisoner. Anwar-ud-din's second son, Muhammad Ali, fled for his life to Trichinopoly, where he had held the post of governor for his father. This was in 1749. His cause was adopted by the English.

French Power with Nizam.—Dupleix had played a double part. While he had backed Muzaffar Jang, he had tried by negotiation and threats to gain the ascendancy over Nāsir Jang, the Nizam actually in power, who was favoured by the English. Nāsir Jang was killed in quelling an insurrection in 1750. Muzaffar Jang was raised to the Subahdarship by the French. He visited Pondicherry, and gave large concessions to his benefactors. He was given a doubtful boon, a body of French troops under Bussy, who practically became masters of the ruler of the Deccan. Bussy was the most capable—the only capable—general the French had in India. On Muzaffar Jang's death in a fight (1751), Bussy raised Salābat Jang, the eldest surviving son of Asaf Jah I., to the Subahdarship. Salābat Jang gave still further concessions to the French, and was formally installed in June 1751, in his capital at Aurangabad, where he held power till 1762.

Fight for Trichinopoly and Arcot: Clive's Brilliant Successes.—When Muhammad Ali fled to Trichinopoly (1749), his successful rival, Chanda Saheb, could easily have crushed him with French help. But Chanda Saheb remained inactive, and wasted time. Muhammad Ali wavered, and his English allies were apathetic. In July 1751, matters came to a head. Chanda Saheb came in force with the French to take Trichinopoly. The small English force sent to assist Muhammad Ali was itself blockaded by Chanda Saheb and his French under the walls of Trichinopoly. Now came the chance of Clive. He was only a young captain of twenty-six, with but indifferent education, but an inborn capacity as a leader of men. With swift decision and unerring strategy he saw that the best plan for the English was to take Arcot, the capital of Chanda Saheb, who with his troops was before Trichinopoly. His plan was approved by the governor, who denuded Madras and Fort St. David of all the available troops, which amounted to a very small force. Clive went straight to Arcot and captured it without a blow.

French Failure, and Dupleix's Disgrace.—This had the desired effect. Chanda Saheb detached large forces, from Trichinopoly and elsewhere, to retake his capital. But Clive was as prudent as he was bold. He had fortified Arcot and prepared himself for a siege. For fifty-three days he sustained a gallant fight, in which his Indian sepoys (soldiers) fought as devotedly as his European force. When the enemy raised the siege (November 1751), he pursued and defeated them. Thanks to Clive's genius, the tide had now turned, and the initiative had passed to the British. By 1752 Chanda Saheb was deserted and killed, Trichinopoly was relieved (although Mysore and the Marathas still hung round it), Muhammad Ali became the effective Nawab of the Karnatik, and Dupleix was foiled in his ambitions. The Governments at London and Paris agreed to suppress this unofficial war in India. In January 1754, Dupleix was superseded by orders of the French Government. He died in France, a poor and broken man, in November 1764.

Firm British Position Established in Bengal, 1757.—There was a short lull in Anglo-French relations in India, during which the British strengthened their position. The Seven Years' War (1756-1763) broke out in May 1756, and the news was known in India by October. But this was to be the decisive contest between Britain and France for sea-power and supremacy in America and Asia, and ample preparations were necessary on both sides. The conflict in the Deccan did not begin till 1758, but in the meantime French agents at Chandernagore had noted the British misfortunes at Calcutta (1756), and given the refugees such assistance as their neutral position permitted them to give. But the avenging hand of Clive had soon turned the tables on the Nawab of Bengal, won the battle of Plassey (1757), and established a firm British position in Bengal. The narrative of these events may conveniently be deferred till after we have finished with the Anglo-French struggles in Madras.

Third Anglo-French Conflict: Lally's Failure before Madras.—In the third Anglo-French conflict in India there was no leader of strength or spirit in the French settlements in India itself, except Bussy, and he was recalled from the dominating position he occupied in the court of the Nizam. The local French in India were cowed down after Dupleix's undeserved disgrace, and had made no preparations for the contest. They were impecunious also, and were not taken seriously by the great general, Comte de Lally, who had been sent out after great preparations at home. He was an Irish-Frenchman, who had proved his capacity in Europe, but who was wholly incapable of grasping the position in India. He arrived at Pondicherry in April 1758, captured Fort St. David after a month's siege in June, and prepared for the siege of Madras. But he won the confidence neither of the local French officials nor of his Indian allies. His armies starved, and were mutinous, and he was provided with no resources wherewith to push on the war. The French admiral, after a faint-hearted fight with the English fleet, sailed away to Mauritius, in spite of Lally's protests. On the British side the preparations had been made steadily with great forethought. Though Clive remained in Bengal, there were in the south sound soldiers, like Stringer

Lawrence (the commander-in-chief) and Eyre Coote, who had been trained under Clive; the navy was well handled, and the Bengal successes had raised the credit of the British. The siege of Madras by the French began in December 1758, and was abandoned in February 1759.

Siege and Destruction of Pondicherry.—The failure before Madras made the French cause hopeless in Indian eyes. Their supplies were cut off. All the districts in which their influence had been established turned against them. The Nizam whom the French had installed was insecure on his throne after Bussy's departure. Colonel Coote defeated the French under Lally at Wandiwash,* January 1760, after which he rapidly took Arcot and other places of importance. Such of the French troops as Lally had been able to save were besieged in Pondicherry, which surrendered in January 1761. The fortifications were demolished, and Lally was sent as a prisoner to London. He returned on parole to France to meet the charge of treachery levelled against him by his own countrymen, by whom he was unjustly beheaded, May 1766. The fall of Pondicherry in 1761 decided the French war in India. Chandernagore, in Bengal, had already been captured by Clive in 1757, and the dream of French dominion in India was over. In America, during the same war, the French had been expelled from Canada, and the Spaniards from Florida, and these losses were confirmed by the Peace of Paris, 1763.

Birth of Anglo-Indian Army.—The birth of the Anglo-Indian army dates from these Anglo-French wars. It consisted of three parts: (1) the Company's Indian troops, drilled and equipped in the European manner, and led by European officers; (2) the Company's European troops; and (3) the troops of the King's British army sent out to serve in India. Some African soldiers were at one time also employed, both by French and British, but they played no important part. The European troops of the Company were rightly so called; they were recruited from the drifting European population of the many nationalities that found their way to India. There were deserters or adventurers of French, German, Dutch, Italian, Swiss, and other nationalities, who fought for the Company

* About seventy miles south-west of Madras.

although the greater proportion of the Company's European troops were British, and some men, like Clive, were recruited from the Company's " writers " in India. The British troops, properly so called, were regiments of the King's army. The first such regiment was the 39th Regiment, to which Eyre Coote belonged, which landed in India in 1754.

Stringer Lawrence, Father of Indian Army.—The father of the Indian army was Stringer Lawrence. He arrived in Fort St. David in January 1748. He was appointed commander-in-chief in 1751, the first officer to hold that rank in India. From the date of his arrival he addressed himself seriously to the task of organizing a good mixed force, of real fighting value. He reorganized seven companies of Europeans. The Indian sepoys (or soldiers) were then called peons; he organized them also in companies, and in 1759 in battalions. Clive, in 1765-1766, created brigades and stations or cantonments for the Bengal army. The growth of three separate presidential armies has already been referred to. The Indian army has stood the test of time for over a century and a half—from the Karnatik campaigns to the Great World War, in which it shared in the fighting in Europe, Asia, and Africa. Stringer Lawrence himself was a modest man in private and public life. He was a capable organizer, a good judge of men, and a sound soldier.

Fourth Anglo-French Conflict.—The Treaty of Paris (1763) restored Pondicherry and Chandernagore to the French, but they were now without fortifications, and even the cities were in ruins. They were centres of subsequent French intrigues, but never raised their heads seriously in Indian politics again. The fourth Anglo-French conflict in India (1778-1782) was merely a series of naval demonstrations in Indian waters on the part of France, in connection with the War of American Independence. There was very little land fighting. The British had no difficulty in taking Chandernagore and Pondicherry. The powerful fleet which the famous French admiral, Suffren, brought out in 1782 did nothing decisive. Bussy's reappointment to India in the same year led to no results, as the Peace of Versailles (1783) put an end to hostilities between the two nations. In this Indian episode the French were merely playing a subsidiary part. The principal fight against the English was waged by Haidar Ali, ruler of Mysore, whose character and career will claim our attention later. In the Revolutionary Wars France had communications with Tippu, the son and successor of Haidar Ali, which led to Tippu's own undoing.

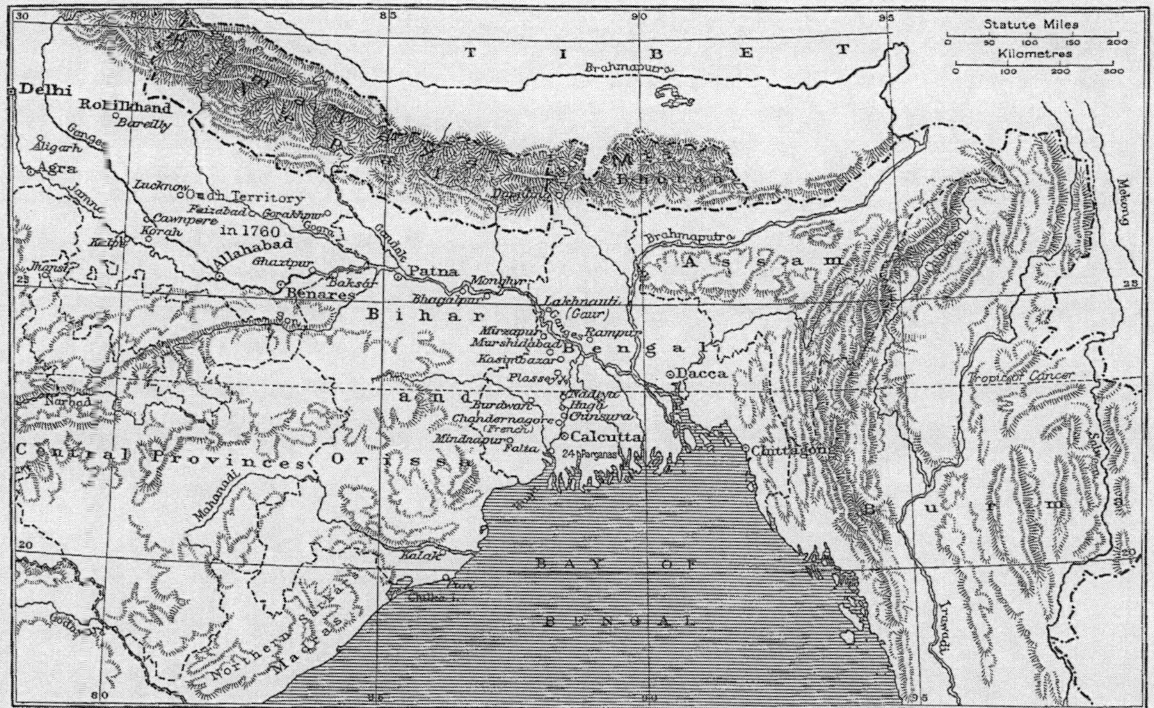

MAP OF BENGAL AND UPPER INDIA

To accompany "THE MAKING OF INDIA," BY A. YUSUF ALI (A. & C. BLACK LTD., LONDON)

CHAPTER XVI

ACQUISITION OF BENGAL

Siraj-ud-daula, Nawab of Bengal, 1756.—In reviewing the Subahs of the Mughal Empire which became semi-independent during the Great Anarchy (1707-1773), we traced the history of Bengal to the accession of Nawab Siraj-ud-daula to the Subahdari in April 1756. Siraj-ud-daula was a youth of barely eighteen years—inexperienced, vain, and headstrong. His fifteen months of nominal power witnessed a series of disasters to himself and his Subah, which were but a prelude to an unparalleled political revolution throughout India.

His Character and Grievances against the English.—He had many enemies. His uncles and relatives, who were in high posts in the Subahdari, were not well-disposed towards him, and he did nothing to conciliate them. His army was discontented, and so were many of his civil officials at distant points in his triple Subahdari (Bengal, Bihar, and Orissa). Some of the rich bankers in his capital at Murshidabad had big financial interests in the trading concerns of the Dutch, French, and English close at hand. Any of his defaulting officials could find an easy asylum in these foreign settlements. One of them had actually fled to Calcutta, and remonstrances had been vainly addressed to the English governor. The abuse of private trade by the Company's servants without payment of duties had been a standing grievance, to which was added the Company's attempt at strengthening the fortifications at Calcutta, in view of the expected hostilities between France and England in Europe. The Nawab captured the English factory at Kasimbazar,* and made up his mind to attack Calcutta.

He Captured Calcutta and Drove the English out of Bengal.—The British had no strong leader at Calcutta. Mr. Drake, who

* Five miles south of Murshidabad.

was governor, was in a panic, and with the commandant and principal officers, shamefully deserted the settlement when the Nawab's army came near. They took to their boats, and sailed down the river, where many of them perished. On June 20, 1756, Calcutta capitulated. The women (except one, probably left by oversight) and the valuable property had already been taken away in the boats. But not a thought was given to those left behind, few of whom survived to tell the tale. The Nawab thought that he had achieved a triumph and that he had driven the English into the sea.

Clive sent to Bengal with a Fleet and Troops.—But his triumph was short-lived. The news reached Madras early in August 1756. The Company in England and the Government had strengthened the sea and land forces in India, in anticipation of hostilities with the French in the Seven Years' War. Clive had left Madras for reasons of health in February 1753, and had been given a diamond-hilted sword by the Directors of the Company in public recognition of his brilliant services in Madras. He was made Lieutenant-Colonel in the King's service, and returned to India as governor of Fort St. David early in 1756. Before joining his post in the Madras Presidency, he landed in Bombay with some King's troops, artillery and infantry. He, with a large land force, and Admiral Watson, with a powerful fleet, destroyed the nest of a Maratha pirate, Angria, who had made himself obnoxious both to the Maratha authorities in Poona and the English authorities in Bombay. Clive then went to his governorship of Fort St. David, from which he was summoned to Madras in August for consultations about the recovery of Calcutta. In December Admiral Watson's fleet arrived at the mouth of the Hugli with Clive and his troops, 900 Europeans and 1,500 sepoys.

He Retook Calcutta and Captured Hugli and Chandernagore.—Calcutta was retaken on January 2, 1757, mainly with the ships' guns. Hugli, higher up, was captured on January 10. The Nawab marched down to Calcutta early in February, but Clive's reputation and his bold tactics saved the situation, and a treaty was concluded by which the Nawab restored all the Company's factories and paid compensation for losses, besides permitting them to fortify Calcutta. Both the Nawab and

Clive wanted peace; the Nawab because the Afghan invasion of Delhi was throwing the pressure of the Imperial family on his western frontier in Bihar; and Clive, because the Anglo-French war made Clive's position difficult unless he could expel the French from their neighbouring settlement in Chandernagore. As soon as his hands were free, Clive and Admiral Watson, against the wishes of the Nawab, took Chandernagore (March 1757), and expelled the French, who joined the Nawab.

Plot to Depose Siraj-ud-daula and make Mir Jaafar Nawab. There was practically open hostility again between Siraj-ud-daula and Clive. The treachery of the Nawab's own men made the fight one-sided. The Nawab's Bakhshi (paymaster of the forces) was a connection by marriage of the Nawab's family, and much older than the Nawab. His name was Mir Jaafar. He controlled the Nawab's army, and had no love for the Nawab. He entered into a secret plot with the English agent at Murshidabad, with the cognizance of Clive and his council at Calcutta, by which he stipulated that, if the English made him Nawab in place of Siraj-ud-daula, he would pay enormous sums of money, not only to the Company and the inhabitants of Calcutta (English, Indian, and Armenian) for their losses on account of the Nawab's invasion, but also pay huge sums (specified) to the army and navy, and to individual Englishmen, such as Colonel Clive and the governor and members of council. The Company was to receive further grants of zamindari, and the French were to be excluded for ever from Bengal. The terms were reduced to writing. It was arranged that Clive should take the field, and Mir Jaafar should join him.

Battle of Plassey.—The Nawab marched in person from Murshidabad with a large army to meet Clive. The battle (such as it was) was fought at the village of Plassey, about thirty miles south of Murshidabad and one hundred miles north of Calcutta, on June 23, 1757. Clive had taken every precaution in case Mir Jaafar did not keep his promise to desert his own side. The only part of the Nawab's army which fought for him was the contingent led by the faithful Mir Madan, and Mir Madan died at an early stage of the engagement. The small contingent of forty to fifty gallant Frenchmen made a brave fight with their light artillery, but Mir Jaafar, with the whole of his troops, moved over to the English side. By two o'clock the Nawab's army had decided to retreat. By five o'clock the betrayed army was a routed rabble, which abandoned its camp, baggage, stores, and transport, and was severely punished by the energetic pursuit of Major Eyre Coote. The betrayed Nawab fled, but was captured and assassinated by Mir Jaafar's son.

Destruction of Authority in Bengal.—Mir Jaafar was now installed as Nawab, but he had an empty treasury, and no real power. The revolution consisted, not in the change of Nawabs, but in the destruction of all authority. It took many years before British authority was established, and before the constructive genius of the British nation could understand the situation. At the present juncture they were represented on the spot by a set of men who were bent on getting rich quickly, and used the Nawab merely as an instrument by which they could personally acquire money. Clive was the only man who had any large views, and he was at one with them in the race for riches, though he did not desert the interests of his nation. He did all that he could to enlarge the area of English influence, and defeat all possible combinations that could be brought against the Company. The new Nawab, Mir Jaafar, was a mere cipher. He could not even meet the extensive money obligations he had incurred to gain the Nawabship, and every default brought him more and more into the toils. His agents and governors sent him no revenue, and he had to ask Clive to use his military force to punish his own refractory officials and zamindars, as well as his enemies. The scattered and defeated army of Bengal must of necessity have lived on plunder. The French forces ejected from Chandernagore must have followed the same course in the interior. And the unhappy officials to whom the screw was applied to meet the exorbitant demands to which Mir Jaafar's promises had committed him must have added to the misery of the people.

Conquest of Northern Sarkars and Elimination of French Influence from Nizam's Court.—Clive was to have gone back to Madras to take part in the fighting there in connection with the Seven Years' War, which began in the southern Presidency in the spring of 1758. But the developments in Bengal kept him there, and the Madras authorities were able, as we saw, to destroy French authority there by 1761. In one important direction Clive was able to help them from Bengal. Colonel Forde, whom he detached for the purpose, did his work thoroughly and effectually. He was assigned the task of occupying the Northern Sarkars, the coastal region between Orissa and the Krishna. This region was originally (1753) granted by Nizam Salābat Jang to Bussy for the support of French troops with its revenues. In 1754 it had to be given up by the French to the Nizam under the terms of the agreement then concluded with the English. On the outbreak of the new war the French had tried to penetrate there again, and Salābat Jang himself had appeared there to check some rebels, who had appealed to Clive in Bengal. Colonel Forde's skilful use of his forces, as well as tactful diplomacy, won the Northern Sarkars for the British in 1758, and the acquisition was confirmed by the Mughal emperor in the arrangements of 1765. Further, Colonel Forde entered into relations with the Nizam, and eliminated French influence from his court.

Invasion of the Prince Imperial: Clive's Jagir.—While Bengal had enough dangers to meet from within, it was also threatened in 1759 from its western frontier. Its neighbour there was the Subahdar of Oudh. The Prince Imperial of Delhi, who afterwards (December 1759) became the Emperor Shah Alam, had left Delhi for fear of his life from hostile factions, and come to Oudh. The Nawab of Oudh instigated him to invade Bengal, whose Subahdari was vacant, the emperor never having recognized Mir Jaafar. This he did early in 1759, but he had to meet the English forces who came in support of Mir Jaafar, at Patna, and he prudently retreated before Clive. But Clive's conversations from Patna, before he returned to Calcutta in June 1759, had convinced him of the feasibility of the plan, which he afterwards adopted, of getting the emperor's sanction for formally conferring the revenue administration of the three provinces on the Company, thus reducing the Subahdar's authority by formal process of law as recognized in India. Mir Jaafar had already, after Plassey, granted the Company the zamindari of the Twenty-four Parganas, a large district south of Calcutta. The zamindari right meant the right to receive rents and profits, but was subject to the payment of the Government revenue assessed on it to the Nawab's treasury. The Nawab now transferred, or assigned, this right to receive revenue to Clive personally. To use the Indian term, this became Clive's jagir; and Clive, the servant of the Company, became its immediate landlord. Later, the Company contested Clive's right to receive such a grant, and claimed its benefit for themselves; it amounted to £30,000 per annum. By a compromise Clive was allowed to retain it during his life.

Conflict with the Dutch.—In October 1759, there was a conflict with the Dutch at Chinsura. During the Seven Years' War the Dutch were neutral, but the local Dutch in India were annoyed at the right of search exercised by the British; jealous at the privileges and monopolies which the British had so easily won in Bengal; and also fired with ambition for themselves. They brought strong naval and land forces into the struggle. But Clive acted with his usual promptitude and decision, and made short work of them. The directions and plans were his own, but the thoroughly workmanlike spirit of the British navy deserves a word of mention. Sailors and naval guns were employed not only on the water, but in some land fights in Bengal during this period, and always with brilliant success. After that the Dutch did not enter Indian politics again. Their trade settlement in Chinsura remained in their hands till 1825, when it was exchanged with the British for some concessions in Sumatra. A few eighteenth-century houses in the Dutch style still testify to their influence in the region of the Hugli.

Clive in England.—In January 1760, Clive returned for the second time to England. He had now a fortune of £40,000 a year, besides £50,000 obtained for relatives. And he had amassed all this wealth at thirty-four in circumstances in which (as he afterwards put it) he was "astonished at his own moderation." He had hoped for a peerage, with a seat in the House of Lords, but when he got only an Irish peerage, he entered the House of Commons. Those were days of pocket boroughs, and a wealthy man could not only buy his own seat, but seats for his nominees. He also purchased sufficient East India stock to give him a large interest in the directorate of the Company.

The voices that were raised against him were soon silenced, and the news from Bengal within the next four years showed the disorders that raged in that unhappy country, with which Clive alone was able to cope. Both his knowledge and his character made him the one indispensable man. Lord Clive set out again for his second mission in Bengal in June 1764, armed with full powers, civil and military, and assisted by a select committee of four, practically of his own choosing. He reached Calcutta in May 1765, and his twenty-one months of administration on this occasion (to January 1767) are the most memorable part of his career. But let us first see what had happened in Bengal in his absence.

Mir Kasim raised to Nawabi, 1760.—All the forces of disorder which Clive had in some measure kept in check broke out unrestrained in Clive's absence. The Council in Calcutta were not united, or only united for purposes of plots and corruption. While the Company's troops successfully defended the western frontier of Bengal against Shah Alam (now emperor) assisted by French refugees, another revolution was carried out at Murshidabad. The Nawab's son-in-law, Mir Kasim, had already plotted with the English at Calcutta. A proposal was made to Mir Jaafar, who could not, out of his depleted treasury, supply money either to the Company or to its servants, that Mir Kasim should be appointed as his deputy, but with power, backed by the English. Mir Jaafar preferred to retire to private life in Calcutta, and Mir Kasim was installed as Nawab, September 1760. He granted the districts of Burdwan, Midnapur, and Chittagong to the Company for the expenses of their troops; to the servants of the Company he made handsome presents; and by his energy improved his own finances, and paid off some of the arrears due to the Company from Mir Jaafar.

His Disputes with the English, and Flight to Oudh.—But Mir Kasim had not a happy time. A portion of the Council had been against his elevation from the beginning. The Company's commanders had been in friendly communication with Shah Alam, whom they had received ceremoniously at Patna, and Mir Kasim was jealous of the events in that quarter. But the chief complaint of Mir Kasim was that his authority was undermined; that his servants were interfered with; that the Company's servants abused the right of private trade, and even issued or sold passes to their Indian dependents and friends, to enable them fraudulently to claim exemption from duties; and that they used violence against his own servants and subjects, and ruined the legitimate trade of Bengal. The friction continued to increase. The Nawab proposed to remit the duties on his own subjects to put them at least on an equality with the foreigners, but the Calcutta council treated this as an infringement of their own privileges, and insisted that no one but the Company's servants should enjoy the exemption. The rupture came in June 1763. There was a massacre of the British at Patna in October. Mir Kasim fled to Oudh, whose Nawab was now the Wazir (prime minister) of the empire. The Emperor Shah Alam was also with his Wazir. They espoused the cause of Mir Kasim.

Munro Fights the Decisive Battle of Baksar.—Meanwhile the Calcutta Council had re-elevated Mir Jaafar to the Nawabi, with the usual repetition of presents and concessions. Only, the Nawabi had now become an empty shell, the one which he had refused less than three years ago. He lived an inglorious life, and died in January 1765, after which, though there was another succession and the usual presents, the Nawabi passes practically out of history. But the Calcutta authorities had now to meet the emperor and the Nawab-Wazir of Oudh, who were preparing to invade Bengal. In February 1764, some of the Company's European troops mutinied. They included some French and Germans, who crossed over into Oudh territory. In April the Oudh army crossed into Bihar (as part of Bengal), and threatened Patna. The temper of the Company's troops was still uncertain, and the utmost that could be expected was that they should repel the invasion, which they did, mainly through the gallantry of the sepoys. Major Hector Munro arrived at the front with fresh reinforcements in May. He put down the mutiny with a strong hand, and on October 22, 1764, fought and won the decisive battle of Baksar.

Results of the Victory: Terms arranged by Clive.—The Oudh forces were defeated, and the emperor saw that his Wazir was only a broken reed. The emperor had really very little choice,

He had been with his Nawab-Wazir more as a captive than as a liege-lord, or even as an honoured guest. He opened negotiations with the English, but the terms were not settled till after Clive arrived, and the Nawab-Wazir felt that the British had him completely in their grasp. They pursued him into Oudh. They took Lucknow and Allahabad, and before May 1765, had driven back the Marathas, whose aid the Nawab-Wazir had invoked, across the Jamna. The Nawab was now ready for peace, which was arranged by Lord Clive personally (August 1765). Three matters required settlement: the territory of Oudh, the position of the emperor, and the position of the Company in Bengal and the rest of India. Oudh was practically in British occupation, but it was felt that to take it would be "full of burden but destitute of profit" to the Company; moreover, Oudh would be a useful buffer between Bengal and the disturbed territory of Delhi; it was restored to the Nawab on the payment of an indemnity, and with stipulations for safeguarding the feudatory interests of a Raja who had been friendly to the British, an ancestor of the Maharaja of Benares. With regard to the emperor, he was assigned two special districts, Allahabad and Kora,* out of what was then Oudh territory, for his maintenance, besides certain sums from the revenues of Bengal.

The Diwani and its Meaning.—The most important provision was as regards the Diwani of Bengal. In Mughal administration the Diwan of a province was the officer who was responsible for the collection and disposal of the revenue. He had to account for all the receipts, and after defraying the expenses of the civil and military administration, to remit the surplus revenue to the Imperial treasury in Delhi. The Diwani was the office of a Diwan, and this office was now conferred on the Company "in consideration" (so runs the Farman of the emperor, dated August 12, 1765) "of the attachment and services of the high and mighty, the noblest of exalted nobles, the chief of illustrious warriors, our faithful servants and sincere well-wishers, worthy of our royal favours, the English Company." They were to be exempt from customs duties, and as they were "obliged to keep up a large army for the protection

* Roughly the modern districts of Allahabad and Fatehpur.

of the provinces of Bengal," etc., they were to keep the surplus of the revenue also, except a certain sum reserved as tribute for the emperor. The provinces concerned were Bengal, Bihar and Orissa. All territorial concessions which the Company had hitherto obtained from Nawabs were expressly confirmed, both in Bengal and elsewhere, and Clive's own jagir was not forgotten. Whatever the British had hitherto obtained by force of arms was now regularized in all the forms of Mughal law. What was even more important, they practically became custodians of the emperor's person, through their agent in Allahabad, and could get any new orders they desired signed by him.

Problems of Inner Organization.—This was the great stroke of Lord Clive's diplomacy, but he had sterner matters to deal with. In September 1765 he returned to Calcutta. He had no difficulty in establishing a grip over the public servants of the Nawab. In virtue of the Diwani the Company had the right now to control their appointments and dismissals. But it was more difficult to control the Company's own servants, both civil and military. They had been demoralized with the enormous wealth which they had the chance of acquiring in the absence of any legal, moral, or social checks, and by the fact of their wielding the only efficiently organized power of coercion; discipline was at a low ebb; and the orders sent out by the Directors in London, though they adopted a lofty moral tone, were not accompanied by an understanding of the problem as it presented itself to the men on the spot, and were frequently flouted. The evils may be grouped under three heads: Mutiny in the troops, receipt of presents, and private trade by the Company's servants.

Mutiny of European Officers.—The mutiny of the European officers came to a head in 1766. In the rush of events in Bengal since Plassey, they had received various allowances and perquisites, which were stopped after the settlement of 1765, when the troops were organized in three brigades, and regular cantonments were established. The field allowance (*bhatta*) had been doubled by competing Nawabs in whose interests the troops had been ostensibly employed. It was now ordered that only single *bhatta* should be allowed when the troops actually took the field (with some exceptions), and that no *bhatta* should be admissible in cantonments. The European officers in a body, including their commanders, resented this, and organized a conspiracy to throw up their commissions together. Lord Clive acted with the utmost coolness and courage. He took the conspirators in detail. He had to employ his sepoys to avert a dangerous situation, but his firm attitude put an end to the mutiny, without further punishment than that awarded to the ringleaders.

Presents, Voluntary and Otherwise.—Of the enormous presents taken from Indian competitors for power or position some idea can be formed from Clive's own example. A Committee of the House of Commons, in 1773, estimated that between 1757 and 1766 the presents proved or acknowledged to have been made to the Company and its highest officials, civil and military, amounted to very nearly 6 millions of pounds sterling. If we allow that a third of this sum was for the Company itself and was so credited, we must also remember that these sums were only those which could be proved in London, and take no account of the presents received by smaller men in India, or those which were not known in London. The favourite mode of remittance from Calcutta in those days was to pay cash in India, and receive a bill payable in Europe. The English Company found that these transactions had so outgrown the Company's own resources that they strictly limited the amount, and the French and Dutch Companies in India were glad of the capital thus put into their hands for their Eastern trade. The "presents" were often extorted with threats. Of one prominent case, in which the point at issue was whether the sums were *voluntarily* given, an experienced official of the Company, who succeeded Lord Clive as governor, Mr. Verelst, drily wrote afterwards: "Perhaps the reader, who considers the increased power of the English, may regard this as a *verbal* dispute." Presents above 4,000 rupees were forbidden to the servants, and directed to be credited to the Company, from May 1764. Lord Clive had the less difficulty in enforcing the order, as the occasions which had called them forth—the revolutions rapidly succeeding one another—ceased under more settled government.

Private Trade.—The question of private trade was not, however, so easily solved. This had two sides. One was the exemption from duties as against the Mughal Government because of the exemption granted to the Company. This became of little importance after the Company got the upper hand, and its servants safeguarded their own rights in the treaties with the Nawabs. The other was the right of the Company's servants to engage in private trade at all. The Company claimed the monopoly of India's foreign trade. But its servants took up the inland trade, in such articles as oil, fish, straw, bamboos, rice, paddy, betel-nut, tobacco, salt, etc. As they got the use of military force they and their agents even began to buy and sell forcibly at their own prices—what the Directors, in February 1764, called "the unwarrantable and licentious manner of carrying on the private trade." They accordingly forbade it altogether. But the vested interests intervened, and within four months (in June 1764) they cancelled the peremptory order, and only instructed the Governor and Council, after "consulting the Nabob" (Nawab), "to form a proper and equitable plan for carrying on the inland trade." This was interpreted by the Company's servants, including Clive, to permit a sort of trading trust or monopoly.

Salt Monopoly.—In August 1765, a monopoly was formed of the trade in salt, betel-nut, and tobacco, to be carried on exclusively for the benefit of the superior servants of the Company. A certain percentage of the profits was to be paid to the Company, and the surplus was to be divided among the Governor, members of council, colonels, lieutenant-colonels, majors, surgeons, and others, including a chaplain, in specified proportions according to ranks. This was to be a sort of company within the Company, and the profits of a colonel or of a member of council were estimated to yield at least £7,000 a year. The Trade Society was formed in the first instance for a year. In spite of the Company's disapproval it was extended for another year. It was so lucrative that Lord Clive was able to sell his five shares to his colleagues in 1767 for £32,000. In 1768 the Company peremptorily forbade inland trade by its servants, though this was modified in 1770. In order to compensate them the Company set apart 2½ per cent. of its net income from the Diwani, to be divided among its superior servants in specified proportions. Open private trade thus ceased. But the Company's monopolies of salt and opium (now State monopolies), instituted by Warren Hastings in 1773, still remain, and are subjects of violent controversy to the present day—salt in India and opium in international politics.

Clive's After-Career.—In January 1767, Lord Clive laid down his office, and sailed for England. His health was bad, but he had hoped to fill a large part in English public life. As early as 1758 the elder Pitt, who was virtually prime minister, had spoken appreciatively in Parliament of his services in Bengal, and had called him a "heaven-born general." Now he was Lord Chatham, and actual premier, but in his decline. Clive entered Parliament again, but the atmosphere in the country and the House was against the Company and its "Nabobs," as its officials were called, who returned wealthy from India. In the reforms which Clive had tried to introduce in his second administration in Bengal he had made many enemies. These took advantage of the strong impression that was now gaining ground in the English mind and in the House that there was something wrong in India. They engineered an attack on him personally, which failed. The evils in India were condemned, but the House resolved (1773) that Lord Clive "did at the same time render great and meritorious services to his country." He committed suicide in 1774.

CHAPTER XVII

THE COMPANY'S POSITION AT HOME: PARLIAMENTARY REGULATION (1765-1781)

Economic Deterioration in Bengal.—Though Clive had done much to re-establish discipline in the civil and military services of the East India Company, and his native genius showed to advantage in diplomacy, his training had been too much in the money-grabbing atmosphere of the old servants of the East India Company to enable him to work out a scheme of Indian administration on broad lines of policy. The economic conditions of Bengal deteriorated rapidly. Trade was dull in the anarchical conditions which we have reviewed. Agriculture suffered on account of the large army of hungry locusts which descended on the cultivators, urged by the demands for money made by various grades of men from above. There was the old tribe of Nawabi officials who had now no responsibility to any one, as the Nawab was reduced to a cipher. The superior officials of the Company scarcely yet understood the intricacies of the Indian social or economic structure, on which successful Indian administration depended, with agriculture as its corner-stone. The Bengal famine of 1770 was the worst of which we have any detailed records. One-third of the population perished as a whole, but in the worst tracts the mortality was as high as 50 per cent.

Company's Dividends.—Without production on normal lines, without efficient trade and agriculture, without a reasonable amount of peace and security, ruin was inevitable. The enormous wealth acquired by the Company's servants contrasted with the deterioration in the Company's own finances. The legend of the fabulous wealth of India was fostered in the public mind, and East India stock rose in value 263 per cent. during the transactions connected with the Diwani. The proprietors of the stock naturally expected increased dividends, and the Directors urged their servants in India to send more money. But the expenses in India more than swallowed up the income, augmented though it was by the "presents" which the Company instructed its servants to credit to them from May 1764. The legitimate profits of trade were really insignificant, and the Company borrowed money to keep up and raise their dividends. In May 1767, a dividend of 12½ per cent. was declared, but it was stopped by Parliament.

Public Opinion in England.—While the Company in India was becoming a great political power, the Company at home was heading towards bankruptcy. It had now a large vested interest behind it. Its servants who had brought wealth from India became proprietors of its stock on a large scale. Its establishments and patronage expanded enormously, and many persons bought the stock for the influence it gave them in procuring or nominating to offices which were supposed to be avenues to wealth. But the heart of the English nation was sound, and English public opinion was determined to find a remedy for what it considered to be a public scandal. Both in Church and State there was a newer and healthier spirit. Wesley's life illustrates the vivifying influence of an appeal to the average conscience instead of to mere traditions and institutions—the exchange from the "faith of a servant" to the "faith of a son." In politics Walpole's methods—of "management" and corruption—had gone out of date, and the position of Chatham was due to his influence in the country at large, based on real talents, integrity, and industry. The British nation was puzzled at the transactions carried on in India in its name, and looked with a critical eye on the Company and its agents in India.

Points at Issue: (*a*) *Territorial Rights and the Company.*—Parliament passed an Act in June 1767, regulating the Company's dividends and compelling the Company to hand over to the national exchequer £400,000 out of its territorial revenues in India. The issues before the public may be stated thus. A large portion of the Whigs considered that the rights of property were sacred, and that the Company under its charter had absolute rights of disposal, whether by dividends or otherwise; and that its income could not be confiscated to the State.

The Tories, who were then in the majority, held that territorial rights and acquisitions could not accrue to a private corporation, but only to the King as sovereign, to whom his subjects were bound to yield them up. This view prevailed, but as a compromise an Act was passed in April 1769, allowing the territorial revenue to the Company for five years, subject to the payment of an annual sum to the exchequer, varying according to dividends, which were themselves regulated; and providing for the export of British merchandise by the Company, exclusive of naval and military stores, to the value of £380,837.

(*b*) *Patronage;* (*c*) *Political Powers, and those of Peace and War.*—Two other questions were violently agitated. First, who was to have the patronage, the appointments to India—the Company or the ministers of the Crown? Secondly, were political and military and naval powers to be exercised in India through the Company, or independently of the Company? On both these points the Company fought hard for its own powers. On the question of patronage there was one important argument which prevailed. If the patronage got into the hands of the King or his ministers, with Parliament as it was then constituted, it would mean such an enormous accession to the resources of the Party in power in England as to upset the balance of parties, and clog the working of the purified Constitution. At that particular time King George III. was trying to get power into his own hands, and patronage in his hands meant danger to constitutional government. On the question of political control and the control of hostilities, a compromise was arrived at, which we shall notice presently.

(*d*) *Justice.*—The question of justice and Courts of Law was no less important. By the charter of 1753 Mayor's Courts had been established for the Presidency towns, with civil, criminal, and ecclesiastical jurisdiction, between Europeans in those towns or in factories dependent on them. The position of Bombay was not much altered since 1753; that of Madras only slightly altered. But the position in Bengal, Bihar and Orissa was now wholly different. There were probably more British in the Mufassal (or outlying parts) of the triple province than in Calcutta, and the Company had no authority by the law of England to punish them outside the jurisdiction of the

Calcutta Mayor's Court, unless they came to England, in which case the evidence of witnesses might not be available. A High Court with plenary plowers over British subjects in the triple province of Bengal was necessary, and this was hardly disputed in any quarter.

The Regulating Act, 1773.—While these questions were being debated in public, the finances of the Company were getting worse and worse. In July 1772, the Company had to apply twice to the Bank of England for loans, and in August they applied to the Government for a public loan of at least a million pounds. The Government of Lord North now had their opportunity for bringing the Company under complete public control, and two Acts were passed in 1773, one (in June) for the financial relief of the Company, and the other (the Regulating Act, July 1773) for a modification of their constitution and the correction of the various abuses which, as then understood, had prevailed in the administration of the Company at home and in India. At home the Directors' term of office was increased from one year to four years, and small proprietors were deprived of votes in the affairs of the Company. In substance the Company became oligarchical, but for that very reason it became more amenable to the ministers' control. But it retained its trade monopoly.

Administrative Machinery.—For India the Regulating Act gave statutory sanction to some principles that had already been decided on—viz., the prohibition of presents and of private trade for the Company's servants. But the importance of the Act lies in the fact that it created administrative and judicial machinery in a form which, in spite of enormous changes, still forms the basis of the modern Government of India. For the Presidency of Fort William in Bengal, there was created a Governor-General, with an Executive Council of four members. The other two Indian Presidencies (Madras and Bombay), as well as a Presidency in Sumatra, were made (but not wholly) subordinate to the Governor-General, whose previous sanction was required in questions of war or peace or treaties, except in cases of extreme urgency. Everything was to be reported by the subordinate Presidencies to the Governor-General and Council; by the latter to the Court of Directors; and by the

Court of Directors to the Ministry. The Ministry's control was thus indirectly established, although the Ministry did not yet give direct orders to the authorities in India. The names of the Governor-General and the four Councillors were inserted in the Act itself, and also show a compromise on the question of patronage. The governor-generalship and one of the memberships of Council were given to the Company's well-tried servants, Warren Hastings and Barwell, presumably on the Company's advice; the other three members of Council were men fresh from England—viz., General Clavering, who was also to be Commander-in-Chief, the Honourable George Monson, and Philip (afterwards Sir Philip) Francis, the probable author of the anonymous *Letters of Junius*. The salaries were fixed on a liberal scale: the Governor-General was to have £25,000 a year, and the members of Council £10,000 a year each—charged on the Company's revenues.

Supreme Court of Justice.—The judicial machinery created aimed at supplying the defects of the earlier charters, but it was not adequate; the provisions were vaguely worded; and it was not quite clear to whom the jurisdiction of the new Court extended, what law was to be applied, and what precisely the relations of the Executive and Judiciary were to be. Some of the more flagrant of the doubts and difficulties were removed by an amending Act of 1781. What was contemplated in 1773 was that a Supreme Court of Judicature was to be established in Calcutta, with a Chief Justice and three barrister judges, all appointed by the Crown, with full civil, criminal, admiralty and ecclesiastical jurisdiction. The jurisdiction was to "extend to all British subjects who shall reside in the kingdoms or provinces of Bengal, Bihar and Orissa, or any of them, under the protection" of the Company; the Court could hear complaints for "any crimes, misdemeanors, or oppressions, committed, or to be committed," and entertain actions against the servants of the Company or any of His Majesty's subjects. British subjects probably then meant what "European British subjects" means in Indian law now. As the Mughal's sovereignty over Bengal was recognized, and the limited jurisdiction of the Nawab also, the "inhabitants of India" were probably still Mughal subjects, with the possible exception of those who lived in Calcutta. But the Court soon claimed universal jurisdiction. On this point the Act of 1781 was a little more explicit, for it brought all inhabitants of Calcutta within the jurisdiction, and established the principle, still maintained, of the application of Hindu and Muhammadan law to Hindus and Muhammadans in family and personal matters. The Governor-General and members of Council and the judges were exempted from the Court's coercive processes, but not from all its jurisdiction.

Legislative Machinery.—A certain amount of legislative machinery was also provided. The Governor-General and Council were authorized to make and issue such rules, ordinances, and regulations for the good order and civil government of Calcutta and other subordinate factories and places "as shall be just and reasonable," and "not repugnant to the laws of the realm" (presumably of England), but they were not to be valid until they were registered and approved by the Supreme Court. This power was supplemented in the amending Act of 1781 by the similar power of issuing regulations for the nominally Mughal territory outside the settlements, and such regulations did not require registration and approval in the Supreme Court. As the Supreme Court was generally in opposition to the Executive, most of the regulations were issued independently of the Court, under the Act of 1781.

Merits and Deficiencies of the Regulating Act.—This was the first essay at Constitution-making for India, by men who had very little first-hand knowledge of India, and who did not trust the Company's agents in India. If judged in all its bearings, it was a creditable attempt, although its machinery worked with great friction, and had soon to be brought under revision in 1781, and again in more important particulars in 1784 and subsequently. But it established a nexus between the British people and their Parliament on the one hand, and the men who were acting in their name in India on the other. Incidentally Lord North's efforts to support the finances of the East India Company led to the crisis resulting in the loss of the American colonies. There were 17 million pounds of tea lying in the Company's warehouse in London. Lord North permitted its export to America, and the Boston "Tea Party"

(December 1773) was the prelude to the War of American Independence.

Warren Hastings.—The Regulating Act affected very little the actual affairs of the people of India, except in matters of high policy. The humdrum affairs—the questions of trade, finance, and land revenue, the numerous civil and criminal courts that were carried on in the Mughal's name under British supervision in the interior, the organization of rural economy, which is everything in an agricultural country, and the investigation into local customs, habits, and ways of thought—these were patiently carried on by the Company's civil servants—men like Warren Hastings and his less showy coadjutors—whose real work, for India and Britain, is apt to be forgotten. Warren Hastings had been in the Company's service since 1750. In 1772 he rose to be President of Council and Governor of Bengal. To him was due the reorganization of the civil and criminal courts of justice in the whole province, nominally under Mughal authority, which dispensed justice to the inhabitants of Bengal under Hindu and Muslim law. It was this precedent which was adopted by Parliament in its Act of 1781.

His Interest in Oriental Law and Learning, and Careful Study of Revenue Policy.—Hastings was so impressed with the jurisprudence of the country that he forwarded a translation of two books on Hindu and Muslim law in 1774 to Lord Mansfield in England, the famous statesman and Chief Justice who bridged the gulf in English law between its archaic formalism and its wonderful adaptability to new needs. He had found English law inflexible, and made it modern. In writing to him Hastings's object was " the legal accomplishment of a new system which shall found the authority of the new British Government in Bengal on its ancient laws, and serve to point out the way to rule this people with ease and moderation according to their own ideas, manners, and prejudices." Hastings went equally to the root of the matter in his revenue administration, which was based on detailed assessments made on the spot for five years at a time, and aimed at the protection of the rights of the ryots (cultivators), the zamindars, and the Government. Hastings showed a deep interest in Oriental learning, founded institutions for its study and encouragement among the Company's servants, and was the patron to whom many Oriental books were dedicated. He attracted noted painters like Zoffany to India, whose work gives us early glimpses of British life in the East. He corresponded and exchanged books with Dr. Samuel Johnson. He was assiduous in his work, loyal to the Company, acquainted with Indian thought, competent and judicious in official matters, and blameless (as to private greed) in the midst of the race for wealth that was going on around him.

His Difficulties.—Such was the man who assumed in 1774 the office of Governor-General. He was appointed by the Act for five years, but his term of office was extended annually till 1785, when he felt compelled to resign on account of the events in Parliament, which appeared to him to make his position untenable. During his twelve years of office he had an uphill task. He had to build up (to use his own words) "an established form and powers of government," with little support from within, and no landmarks to guide his foreign policy. His internal difficulties may be classified under four heads: (1) divisions in his Executive Council; (2) frictions between the judicial and the executive authority; (3) want of harmony between the Supreme Government and the subordinate Presidencies, which had been newly placed under the vaguely defined control of Calcutta; and (4) want of harmony between Calcutta and London. In the Executive Council the three gentlemen from England were generally opposed to the two Company's men, Hastings and Barwell. Until Colonel Monson died in September 1776, Hastings and Barwell were generally in a minority against the other three, whose point of view was entirely different. Francis had a caustic tongue and pen, and was always a thorn in Hastings's side until he (Francis) returned to England in 1781—not without having fought a duel with Hastings in Calcutta. The differences between the judiciary and the executive were due to the faulty constitution and the unsuitability of the law which the English judges, new to the country, tried to administer, as well as to their desire to extend their jurisdiction. With regard to the subordinate Presidencies, the Supreme Council was jealous, and the Presidencies were impatient. Bombay wanted to assert itself, and its Maratha policy was overruled from Calcutta. Madras had violent disputes in Council, ending in the Governor's (Lord Pigot's) arrest and imprisonment (1776). In 1779 its policy with regard to the Nizam was censured and overruled. In England, also, there were divided counsels. The Court of Proprietors was not in harmony with the Court of Directors, and the Ministry looked with suspicion on both and on the Company's agents in India.

Social Calcutta: Attitude of the Country Powers.—To these difficulties were added the general social difficulties of life in Calcutta. Duelling, intrigues, and loose morals make a picture of British society in Calcutta in those days very sombre. Habits of intemperance combined with the rigours of the climate in producing a disproportionate mortality among the British residents. Through all these difficulties Hastings laboured on. His difficulties with the "Country Powers" were due to their realization, which they naturally did not welcome, that the Company was becoming a ruling power more efficient in war and peace, in trade, finance, and organization than themselves; and that it must soon claim, instead of being a contending power like themselves, to be the predominant power. This will be best understood by the narration of external events in the next chapter.

CHAPTER XVIII

CONSOLIDATION IN BENGAL: EXPANSION IN MADRAS AND BOMBAY

GOVERNORS-GENERAL: WARREN HASTINGS, 1774-1785; LORD CORNWALLIS, 1786-1793; SIR JOHN SHORE, 1793-1798.

It took Time to Achieve Unity of Policy.—The unity which the Regulating Act of 1773 intended to give to British policy in India by placing it in the hands of the Governor-General took some years to realize in practice. We have seen that among the difficulties of Hastings was the faction spirit of his own Council—the Supreme Council in Bengal. On the one side, his schemes and orders were upset by the majority of his own Council. On the other hand, the subordinate Presidencies of Bombay and Madras followed their own policies, and the new control from Calcutta was not accepted by them without demur. The subordinate Presidencies were also allowed to correspond direct with the Court of Directors in London. The time it ordinarily took to receive orders from London on a reference from India was about a year, and often much confusion resulted from cross references. Hastings tried, in 1778, to establish shorter communication by an overland service through Egypt, but it had to be abandoned through political considerations by orders from home. The three London authorities—the Ministry, the Court of Directors, and the Court of Proprietors—were also often at cross purposes. It required all Hastings's tact, energy, nerve, and strength of purpose to carry out his external policy with the success which marked his administration.

Hastings's External Policy, and its Leading Motives.—Hastings's external policy may be considered under the four heads: relations with the Nawab of Bengal, and with Oudh and the territories beyond, and affairs in the Bombay and Madras Presidencies. His guiding principle in all these was to lead up to British supremacy throughout India. He saw clearly that in the conditions with which he had to deal there were only two alternatives before the Company. If it did not expand its political influence it must go under altogether. He was severely hampered by financial limitations. The Directors at home asked for money. He required money for internal developments in Bengal, and for those large schemes of policy which required backing by military force. He had to finance both Bombay and Madras from Bengal. He did not directly take over much territory for the Company, but before he left, the Company was already a great power in India, and his successor, Lord Cornwallis, inherited and dealt with matters which Hastings had set in motion. Many of the events of Hastings's administration provoked a storm of controversy both before and after he had retired. Much of that controversy was due to the personal malice of men like Sir Philip Francis, who had been baulked in India. There was also undoubtedly a feeling in the British public mind that the British name and power had been used in India to cover transactions which the British nation could not approve of. This found expression in the passionate rhetoric of Burke and Sheridan in Hastings's impeachment, and in the support of that impeachment by the otherwise friendly Pitt (the younger).

Practical Extinction of Nawab's Powers in Bengal.—In Bengal the Company had vacillated in its administrative policy ever since the acquisition of the Diwani (1765). At first they had left the old administrative machinery of the Nawabi intact, merely making and unmaking the Nawabs and their immediate deputies. But this was neither fair to the people of Bengal, who were fleeced by men without responsibility, nor to the Company, whose revenue did not improve. In August 1771, they decided "to stand forth as Diwan, and by the agency of the Company's servants, to take upon themselves the entire care and management of the revenues." This change was effected under Hastings as Governor of Bengal in 1772, but the Nawab still (at least nominally) retained his character of Názim—*i.e.*, the authority in charge of the judicial, police, and executive administration. The Nawab was a minor, and practically this branch of the administration also came into

British hands. The Nawab's allowances were at the same time cut down by a half. In 1781 further measures were taken to improve the judicial, police, and executive administration. The extinction of the powers of the Nawabi of Bengal as a practical factor may be dated from the administration of Warren Hastings. The appointment of British Collectors of districts, with miscellaneous executive powers, may be dated from the same period, though the complete reorganization on that basis took place in the time of Lord Cornwallis (1793).

Oudh and Upper India.—Hastings's relations with the Nawab-Wazir of Oudh and with the Emperor Shah Alam, whom we saw settled in Allahabad and Kora by Clive in 1765, were marked by cautious steps; Oudh was brought more under control, and Delhi was put more and more into the background. The emperor was never happy in Allahabad. He looked upon himself as an exile, and when the Marathas offered to restore him to his capital at Delhi, in 1771, he gladly embraced the opportunity, much against the advice of the English. But the "Restoration" gave him no real power; his dependence was now on sterner masters, and he lost the revenues of Allahabad and Kora, which had been assigned to him by Clive. The Marathas got a paper assignment of these provinces to themselves. But Hastings considered that the emperor had broken his part of the bargain in placing himself in the hands of the enemies of the Company and its ally, the Nawab of Oudh. Hastings therefore sold these provinces (1773) to the Nawab of Oudh, whom it was also his policy to assist in other ways. He stopped the Bengal "tribute" to the emperor. In 1774 Hastings lent the Nawab of Oudh British troops to invade the territory of the Rohillas and destroy their power. The Rohillas were an Afghan confederacy which had established itself in Rohilkhand about 1743, soon after the confusion that followed Nadir Shah's invasion of Delhi (1739). Under their leader, Hafiz Rahmat Khan, they maintained peace and order. Threatened by the Marathas they appealed to the Nawab of Oudh, who only saw an opportunity of extending his own power. The Rohilla leader was slain in his gallant fight against the British forces (1774), which did the real fighting while the Nawab of Oudh claimed the glory and the territory. The

Company got 1,500,000 rupees as its share of the Rohilla plunder. The only remnant of Rohilla power that now remains is the Indian State of Rampur (893 square miles), whose chief assisted the British in the Rohilla War.

Screw Applied for Money from Oudh and Benares.—The Nawab of Oudh, whom Hastings found so useful for augmenting his financial resources, as well as his fighting force, was Shuja-ud-daula. He died in January 1775, and was succeeded by his son, Asaf-ud-daula (1775-1797), a ruler more notable for his lavishness and magnificence than for the wisdom of his State policy. He changed the capital of Oudh from Faizabad to Lucknow. His accession was signalized by the cession to the Company of the Benares province, yielding an annual revenue of 2,210,000 rupees, and the augmentation of the financial subsidy for the Company's brigade to the large sum of 3,120,000 rupees per annum. The Nawab's treasury was depleted; he had to reduce the allowances to his own family and dependants; and he complained that he was himself "without a subsistence." In 1781 Hastings struck a bargain with him on behalf of the Company, which was much criticized afterwards. It amounted to despoiling forcibly the two dowager Begams, the mother and grandmother of the Nawab, of their jagirs and treasures, for the benefit of the Company. The Raja of Benares (Chait Singh) was in 1780 coerced for resisting a demand for a heavy war subsidy for the Company; there was some fighting, in which he was defeated; and his son was substituted in his place, on terms very advantageous financially to the Company.

Bombay Presidency and Maratha Affairs.—The Bombay Presidency had so far been quiescent, except as a naval base. It had not yet acquired any fertile territory producing revenue. Even the small island of Salsette, which should have been ceded by the Portuguese along with the island of Bombay, as the two islands really form one settlement, was retained by the Portuguese in 1668. The Marathas captured it (and Bassein not far off) from their effete hands in 1739, thus placing themselves in an advantageous position for an attack on Bombay. The Presidency of Bombay took advantage of dissensions in the Peshwa's capital at Poona to seize the island in December

1774. This led to the first Maratha War* with the Company (1775-1782). At this time the rightful Peshwa was a minor, and the able minister, Nana Farnavis, held the power, and opposed the claims of the Peshwa's uncle, Raghoba, who was supported by the Bombay Government. On this question Hastings was not in full accord with his Council in the Supreme Government at Calcutta, which sent out an agent from Bengal to negotiate with the Regency opposed to Raghoba. The Directors at home supported Raghoba. A series of futile transactions took place, which lowered the name of the British, both from a military and diplomatic point of view.

Hastings Retrieves the Situation.—Hastings eventually unravelled the tangle by a vigorous policy, when he got a free hand. The Maratha Confederacy was but loosely held together. The real power was not in the hands of the Peshwa or his Council of Regency at Poona. It lay with the Maratha commanders—the Gaikwar in Gujarat, Holkar at Indore, Sindhia at Gwalior, and the Bhonslê in Berar, with his capital at Nagpur. The Bhonslê was won over by judicious negotiations; he permitted the march, through his territory, of the Bengal column which Hastings sent to Poona in 1778-1779. This was a wonderful march—the first march of the Company's troops right across the country. The troops, baggage-men, and camp followers numbered 36,000. Assembling at Kalpi, before the rainy season of 1778, this column was delayed in Bundelkhand, but crossed the Narbada into the Berar country on December 1, 1778, and arrived at Burhanpur under Colonel Goddard on its way to Poona on January 30, 1779. But Bombay had not waited for the Bengal column, and had fought and lost before Goddard's arrival. Goddard turned to Gujarat, and made favourable terms with the Gaikwar, whom he detached from the Regency at Poona. Holkar's affairs were then under the guardianship of that great and good lady Ahalya Bai, who was more interested in the arts of peace than those of war. There remained Sindhia. Goddard continued to press him from the south, but a master-stroke was prepared against him in the

* The operations in this war are sometimes divided into two, and the war spoken of as the first (1775-1779) and the second Maratha War (1779-1782).

north. A young and energetic officer, Captain Popham, was sent to stir up the Jats and Rajputs against him. With slender resources but brilliant talents, Popham stormed the almost impregnable rock fortress of Gwalior, the capital of Sindhia, August 1780. This practically ended the war. Sindhia not only made peace for himself, but he undertook to negotiate the peace with Poona, as representing the Maratha Confederacy. The treaty of Salbai* (May 1782) confirmed Salsette to the British, extinguished Raghoba's pretensions at Poona with a pension, and otherwise restored the *status quo*. Thus Hastings, by direction from Bengal, had neutralized the mistakes of the Bombay Government, and restored the credit of the British name. He also released military resources for the fight with Haidar Ali of Mysore in Southern India.

Mahadaji Sindhia (1730-1794).—The further career of Mahadaji Sindhia (also called Madhoji or Madhava Rao) is concerned with the emperor's affairs at Delhi. Sindhia was a man of military, diplomatic, and administrative abilities. He had also large views. Freed from his preoccupations in Central India, he turned towards Delhi. The Emperor Shah Alam was being used as a pawn by rival factions of Pathans, Persians, and Kashmiris. They rose and fell; they made revolutions and counter-revolutions, all in the name of the luckless descendant of Akbar. Mahadaji Sindhia engaged the French officer, Count de Boigne, through Hastings's good offices. De Boigne drilled and led some highly efficient brigades for Sindhia. Unlike the French in the courts of Poona and Mysore, de Boigne did not come on behalf of France, but merely as a soldier of fortune. In India he had seen service with British troops, and he served Sindhia (except for a short interval) from 1782 to 1796. With a strong army at his back Sindhia appeared before the emperor at Delhi in October 1784, and took all the power into his own hands. In order not to stir up the jealousy of the Maratha Confederacy, he got the emperor to appoint the Peshwa (a minor) as deputy of the Empire, and himself (as deputy of the Peshwa) to the chief command of the Mughal army. In this capacity he began to subdue various chiefs. The Jats and Rajputs joined in the fray. At length the Pathans again got the upper hand

* Thirty miles south of Gwalior.

in Delhi, plundered the palace, and put out the wretched Shah Alam's eyes (August 1788). Sindhia rescued Shah Alam, but he had to fight the Rajputs and the Maratha warriors of Holkar and the intrigues of Poona. He went to Poona to arrange matters, but died suddenly and mysteriously in February 1794. With him ended the dream of a Mughal Empire revived with Maratha arms.

Country Powers Dealing with the Madras Presidency.—Since the elimination of French influence from Madras in 1761, events had not moved fast in that Presidency for the British, but great changes had taken place in the balance of the Country Powers. Nizam Ali had become the Nizam in July 1761, and made Hyderabad the capital of his State. He had tried at first to check the British, but had felt their power. By direct negotiation with the emperor in 1765 they had obtained the legal title to the northern Sarkars, and they had got the Nawab of the Karnatik declared free of the Nizam's authority. Whatever resentment he may have felt at this diminution of his territory, he knew that he had to fight with the Peshwa at Poona and the Bhonslê in Berar, and the rising power of Haidar Ali in Mysore, whom his own brother had invested with the dignity of a subordinate Nawab. He entered into treaty relations with the British in 1766. Haidar Ali's rise had been remarkable. From a petty Naik, or corporal, he had practically made himself master of the kingdom of Mysore by 1759-1760. By 1769 he had become strong enough to end a war with the British by dictating a peace under the walls of Madras (first Mysore War, 1767-1769). The worthless Nawab of the Karnatik, although he was nominally a direct ruler under the emperor, transferred his whole military power to the Company in 1770. But by continuing to be responsible for military expenditure, he got more and more hopelessly into debt, and added to his troubles with the Company. After various attempts by the Company (in 1783, 1790, and 1792) to deprive him of the revenue and general administration, Karnatik was finally annexed to the Madras Presidency in 1801. In the time of Hastings and Cornwallis the most formidable power in the Deccan was that of Mysore, which fought in varying combinations with the Marathas, the Nizam, and the Company.

Second Mysore War (1780-1784).—Unfortunately the conduct of the affairs of the Southern Presidency during the last three decades of the eighteenth century was characterized by violent quarrels within the Presidency and with the supreme Government, combined with inefficiency, insubordination, and corruption among the Company's servants. There was, therefore, neither a consistent civil policy nor any vigour in military operations. In connection with the War of American Independence the French were fighting against the British in America and Europe, and the hostilities also extended to India in 1778. Warren Hastings promptly took the French settlements of Pondicherry and Mahé. The latter was on the Malabar coast then under Mysore, about thirty miles north of Calicut. Haidar Ali resented this, took the French officers into his pay, and joined the Grand Confederacy, consisting of the Marathas, the Nizam, and himself against the Company. The second Mysore War was the result (July 1780 to March 1784). In the first Mysore War the Nizam and the Marathas had been allied with the British against Haidar Ali. The events of the second Mysore War must be read in conjunction with those of the first Maratha War (1775-1782) in Western and Central India.

Its Conduct and Conclusion.—Hastings's finance, Hastings's diplomacy, and Hastings's well-thought-out plans prevented disaster, in spite of local incompetence. He got money from Oudh and Benares to finance Madras. He conciliated and detached from hostilities both the Nizam and the Bhonslê of Nagpur. In 1780 he had practically won against Sindhia, Holkar, and the Gaikwar, and taken the sting out of the hostility of Poona. The Treaty of Salbai (May 1782) got the Marathas out of the fight altogether. The British campaigns in Central India had helped the struggle both in Bombay and Madras. Hastings also sent troops by sea and land to Madras from Bengal. Not only did the Bhonslê permit their passage through his territory, but he added a contingent of his own to aid the British. Haidar Ali was isolated, but he was strong, and won many successes. His object was to take the Karnatik from the effete Nawab, whom the Company was defending. His son, Tippu, also showed himself to be a commander of energy and talent, and defeated Colonel Baillie at Conjeeveram, forty miles south-west of Madras (September 1780), and Colonel Braithwaite near Tanjore (February 1782). Against this was Sir Eyre Coote's defeat of Haidar Ali at Porto Novo, 120 miles south of Madras (July 1781), and the gallant though unsuccessful British defence of Mangalore on the Malabar coast (1783-1784). The Franco-British naval operations (1782) were inconclusive. Haidar Ali died in December 1782, and was succeeded by his son Tippu; Sir Eyre Coote, the British Commander-in-Chief from Bengal, died at Madras in April 1783. In July 1783, news arrived of the Peace of Versailles between the French and the British, and the French withdrew from the fight. There was friction between the Company's troops and the King's troops on the British side, and in spite of the combination of military resources from Bengal, Madras, and Bombay, no decisive advantage had been gained. The Treaty of Mangalore (March 1784) closed the war on a basis of the *status quo*, but it left Tippu in a frame of mind which led eventually to his own undoing. He inherited Haidar Ali's energy and capacity, but not his wisdom in statecraft.

British Opinion in Parliament: Pitt's India Act, 1784.—Meanwhile British opinion in Parliament had been much exercised about India. The disasters in America had driven out Lord North's Ministry, and a considerable body of opinion had been formed in Parliament in opposition to Pitt (the younger). The Whigs came into power in 1782, but they were divided. They were driven out of office in 1784 on the very question of India. Parliament was willing and anxious to bring the East India Company under control, but not willing to place the huge patronage of India in the hands of the Ministry to turn the balance in home politics. The Company's finances as a whole had not improved. The vast sums realized by Hastings had been more than swallowed up by military expenditure. The Company's trade in tea was at this time the principal source of their trade income.* The British duties on tea were reduced

* The tea was then imported from China, but the Company was anxious to grow it in its own territories, and Sir Joseph Banks, the botanist, reported favourably (1788) on its cultivation in the districts near Assam. Subsequently the wild tea plant was found in Assam, and by 1840 Assam tea was being sold in the London market. India now produces more than 300,000,000 pounds of tea annually.

in 1784 from 50 to 12½ per cent., which afforded some relief to the Company at the expense of the general British taxpayer. In the same year Pitt's India Act made a constitutional change of great importance. It created a Board of Control presided over by a member of the King's Ministry, and thus established the direct and complete superintendence and control by the Ministers of the whole of the Company's civil and military government and revenues in India, leaving only trade concerns to the management of the Company. Patronage, however, was not taken over by the Ministry, but was left to the Company. The Company's Court of Proprietors was deprived of all power in matters not relating to trade. Even the Company's Board of Directors were left, as a whole, without initiative or control in matters of government. A Committee of Secrecy, consisting of not more than three of the Company's Directors, was constituted, which was to transmit the secret orders of the Board of Control to India without the cognizance of the other Directors. In India the control of the Governor-General and his Council over the subordinate Presidencies was extended and rendered less ambiguous. Stricter measures were also provided for making British subjects more amenable for their conduct in Indian States to British courts in India and England. Schemes of conquest and extension of dominion in India were declared to be "repugnant to the wish, the honour, and policy of this nation." The difficulties which had arisen by the opposition of a majority in Council to the Governor-General were obviated by a later Act (of 1786), which enabled the Governor-General to overrule his Council on his sole authority. This act also made it possible for the Governor-General to combine with his office that of Commander-in-Chief, thus enabling Lord Cornwallis to go out to India with full civil and military powers.

Hastings Resigns: His After-Career and Character.—Warren Hastings felt that he could not count upon the support of Pitt as head of the Government in England. He resigned, and left India in February 1785. His impeachment was voted by the House of Commons in April 1787, and his trial in the House of Lords lasted from February 1788 to April 1795. A number of charges were drawn up against him, but the only ones that were proceeded with related to three matters. The first group was about the receipt of presents and personal corruption; on these he was unanimously acquitted. The second and third related to his undue harshness to Chait Singh of Benares, and to the Begams of Oudh; on these also he was acquitted by an overwhelming majority by the Peers' votes. The charge about the Rohilla War was thrown out by the Commons, and did not go as far as the House of Lords. Hastings lived for many years as a country gentleman, and died in 1818. In private life he was loved by all who knew him, and he was a model husband. As an administrator his career has been the subject of acrimonious controversy. It was a difficult time not only for the British dominion in India, but for the British Empire in the world, then struggling against the revolt of the American colonies, backed by the powerful resources of France, Spain, and Holland, and the Armed Neutrality of continental nations. The Irish movement was also a menace. Hastings devoted all his energies and all his great abilities to the service of his King and country in India, and that service was of more than local value. He met his difficulties in his own Council, and with his subordinate Presidencies, with coolness and patience, and surmounted his personal and political dangers with courage and a steady pursuit of permanent aims. On the other hand, whatever pain and personal loss his impeachment may have cost him, it was good that the national conscience should have been stirred, and that the Company's doings at that formative period of British rule should have been searchingly examined in the light of first principles, which are the ultimate tests for a good or bad policy. The measures which he took for raising money may be questionable, but any criticism on that score raises fundamental questions of policy, and cannot be made the ground of a personal impeachment. The general lines which he laid down for military, political, revenue and administrative organization in India, were the basis on which the fabric of Indian government was afterwards completed. He understood and sympathized with the people of India, and gave a great impetus to the study of their languages, ideas, and institutions.

Lord Cornwallis: Advantages of His Position.—The Company's service supplied a temporary Governor-General who held charge for a year and eight months, before the arrival of Lord Cornwallis in September 1786. He was at the helm in India for seven years. In spite of his not very brilliant performances in the American war, he was also Commander-in-Chief in India, and personally took the field when hostilities broke out in Madras in 1790. His high social position, his contact with the Ministry in power at home, and his detachment from the Company's servants in India, gave him a great advantage in his transactions of peace and war, in his administrative reforms, and in his work in carrying through the great measure of the Permanent Revenue Settlement of Bengal, with which his name is associated in India.

Third Mysore War, 1790-1792.—The second Mysore War had been closed inconclusively in 1784, with exhaustion on both sides. Neither Tippu nor the Company considered the settlement satisfactory. The greater part of the plateau of the Karnatik (Karnatik above the Ghats) was in Tippu's possession, thus depriving the Company of part of the resources which would have been available for them under the name of their protégé, the Nawab of the Karnatik. The Nizam and the Poona Marathas were also smarting under the losses which Tippu had inflicted upon them. In 1786 the Peshwa combined with the Nizam in taking some territory from Tippu. A treaty of offensive and defensive alliance was concluded in July 1789, between the Company, the Nizam, and the Peshwa to invade Tippu's territory, and divide any conquests amongst themselves. Tippu, on the other hand, spread himself out in the south, and invaded Travancore, which had hitherto preserved its independence in all the wars of the Deccan (December 1789). Formal hostilities began in April 1790. Cornwallis ordered the Bombay Government to invade Malabar in the north of Tippu's kingdom, while the Madras forces occupied Dindigal (about sixty miles south-west of Trichinopoly) and the surrounding country. In December 1790, Cornwallis assumed personal command of the southern front. By March 1791, he had established his base at Bangalore, and in May he pushed on to within nine miles of Seringapatam, Tippu's capital. His commissariat difficulties were relieved by the Marathas, but the allies had to retreat to Bangalore. Tippu gained some successes against both the

Marathas and the Company in November 1791. But the tide soon turned. Reinforcements arrived from Bengal. The Company's forces now numbered 24,000 men, while the Nizam sent a force of 10,000 horse, and the Maratha mobile forces swarmed on all sides. Tippu was completely hemmed in. But the Company's two allies, instead of co-operating in a general plan of campaign, began to seek their own several ends. The war was thus prolonged till March 1792, when fresh troops came up from Bombay. Tippu's situation was now hopeless, and he accepted the Treaty of Seringapatam, by which he lost the more fertile half of his dominions, and had to pay a heavy indemnity. The Company retained for themselves Dindigal and the southern portion of the Karnatik Plateau (the Baramahal), together with the overlordship of Coorg, thus enclosing Mysore to the south and south-west. On the north they divided the territory between the Nizam and the Peshwa, annexing Malabar to the Bombay Presidency. What was left to Mysore was the relatively barren district in the centre.

Reforms in the Civil Service and Judicial Administration.— The internal reforms of Lord Cornwallis left the framework of Bengal administration practically what it has remained ever since, and this model was followed in all the territories subsequently acquired. He abolished the perquisites which the Company's servants used to receive, and which were sometimes many times more valuable than their salaries. At the same time he raised the scale of salaries, so as to leave no temptations in the path of those who were working for their Government. The country was parcelled out into areas called districts, and each district was put under the charge of a Collector, who was a member of the Civil Service, and administered the Executive Government as well as collected the revenue.* The district became the unit of administration, and the "District Officer" the backbone of the personnel of the Government. Each district had its own judicial machinery, although sometimes several districts were united under a single British judge. These

* Executive and judicial functions were sometimes combined and sometimes separated in district administration in the early days of the Company. Cornwallis separated them; Lord Hastings afterwards combined them. This combination still continues in a modified form, and is a subject of controversy.

Company's courts were not yet brought into subordination to the Supreme Court in the Presidency.

Land Revenue Administration.—In Land Revenue Administration a new policy was adopted, which had been discussed by the Directors for some years, but which required the strong conviction and driving force of Cornwallis to carry into effect. The revenue of the Government in those days had consisted in the main of the dues they realized from the land. Careful enquiries had been going on for many years into the amount and mode of collection of land revenue in Bengal. For some years after the Diwani was assumed, an annual "settlement," or arrangement, had been made with farmers of the revenue. Some of these farmers were ancient Rajas; some were new dignitaries promoted during Nawabi rule; others, again, were mere contractors, who had no connection with the soil, or with the actual cultivators (ryots), except for the purpose of collecting revenue. These contractors themselves may be divided into two classes: some were men who had collected from year to year for a considerable period during the Nawabi, and had acquired a sort of prescriptive right, while others were new men who had manœuvred themselves into the position in the early years of the Diwani. All these were indiscriminately lumped together as zamindars or landholders. A five years' settlement was made in 1772-1777, and the farms were put up to the highest bidder. From 1777 to 1781 annual farms were given out; but preference was given to old zamindars. From 1781 to 1790 the settlements were again annual, but the preference to zamindars was abandoned. In 1784 Pitt's India Act directed an enquiry into the complaints of dispossessed zamindars, and the framing of permanent rules "for land rents according to the laws and constitution of India." It was not clear what was the nature of the demand made by the State on the land,—whether it was a tax or a rent. It was indifferently termed either a land-tax or the rent of land, but was really neither, according to the strict economic definition of those terms. It was a demand levied by Indian Governments, assessed on land according to well-understood but ill-defined customs. Enquiries into these customs and the relations of the various parties concerned in the management of land from the actual cultivator to the State were diligently prosecuted until 1793, when the Permanent Revenue Settlement was proclaimed by Lord Cornwallis with the consent of the Ministry at home. The figures of this Settlement were based on the ten years' settlement which had been made in 1790.

Permanent Settlement.—The principle of the settlement was that the zamindars (including farmers of revenue) were acknowledged as owners of the land, and the State fixed its demand on the land in perpetuity at certain sums, which were charged on the land. These sums were calculated in such a way that the State received in cash roughly about 45 per cent. of the produce. The total amount fixed for Bengal worked out to about the same figure at which it had stood just before the acquisition of the Diwani. But any increase in cultivation, or any change in the value of money enured to the benefit of the zamindar, as the State had limited its demand for ever. This was the weak point of the Settlement, as it failed to secure future unearned increments for the State or the community. But against this it had some outstanding merits.

Its Merits.—Nearly a third of the *cultivable* land of Bengal before the Permanent Settlement was waste, and inhabited by wild beasts. The absconding cultivator was the problem haunting the zamindar, and the absconding zamindar the problem haunting the Government. The changes in land management from year to year produced no sort of stability, and the deficiency of population produced by the terrible famine of 1770 had not yet been made up. It was hoped that the grant of a permanent heritable interest in the land would stabilize both the population and the Government revenue, and this result was satisfactorily achieved in a few years. After the lapse of a century and a quarter the value represented by the share of the State is a much smaller proportion of the actual produce of the land. But cultivation has improved both in extent and in quality; a large land-holding class has grown up in Bengal, shading off into the landed aristocracy; a large middle class has grown up in Bengal depending upon the landed aristocracy; much capital has accumulated in the province, and famines have occurred less frequently than in other provinces of India.

Its Working.—The working of the Permanent Land Revenue Settlement was attended with many difficulties in the beginning. There was no complete survey of the land, or record of the rights of subordinate tenure-holders. The scheme certainly contemplated some fixity of tenure for the ryots, and some definite rules for the limitations of rent by means of leases (pattas or, according to Bengali pronunciation, pottas), but these matters were not satisfactorily dealt with until the legislation of 1859 and 1885. A statutory Tenant Right, as well as fixity of tenure and reasonable safeguards for all the interests of the actual cultivators, have now been provided. A great many intermediate tenures have also grown up between the ryots and the zamindars, which have been carefully defined, and their relation with other tenure-holders determined by legislation. The minute subdivision of holdings has gone on under the provisions of Hindu and Muslim law, but on the whole the big landed estates in Bengal in which the rule of primogeniture is customary have held their own. The first expectations of the tremendous boon which the Permanent Settlement would confer on the zamindars were disappointed. They had been accustomed to a free and easy mode of rent collection and payment of the Government revenue. In place of it was substituted a rigid system of punctual payments, in default of which the lands were sold by auction, and the zamindars dispossessed. Wholesale expropriations occurred under the sale law. It may almost be said that the first race of zamindars were swept away, and gave place to an entirely new set, who came as strangers to the land, and treated their ryots with little consideration and sympathy. To help them in their collections, rigid powers of distraint were also given to them as against the tenantry, and much distress ensued, which was reflected in the reports of the Parliamentary enquiries that took place during the next twenty years. But, in any case, a social revolution was inevitable in the wake of the political and economic revolution that had taken place in Bengal.

Comparison with Other Provinces.—The Permanent Land Revenue Settlement was carried out in all the territories that were directly British at that time. This included the triple province of Bengal, Bihar and Orissa (that is, such parts of

Orissa as were not then subject to the Marathas), and to the province of Benares. Territory that became British subsequently was settled differently, as we shall see later. After a few decades there was a strong revulsion against the policy of a Permanent Settlement. The result of these different systems in different parts of India has been that the fiscal burdens on the land are assessed at very unequal rates in different parts of British India, and this makes modern inter-provincial finance both intricate and inequitable. The permanently settled tracts pay comparatively small proportions in land revenue. But they are more highly rated for local rates. As the Permanent Settlement cannot be touched without a breach of faith on the part of the Government, the only remedy appears to be to give other provinces a somewhat more favourable treatment as regards their contributions to the State on land, and remodel the entire basis of taxation in the country. The taxation problem is under consideration by a committee appointed (1924-1925) by Lord Reading's Government.

Sir John Shore's Weak Administration, 1793-1798.—The strength and authority with which Lord Cornwallis had been able to deal with the problems of British India, both external and internal, established a precedent for appointing to the office of Governor-General a British peer of public experience and influence, sent out direct from Great Britain. Lord Cornwallis himself left his opinion in favour of this practice, but made an exception for his immediate successor, in favour of Sir John Shore, who had supplied him with all the material facts on which the Permanent Land Revenue Settlement was based. Sir John Shore's administration lasted from August 1793 to March 1798. He followed a weak and colourless policy, both internally and in his relations with the country powers. After the defeat and humiliation of Tippu, the Peshwa came into collision with the Nizam. The Nizam had, in the earlier years of confusion at Poona, extended his territory at the expense of the Poona Government. But the Poona Government, under Nana Farnavis, now made a strong effort to win back its losses, and called to its aid for the last time the great military commanders from Central India. The Nizam, counting upon his alliance with the Company, called for British aid against the Marathas, but Sir John Shore refused to assist him. In 1795 the Nizam lost heavily against the Marathas at the battle of Kharda,* in which his Amazon troops, and those led by Monsieur Raymond made a notable stand. The Nizam was disgusted at what he considered his desertion by the British, and French influence again became predominant in the court of Hyderabad. About the same time the British officers in the Company's service became mutinous. The home authorities became nervous, and sent out the Earl of Mornington (afterwards Lord Wellesley) to replace Sir John Shore. Shore, however, carried out one stroke of policy for the Company before he left. In January 1798, in placing the new Nawab, Saadat Ali, on the throne of Oudh, he made arrangements which were afterwards widely followed in what were known as subsidiary alliances. He stipulated that 10,000 troops should be maintained by the Company for Oudh; that the subsidies hitherto allowed by Oudh should be largely increased; and that no Europeans should be allowed to serve or reside in Oudh except by the permission of the Company. Oudh had also to cede the fort of Allahabad, and became a subordinate instead of an independent ally of the Company. The Company's frontiers were now pushed up westwards to the Doab, that is, the country above the confluence of the Jamna and the Ganges, and between these two rivers.

* Now in a British enclave in the Nizam's Dominions, about twenty-three miles south-east of Ashti.

CHAPTER XIX

FIGHT FOR SUPREMACY. 1789-1819

GOVERNORS-GENERAL: LORD WELLESLEY (EARL OF MORNINGTON), 1798-1805; TWO SHORT APPOINTMENTS; LORD MINTO I., 1807-1813; LORD HASTINGS, 1813-1823.

French Revolution Furnishes the Key to Indian Policy during the Period.—The French Revolution (1789) was a moral, economic, and political cataclysm, and the wars which followed partook of all these characters. Great Britain was involved in the war against France, except for short intervals, from 1794 to 1815. While all landmarks seemed to be disappearing from Europe, she was the only stable factor. Her elastic constitution stood the strain. But all the time she followed a strong definite policy, of which the corner-stone was the defeat of the revolutionary movement which began in France, but spread like a conflagration, in the name of France, throughout the world. The East was also affected both by Napoleon's Eastern ambitions, and by the resistance which Great Britain offered to them. The Revolution is the keynote of the history of India from 1794 to 1819. In the process of resistance Britain enormously added to her Empire in the world, and in India. Outside India proper she added Ceylon (1796), Cape Colony (1806), Mauritius (1810), and Singapore (1819), and temporarily the Dutch colonies in Java and the Indian Archipelago (1811-1817); she strengthened her position in Australia, where the first convict settlement had been established in 1788, and had been fed in its infancy from the Dutch Indies and British India; and she established communications with the furthest nations of the East, including Japan, and more intimate relations with the Oriental powers in the immediate neighbourhood of India.

India the Key to British Expansion in the East.—In all this British expansion India supplied the key to Britain's Eastern policy. The British commander who took the Cape in 1806 was Sir David Baird, who had been in three Mysore wars, and was the hero of the siege of Seringapatam, 1799. The organizer of the Nizam's forces on behalf of the East India Company (1798-1800) and the hero of the second Maratha War (1803) was Arthur Wellesley, afterwards Duke of Wellington, whose dogged tactics in the Spanish Peninsula offered the first check to Napoleon on land (1808), as his Waterloo campaign helped in compassing the final overthrow of Napoleon (1815). The conquest of Ceylon was effected with the East India Company's forces, and the island was attached to the Madras Presidency (1796-1798) until it was made a Crown Colony in 1798. Singapore (1819), the key to the Pacific and the pivot of Far Eastern commerce, as well as Java (1811), were conquered with the East India Company's resources and on the initiative of a remarkable servant of the East India Company, Sir Stamford Raffles. Singapore remained attached to Bengal until 1867. British influence in Borneo also dates from the time of the Javanese expedition of 1811, though its consolidation under Raja Brooke, himself an ex-servant of the East India Company, came later (1838-1841). An Indian expedition was sent to Egypt under Sir David Baird (1801-1802), and marched across the desert from Kosseir to the Nile, and afterwards to Alexandria, to help in the expulsion of the French and the establishment of British influence with Egypt and the Turks. At the same time communications were opened from India by Lord Wellesley with the Sharif of Mecca, the Imam of Sanaa (Yemen), and the Sultan of Aden (annexed to India, 1839), establishing the first relations with the peninsula of Arabia. The embassy of Captain (afterwards Sir John) Malcolm, one of the most brilliant diplomatists of the East India Company, to Teheran (1799), not only kept Persia out of French influence, but resulted in political and commercial treaties with Persia. Even more important still, by turning Persian arms against Afghanistan, he averted an Afghan invasion of India in force under Zaman Shah.

Nizam in the Subsidiary Scheme, and Tippu's Destruction: Fourth Mysore War (February to May, 1799).—Lord Wellesley went out to India with large ideas, which he successfully carried out, in many instances in defiance of the Company's narrow commercial policy. He had studied Indian affairs as a whole as a member of the Board of Control in London, and his warm advocacy of Pitt's foreign policy in Parliament furnishes the clue to the foreign policy which he pursued in India. First he disarmed the French in the service of the Nizam, and induced the Nizam to accept a subsidiary alliance, under which the Nizam was to receive and pay for a force of 6,000 from the Company, under British officers (1798). Next he dealt with the ambitions of Tippu Sultan. Ever since the close of the third Mysore War (1792) Tippu had realized his untenable position as against the growing power of the Company. He had sought to win French aid against the British, and to that end had sent envoys to Louis XVI. at Versailles (1787-1788), and afterwards enthusiastically joined the French Revolution as "Citoyen" Tippu. He had written to the French Directory, and sent agents to Mauritius. He had tried to get into touch with Shah Zaman, the ambitious ruler of Afghanistan, whose designs against Persia were frustrated by the Anglo-Indian embassy to Teheran. He had also sent an emissary to the Sultan of Turkey, to get a Musalman coalition against the British, but the Turks had their own troubles in Syria and Egypt. Tippu had also large plans in his own State. He entertained French officers, tried to get a navy and a mercantile marine, and sought to undermine the loyalty of the worthless Nawab of the Karnatik to the British connection. The British were aware of his plans, and Lord Wellesley was able to crush him by a short and swift stroke. The fourth Mysore War (February to May, 1799) ended with the fall of Seringapatam and the destruction of Tippu and his dynasty.

Partition of Tippu's Kingdom, and Creation of the New State of Mysore.—The kingdom of Mysore was partitioned; the seaboard and the southern portion were taken by the British; an equal portion touching on the Nizam's territory was allotted to the Nizam as an ally; and a small portion was given to the Peshwa, who had been a nominal ally, though he had done nothing to help in the war. The Mysore territory given to the Nizam in 1799, as well as that given in 1792, was annexed by the Company under the treaty of 1800 with the Nizam, when the subsidiary force of the Nizam was largely increased, and the integrity of his dominions was guaranteed. The remaining portion of the Mysore kingdom was made over to a boy, aged five, of the extinct Hindu kingdom, on terms which made it completely subordinate to the Company. Thus was created the new Protected State of Mysore. It was under British administration from 1831 to 1881, and has maintained a high standard of government under the Maharaja ever since.

Completion of the Madras Presidency; Extension in the Bombay Presidency.—Hyderabad and Mysore being settled, Lord Wellesley turned his attention to the effete Nawab of the Karnatik (also called Nawab of Arcot), and annexed his territory (1801). The small Maratha principality of Tanjore had already been annexed in October 1799. Madras was now a solid Presidency, substantially as it is now, with the whole of the eastern sea-coast from Orissa to Cape Comorin, and the western sea-coast from Cape Comorin to Malabar (with the exception of the comparatively minor States of Travancore and Cochin), and detaching the two great States of Hyderabad and Mysore from the sea. The annexation of Surat in 1800 added a small but important piece of territory to the Bombay Presidency. The troubles in Surat had been of old standing: the divided authority as between the Fort and the City, dating from the days of Mughal vigour, had given rise to constant disputes, in which the Marathas and the Sidi Admiral of Janjira had taken part; in these disputes the Company had already established their hold on the Fort, and now the Nawab of the City was pensioned off.

Oudh Curtailed; "Ceded Districts"; Lord Wellesley's Differences with the Home Directors.—In 1801 Lord Wellesley carried out a "reform of the military establishment" of Oudh. Oudh had already been reduced to a subsidiary alliance, but it was proposed to increase the Company's troops in Oudh, and to annex territory for their expenses. The territory in the present province of Agra (in the United Provinces), east and south of Oudh, along with Rohilkhand, and certain tracts of the Doab (the tract between the Ganges and the Jamna), was annexed by the Company under the name of the "Ceded Districts." Oudh was reduced to practically a third of its former size, and even its internal powers of civil administration were curtailed. The Governor-General's agent in these Oudh transactions was his youngest brother, Henry Wellesley (afterwards Lord Cowley, British Ambassador in Vienna). The simultaneous employment of three brothers in the highest posts in India was commented on, and Lord Wellesley's rapid extension of troops, expenses, territory, and the Company's political responsibilities, as well as his neglect of their commercial interests, caused friction between him and the Company's Directors in London. His whole conception of the training and position of the Company's civil servants as diplomatists and administrators, rather than commercial agents, was different from that which could find favour in the City. In 1800 he established Fort William College in Calcutta (abolished 1854, and practically superseded by the foundation of Haileybury in 1805) for the study of Indian and Eastern languages and institutions by the Company's servants. In 1802 he sent in his resignation, but he stayed on until 1805, and directed the greater part of the second Maratha War (1802-1805).

The Second Maratha War (1802-1805) and its Results.—The Maratha States were not easily brought into the Subsidiary Alliance scheme. Their internal affairs were in a very confused state. After some pressure Baji Rao II., in order to secure his position as Peshwa against the opposition of his own people, signed the Treaty of Bassein (December 1802), by which the Peshwa received a subsidiary force, ceded territory, and resigned his foreign policy to the Company. The Gaikwar also soon came into line, but Sindhia, Holkar, and the Bhonslê refused, and extensive military operations had to be undertaken. Those in the south were under the command of General Arthur Wellesley (afterwards Duke of Wellington). In September 1803, he defeated the combined armies of Sindhia and Bhonslê at Asāi* (Assaye), and by a masterly display of force and diplomacy soon succeeded in closing the southern campaign. The northern operations were equally successful under General Lake, who defeated Sindhia's troops under French officers near Aligarh (August 1803) and Delhi (September 1803). This

* Now in the Nizam's Dominions, forty-five miles north-east of Aurangabad, and near the famous Ajanta Caves.

gave the Company the western districts of the present United Provinces, and Delhi and the territory around it, together with the person and the nominal authority of the Mughal Emperor, in whose name Sindhia had been acting. The British victory at Laswāri (in Alwar State), November 1803, prepared the way for the Treaty of Surji Arjungāon (December 1803) with Sindhia. Holkar was not yet subdued, and he won some successes against Colonel Monson (July 1805), but was repulsed from Mathura (September 1804) and Delhi (October 1804). He was besieged at the fortresses of Dig (December 1804) and Bharatpur (January 1805), and pursued into the Panjab (September 1805). He made peace in December 1805. The net result of this Maratha war was that all the chiefs except Holkar entered into subsidiary alliances; that all of them agreed to entertain no European officers in their service; that, besides the territory already mentioned, the provinces of Bundelkhand and Katak (the portion of Orissa that had been in the possession of the Bhonslê) and the district of Broach were added to the Company's territory; that Berar, with the tract round Ajanta, was restored to the Nizam from the Marathas; and that British supremacy was acknowledged throughout India, with the exception of Sindh and the Panjab. The more favourable terms granted to Holkar were due to a change of person and policy in the Governor-General.

Lord Minto (1807-1813): Embassy to Amir of Afghanistan.—As we saw, the Directors were alarmed at the Marquis of Wellesley's forward policy, and sent out Lord Cornwallis a second time to pursue a policy of peace. He arrived in July 1805, old and feeble in health, and proceeded immediately to Upper India to be near the scene of Holkar's war, but died at Ghazipur in October 1805. Sir George Barlow as senior member of Council, held the reins temporarily until Lord Minto took over charge (July 1807). During Lord Minto's term of office (July 1807 to October 1813) India was at peace within, but was the base for a vigorous British policy in the Pacific, which we have already reviewed at the beginning of this chapter. Napoleon's Treaty of Tilsit (1807) with the Tsar Alexander I. was a Franco-Russian threat to Britain in the East, and Lord Minto took diplomatic precautions to safeguard the north-western frontier of India. Mountstuart Elphinstone was sent from Delhi on an embassy to the Amir of Kabul (then Shah Shuja) (1808-1809), whom he met at Peshawar. A treaty was concluded, but Afghan politics were in a very unsettled condition, and Shah Shuja was a fugitive from his own people by June 1810.

Panjab and the Sikhs: Rise of Ranjit Singh.—Another embassy, that of Mr. (afterwards Sir Charles, and Lord) Metcalfe, to Ranjit Singh (1808-1809), gives us an opportunity of reviewing the state of the Panjab and the progress of the Sikhs. After their suppression in 1714-1716 the Sikhs formed bands of plunderers, and in the confusion of the eighteenth century Mughal and Afghan governors of the Panjab sought the assistance of such bands. Ahmad Shah Abdali in 1762 made the head of the house of Patiala a Raja, and five years later a Maharaja, under himself. In or about 1764 the Sikh chiefs met in Amritsar and established a union of political confederacies, and in imitation of the Maratha *chauth* they began to levy *rakhi* on the villages they spared from plunder. The Confederacies were called Misals. In addition a militant Order, that of the Akālis, was instituted, which represented the religious side of the militant movement. In the latter part of the eighteenth century the Afghans nominally held the Panjab, but their own country was unsettled, and the Sikhs, the hill Rajputs (Dogras), and the Marathas contended for mastery with the Muslims in the Panjab. Zaman Shah came from Kabul to Lahore in 1797, and again in 1798-1799, and at the latter visit appointed one of the Sikh chiefs, Ranjit Singh, governor of Lahore. Ranjit Singh now began to fight with the other Sikh chiefs to gain the whole power into his own hands. His strongest opponents were the Sikhs to the south of the Satlaj river, who had been harried by the Marathas, but who had come under British protection after the Company had expelled the Marathas from the Panjab. These cis-Satlaj chiefs, whose States are also known as the Phulkian States,* from the Phulkian Misal, came formally into the system of Protected States when Metcalfe made the Treaty with Ranjit Singh (1809), by which he was left a free hand beyond the

* The Phulkian States are Patiala, Nabha, and Jind.

Satlaj, but he agreed to recognize that river as the boundary of British influence.

Charter of 1813: New Principles Introduced.—In July 1813, the Company's charter was renewed for a further period of twenty years. A searching Parliamentary investigation, extending over four years, culminated in the "Fifth Report" (July 1812), which gave an admirable summary of land, judicial, and police administration and the connected problems in the early years of British rule. The European ports having been closed to British commerce in the Napoleonic war, strong pressure was brought to bear in Parliament to open the Asiatic trade to the nation, and abolish the Company's monopoly. The Company fought hard for their monopoly, but the new charter only gave them the monopoly of the China trade, and opened up the trade of India, except as regards tea. That meant free trade for Britain's manufactures in India, but British markets were protected against Indian manufactures. Independent Europeans were now to be admitted to India, but under a system of licences. This provision was mainly inserted in the interests of Christian missionaries. A bishop and archdeacons were appointed to look after the Company's military chaplains and Christian servants. The missionaries, hitherto discountenanced by the Company in Bengal, had already settled in the Danish settlement of Serampur, fifteen miles north of Calcutta. Here the Baptists, Marshman, Carey, and Ward, had carried on their work of education for Bengal, with marked effect on the modern growth of the Bengali language. The Serampur work remained, but missionary effort now spread itself over British India. William Wilberforce also got a provision inserted for the allotment of a lakh (100,000) of rupees for the encouragement of education and learning among the natives of India. The Company's territorial and commercial accounts were separated. As far as India was concerned, the Company ceased to be a trading body, and became a trustee for the government of India under the Crown and people of Great Britain.

Lord Hastings (1813-1823); Conquests and Pacification; Nepal War (1814-1816).—The Earl of Moira (Marquess of Hastings) succeeded Lord Minto in October 1813. He was

Governor-General till January, 1823, and completed the work of unification and pacification. He also held the office of Commander-in-Chief. There was a war with Nepal (1814-1816). The Nepalese had spread themselves in the hill districts of the Himalayas, from Sikkim to the Panjab, but their rule was not popular, and they began to encroach on British territory. As a result of this war the hill tracts of Kumaun Division (including Garhwal) and Dehra Dun were conquered from them and annexed to the territory of what are now called the United Provinces. Some small tracts round Simla were also then acquired, and became the nucleus for the subsequent formation of Simla district. Apart from the acquisition of this hill territory, in which numerous hill stations have grown up, the relations between Nepal and the Government of India were cemented on a firm and frank basis. Nepal enjoys greater independence than the subsidiary Indian States. She rendered valuable assistance to the British Government in the Mutiny of 1857 and in the Great War (1914-1918), and her hardy mountain sepoys, the Gurkhas, still supply, under treaty, some of the best fighting material to the Indian army.

Extirpation of the Pindaris.—The chief work of Lord Hastings's administration was the rounding up of the Pindaris, the final settlement of the Maratha question, and the completion of the treaty structure on which the whole system of Protected States in India is based. The Pindaris were bands of mixed robber organizations, which had fought in Maratha armies from the first rise of the Maratha power, but which became more independent and troublesome when the Maratha States were curbed and shorn of territory in Lord Wellesley's wars. Their depredations in Central and Northern India and Rajputana became intolerable from 1812 onwards. After some negotiations, by which certain minor States were brought into British alliance, a comprehensive military drive was undertaken by Lord Hastings with an army of 120,000 men. The Pindaris and their confederates within a circle some 700 miles in diameter were hemmed in, and their nests destroyed.

Third Maratha War (1817-1819) : Pacification and Settlement of Central India, Malwa, and Rajputana.—The Grand Army suffered much from cholera. The operations lasted from 1817 to 1819. The Peshwa of Poona had been suspicious and unfriendly, and the Bhonslê and Holkar had also been hostile. The third Maratha War (1817-1819) ended in the extinction of the Peshwa and the annexation of his territory to the Bombay Presidency; the curtailment of Bhonslê territory by the annexation of the Sāgar and Narbada districts, which afterwards formed the nucleus of the Central Provinces; the reduction of Holkar to the position of a subsidiary chief; his cession of Khandesh and its annexation to the Bombay Presidency; and the release of Rajput and Central India States from Maratha control. Sindhia had early been detached from any active fighting in the war, and his position remained unaffected, except that certain exchanges of territory were effected for administrative convenience, which gave Ajmir to the British. A number of treaties were drawn up with Rajput chiefs, among whom may be mentioned Jodhpur, Udaipur, Jaipur, and Bikanir, and chiefs in Malwa and Central India. The Pathan State of Bhopal, which had rendered generous assistance, was recognized and protected, and its position defined by treaty. The famous Pindari leader, Amir Khan, was pacified by the creation of the State of Tonk. The primitive tribes of Bhils and Gonds were brought into subjection. Henceforward, the intricate, and in some cases interlacing, boundaries between the various States in Central India, Malwa, and Rajputana were no longer in dispute, and protection was afforded to minor chiefs in relation to direct Feudatories of the Indian Empire, as well as to the Feudatories themselves in relation to the Empire. The *Pax Britannica* was established under the guarantee and supremacy of the British Government, as represented by the East India Company. The finances of India were also rehabilitated, and Lord Hastings left the country (1823) in a flourishing condition.

GEORGE PHILIP & SON, LTD. THE LONDON GEOGRAPHICAL INSTITUTE

MAP OF THE PANJAB

To accompany "THE MAKING OF INDIA," BY A. YUSUF ALI (A. & C. BLACK, LTD., LONDON)

CHAPTER XX

REFORM AND PHILANTHROPY: MOVEMENTS, MORAL, SOCIAL, AND RELIGIOUS. 1819-1836

GOVERNORS-GENERAL: LORD AMHERST, 1823-1828; LORD WILLIAM BENTINCK, 1828-1835; SIR CHARLES METCALFE (TEMPORARY) MARCH 1835 TO MARCH 1836.

Indian Treaty System of 1819 and Enthusiasm for Reforms related to Policies in Europe and Britain.—The Reform Bill of 1832 may be called the central pivot of British parliamentary history from 1821 to 1841, although the Tories were in power within that period till 1830. In spite of the discontent and repression that attended the Industrial Revolution and the effects of the Napoleonic Wars, there was a steady movement towards reform, of which Catholic emancipation (1829), middle-class franchise (1832), abolition of slavery (1833), the East India Company's charter (1833), various measures of Irish relief, and Lord Durham's famous Report about Canadian self-government (1839), are different phases. In foreign policy the Grand Alliance (1815-1822), by which the four strong Powers endeavoured to maintain the peace of Europe and the world after Napoleon's downfall, was a dream for the confederation of Europe, the Great Powers imposing on themselves the task of keeping the small Powers in order. Castlereagh, Britain's Foreign Minister (1812-1822) called the Alliance "a piece of sublime mysticism and nonsense," and it broke down in Europe. But the treaty structure erected in India in 1819, by which one overwhelmingly strong Power undertook to regulate the constitution and external position of a number of small Powers of various grades, which could not possibly compete with it, was eminently successful, and endures to the present day as a monument of Anglo-Indian diplomacy, backed by military force. The Liberalism of England became the pattern for the Liberalism of Europe in the Liberal Empire of Louis Philippe (1830) and the widespread movements that followed.

It was the direct parent of the many Liberal movements which came to the surface in India between its pacification and the Imperialism of the two decades before the Mutiny.

External Events: First Burmese War (1824-1826).—We might take a rapid glance at the external events before considering the less tangible movements that were taking shape in the country. The first Burmese War (March 1824 to February 1826) was a consequence, on the one hand, of the overweening ambitions of a locally successful and expanding dynasty, and on the other, of the necessity of strengthening the Company's eastern frontier. About the time that the Company was consolidating its position in Bengal, the Burman kingdom of Ava (near Mandalay) had won remarkable successes over its neighbours. It had successfully fought the Chinese and Siamese, subdued its suzerain kingdom of Pegu, and founded a Burman Empire. In the first two decades of the nineteenth century it had annexed Manipur and Assam. In 1824 it came into conflict with the Company's troops. The war that ensued was primarily aimed at turning out the Burmese from Assam. By May 1824, Rangoon was occupied from the sea, but when an attempt was made to invade the interior, the enemy made a stout and skilful resistance. Peace was not made till the British were at Yandabo, sixty-three miles south-west of Ava, February 1826. The Company obtained an indemnity and annexed Assam, as well as the coast districts of Burma, except Rangoon and the delta of the Irawadi from the Salween river to Bassein. Martaban was included in the Company's acquisitions. The British troops suffered from cholera and scarcity of provisions.

Bharatpur the Jat Principality: Who are the Jats?—The storming of the Jat fortress of Bharatpur (near Mathura) by the Bengal army under Lord Combermere deserves passing mention. It was considered impregnable, and had defied Lord Lake in 1805 when he was pursuing Holkar. It was now mined and stormed with great gallantry, on account of the chief having defied the Company's authority in some internal disputes. The rightful heir was reinstated. This is one of the two Jat principalities left in India, the other being the State of Dholpur. The Jats are an interesting race allied to the Rajputs. Ethnically they form the chief element in the Sikh people.

Jats are found in the Panjab, the western portion of the United Provinces, Rajputana, Sindh, and Baluchistan. Many of them are Muslim by religion.

Mysore, Assam, and Coorg.—The chief external events of Lord William Bentinck's administration may be briefly mentioned. In 1831 the disorders in Mysore State compelled the Company to take over the administration, which remained in its hands for fifty years. The position was consolidated in the outlying province of Assam, where tea cultivation and manufacture were systematically undertaken by means of a Government plantation and (after the abolition of the Company's monopoly in 1833) by private enterprise. Skilled Chinese workmen were imported into India in this connection. The annexation of Coorg in 1834 added a picturesque community to the composite sociological fabric of British India.

Finance: How the Opium Question Grew to be an International Question.—The Burmese war had drained the Indian treasury, and financial retrenchment was one of the tasks entrusted to Lord William Bentinck, which he performed without showy results, but which earned him much unpopularity in the services. He curtailed certain allowances to military officers; regulated the exports of Malwa opium from Protected States, so as to give better financial control to the Company; and resumed many revenue-free tenures of land. Warren Hastings had placed the monopoly of Bengal opium in the Company's hands. The opium produced in the Indian States of Malwa was now brought within the Company's regulation in its export trade through Bombay, mainly to China. This big opium interest led up to what has been called the "opium war" with China in 1840. The opium revenue of the Indian Government became a bigger and bigger item in the Indian budget, mainly from the export trade, until it was severely restricted by agreement from 1907. The export trade to China would then have been extinguished altogether in ten years, had not Chinese provincial governors themselves started production on a large scale in China for revenue purposes. The opium question is now (1925) mixed up with the question of cocaine and other drugs, and is in the hands of the League of Nations for solution by international agreement.

Administrative and Judicial Reforms.—The administrative and judicial reforms of the period are at least as important as the "philanthropical" reforms which are usually thrown up so much into relief. The land revenue administration was further developed, and newer systems were devised to supplement the one adopted in Bengal by Lord Cornwallis. These will be noticed later in describing the growth of provincial administration. The judicial machinery was tightened up, and brought more into harmony with the general administration. Madras had had a Supreme Court since 1800, and Bombay since 1823. In 1829 the Bombay Supreme Court came into open conflict with the Bombay Government on a question of jurisdiction, which was decided by the Privy Council in London against the contentions of the Bombay Court. Indian agency began now to be employed more and more in the middle ranks of the administrative services; in the lower ranks it had always been indispensable, and the higher ranks were opened to it by gradual steps much later.

Suppression of Sati and Thagi.—The practice of *sati* immolation—that is, the theoretically voluntary burning of Hindu widows on the death of their husbands—was suppressed by law (1829). This measure had been carefully considered for many years, as the practice seemed to have increased in Bengal and in the neighbourhood of Calcutta. Careful preliminary enquiries had been made as to the possible political effects of legislation, and the active support of the new school of Hindu thought educated in English had been secured. The criminal bands of Thags, or secret societies for robbery by deceitful murder, were suppressed. These bands had operated in large areas of the country, in Northern and Central India. They had the terrible goddess Kali for patron, and used scouts, a criminal *patois*, and a system of quiet strangulation or poisoning for those travelling with money. To meet their underground operations a special Department had to be created—the Thagi and Dacoity Department, a carefully organized detective force in plain clothes, also working in secret, and by means of informers. Major (afterwards Sir William) Sleeman was appointed Superintendent (1835) and Commissioner (1839) of Thagi and Dacoity Operations. The department afterwards developed into the modern Criminal Investigation Department, now charged with the duty of tracing political crime.

English Education: Freedom of the Press.—English education had been proceeding at a rapid pace in Bengal. The missionaries had given some attention to it, although they also sought to reach the people through the vernaculars. They had in addition started girls' schools. Private agencies also ardently took up English education. In 1816 the English watchmaker David Hare co-operated with the Brahman Raja Ram Mohan Roy* in founding the Hindu College in Calcutta for teaching natural science, history, geography, Milton, and Shakespeare. Freemasons were actively supporting the English movement. In philosophy it followed the utilitarian English school of Jeremy Bentham and James Mill. The Company's government took it up in 1835 with the enthusiastic support of Macaulay, who contemplated the employment of public funds for English education alone. Fortunately, village education (in the vernacular) seems to have been organized a few years afterwards, but English became the vehicle for higher education. The Calcutta Medical College was started in 1835; similar colleges were started in Bombay in 1845, and in Lahore in 1860. English newspapers, conducted by Englishmen, had appeared since 1780, but they had retailed scandal and been against authority. Editors had been deported. An official censorship was instituted in 1798 during the war, but was abolished by the Marquis of Hastings in 1818. All restrictions on the Press were removed by Sir Charles Metcalfe in 1835. Among vernacular papers, the first Bengali paper had been published (by the missionaries) in Serampur in 1818; the first Gujarati paper in Bombay in 1822; and the first Urdu paper in Delhi in 1836. But the vernacular press was still in its infancy.

Charter Act of 1833; Company Ceased to be Commercial; Changes in Constitution and Legislation; no Colour Bar.—We have somewhat anticipated the chronological sequence of events. Thomas Babington Macaulay's presence in India, and his educational pronouncements and activities in legal codification, were rendered possible by the Charter Act of 1833. It

* His title of Raja was bestowed by the Mughal Emperor, who sent him as his envoy to England.

17

bears the impress not only of the idealism of the Whigs then in power, but of Benthamite theories of legislation and of the Clapham school of Evangelical enthusiasm, of which William Wilberforce and Zachary Macaulay had been leaders. The Company's tea monopoly and monopoly of the China trade were abolished. The Company ceased to be a trading body, and were directed to wind up their commercial concerns. But they were still to govern India, in trust for the Crown, for twenty years; the term was renewed indefinitely in 1853, and terminated in 1858. The Governor-General of Bengal, who had previously been vested with supervision over the other Presidencies, was made into the Governor-General of India, and a fresh Presidency was contemplated for Agra; but in actual fact the Agra province was made into the North-Western Provinces (which, with Oudh, now form the United Provinces) under a Lieutenant-Governor. Bengal still continued to be under the Governor-General direct until a Lieutenant-Governor was created in 1854. The Governor-General's Council was strengthened by the addition of a fourth member, the Law Member, for purposes of legislation. The country was thrown open to Europeans without licence. The legislative power was concentrated in the Governor-General in Council, and the other two Presidencies were (until 1861) deprived of legislative authority. The Council's Acts were to be like Acts of Parliament—valid for all places, over all persons, and in all matters in India as limited by the statute—and not restricted like the Regulations which the Governor-General had hitherto issued. A codification of laws was foreshadowed. The Company's civil service was to be recruited by competition confined to nominations amounting to four times the number of vacancies. Macaulay was then Secretary of the Board of Control, and expounded the Bill in Parliament, and was then appointed the first Law Member to carry out its legal provisions. No subject of the King was to be disqualified for office in India by reason of his birth, creed, or colour; the Directors explained the meaning of this to be "that there shall be no governing caste in British India."

Sympathetic Provincial Administrations.—The strength and character of provincial administrations during this period require a brief notice. The real work of what Macaulay called

" enlightened and paternal despotism " fell to the rulers of the provinces. A set of particularly able and sympathetic men distinguished themselves in this line; we may mention Mountstuart Elphinstone, Sir Thomas Munro, and James Thomason. Elphinstone was Governor of Bombay from 1819 to 1827. He supported indigenous institutions like the village system of watch and ward; the system of Panchayets, or people's councils for settling disputes; and the education of Hindus by means of Hindu tales with sound morals. Munro was a military officer who had acquired extensive civil and diplomatic experience; he was Governor of Madras from 1820 to 1827, and frequently compared notes with Elphinstone. He believed in saving the people from novel and intricate judicial machinery; in the employment of qualified Indians in offices of trust; in winning the confidence of Indians by maintaining their ancient institutions and usages; and in land revenue assessments with individual cultivators, instead of (ordinarily) with large zamindars, as in the United Provinces, and on twenty or thirty years' terms of settlement, instead of the Permanent Settlement of Bengal. James Thomason came a little later; he was (1843-1853) Lieutenant-Governor of the North-West Provinces* (Agra province in what is now the United Provinces), where the principles of thirty years' settlements were worked out with great care and accuracy, before him and during his term of office; but the settlements were with zamindars or village communities, according to the prevailing usage of that part of the country. He worked out a complete system of village vernacular schools, and converted the great Ganges canal scheme from being one merely for navigation to one for the irrigation of crops and the benefit of agriculture; and he founded the Engineering College at Rurki (1848). In dealing with provincial governments we get at once into the atmosphere of the people, instead of the high politics of the Government of India. We also realize the necessity, for the growth of India, of variety in methods no less than of unity of administration.

Attitude of Hindus.—While all these noble sentiments were being declared, and beneficent schemes of administration and

* The North-West Provinces were constituted into a separate province in 1835.

social amelioration were being carried out, what movements swayed the masses of the Indian people? What leaped to the eye of British observers was the Liberal movement in religion and social life, led enthusiastically by men like Raja Ram Mohan Roy (1774-1853), who wrote against idolatry as a lad in his teens, and later (1828) founded the Hindu Unitarian Church. He strongly supported the Government action against *sati* immolations. But there were other Hindus who were educated in English, and enjoyed rank and consideration in English society, whose social opinions were reactionary. For example, Radha Kant Deb proposed at the Hindu meeting for an address to Lord Hastings when he was leaving India (1823), that he should be particularly thanked for "the protection and encouragement which he had afforded to the ancient and orthodox practice of widows burning themselves with their husbands' bodies"! This was merely because Lord Hastings, for political reasons, had taken no steps against the practice. The motion was seconded, and though it was not carried, it showed that moral evolution required time for its accomplishment, as well as English education. The vast mass of the people still went to the Jagannath Car, tortured themselves in the hook-swinging festivals in honour of the goddess Kali, and performed the time-honoured rites and superstitions of the countryside.

Attitude of Muslims.—The case of the Muslims was tragic. They were the people who had suffered and lost most from the revolutions which had placed the British in power. Their attitude was sullen and in the early stages full of irreconcilable despair. Saiyid Ahmad of Bareilly* (1782-1831) acquired an enormous following by preaching the purification of the faith, back to its primitive simplicity. His teaching raised a storm of theological Muslim controversy. He emigrated to the Afghan frontier with a large body of men, and died fighting a holy war against the Sikhs who were oppressing the Muslims in the Panjab. Apart from this militant movement, which was hostile to all

* Not to be confounded with Sir Saiyid Ahmad, the founder of Aligarh College, and identified with the Liberal educational and religious movement among Muslims, which led to the foundation of Aligarh College, 1877.

non-Muslims, pessimism and an utter sense of helplessness were the dominant notes of Hindustani poetry. In the Delhi court poet Zauq (1790-1855) it is unrelieved by any lighter vein, and thus reflects the mood of the overthrown dynasty. The poet Insha, who migrated to Lucknow, and died there in 1818, reflects the Lucknow mood. It presented a certain show of brilliancy combined with recklessness and irresponsibility. The Nawabs of Oudh had lost all real power long before Lord Hastings encouraged Ghazi-ud-din Haidar to assume the title of King of Oudh (1819). But there was some artistic gaiety in the court of Lucknow, though it barely concealed the gloom, despair, and futility which prevented its people from welcoming the new light rising from Calcutta.

CHAPTER XXI

PUSH TO THE NORTH-WEST: PANJAB, SINDH, AND AFGHANISTAN. 1836-1856

GOVERNORS-GENERAL: LORD AUCKLAND, 1836-1842; LORD ELLENBOROUGH, 1842-1844; SIR HENRY HARDINGE (LORD HARDINGE I.), 1844-1848; LORD DALHOUSIE, 1848-1856.

India under Lord Auckland (1836-1842).—Lord Auckland, at the Directors' banquet on his departure for India, spoke of his mission as that of "extending the blessings of good government and happiness to millions of her people." The country over which he was going to assume the reins of an "enlightened and paternal despotism" (the words are Macaulay's) had a revenue of 20 millions, an army of about 200,000, and a population estimated at 100,000,000. He certainly directed his attention to education and medical organization, as well as canal irrigation, but he inaugurated a period of wars which lasted twenty years, and a Central Asian policy which dominated Indian finance and politics throughout the nineteenth century, and whose effects persist to our own day.

Russian Advance in Asia, and Problem of the North-West Indian Frontier.—Lord Palmerston had become Foreign Secretary in England in 1830. He viewed with a jealous eye the advance of Russia in Asia, and tried to extend British influence in the Near and Far East as a counterpoise to that of Russia. It cannot be said that his policy was wrong. But the methods employed in carrying it out led to disasters in the early stages, and added complications to the troublesome question of the defence of the North-West frontier of India, which is both Imperial and Indian, and which, in spite of many different modes of approach already tried, still remains unsolved. In the eighteenth century the Russian Tsars, with the resources of European warfare, began to expand eastwards. Their encroachments on Turkey do not concern us here, but their pressure on Persia (Treaty of Turkmanchai, 1828) and their entry into the region between the Caspian and the Oxus could not be a matter of unconcern to India. The Afghans were at that time in a chronic state of civil war, and Persia could easily become the cat's-paw of Russia for bringing the Tsar to the Indian region. The Panjab and Sindh, which lay between British India and these storm centres, were themselves sources of anxiety; the one on account of its seeming strength, and the other on account of its weakness.

Ranjit Singh and the Panjab.—We left Maharaja Ranjit Singh in 1809 (Chapter XIX.), at the stage at which his treaty with the British left him a free hand in the Panjab beyond the Satlaj. His military genius, aided by the army of the Khalsa (Sikh army), made him master of the trans-Satlaj Panjab and the territories on its borders (1820). He annexed Kashmir in 1819, and cast longing eyes towards Afghanistan and Sindh. He had drilled a fine army under French and Italian officers, and was well supplied with heavy artillery. Generals Ventura and Allard, in his service, were Napoleon's officers. After the final fall of Napoleon their occupation was gone, and they sought openings in the East. The British naturally objected to Maharaja Ranjit Singh's ambitions in the direction of Sindh and Afghanistan, for which they had their own plans. But when Dost Muhammad, the actual Amir of Kabul, rejected their overtures and favoured Russia (1837) they sought and obtained the Maharaja's alliance (1838) in a scheme to substitute for Dost Muhammad an Amir of their own, Shah Shuja, who was then in exile from Afghanistan, and under British protection. The alliance was of doubtful value to the British. The Maharaja was in ailing health, and died in June 1839, and the Sikh troops employed in the Afghan expedition and the subsequent withdrawal (March 1839 to November 1842) played for their own hand, and were often a source of danger to the British troops.

First Afghan War (March 1839 to November 1842).—The Bombay contingent marched through Sindh to Kandahar. The Bengal army marched from Firozpur and also met at Kandahar. Shah Shuja was installed at Kabul in August 1839, Dost Muhammad having fled. But the Afghans did not like an Amir forced on them with foreign bayonets. Risings occurred in 1841, and the two political officers, Sir Alexander Burnes and Sir William Macnaghten, were assassinated in November 1841. The British garrison of 4,500 men with 12,000 camp-followers attempted to retreat by the shortest route, the Khaibar Pass, into India, but were annihilated (January 1842). Shah Shuja was himself assassinated. An army of retribution was sent to Kabul, which relieved the heroic garrison of Jalalabad (April 1842), and reached Kabul (September 1842), where it was joined by the Kandahar garrison. After blowing up the Kabul bazaar, and recovering the British prisoners, it returned to Peshawar (November 1842), and Dost Muhammad resumed his throne at Kabul. The expedition had failed, having resulted in the destruction of many lives, the waste of much treasure, and the loss of British prestige.

Lord Ellenborough (1842-1844): Napier and the Conquest of Sindh, 1843.—Meanwhile (February 1842), Lord Ellenborough had succeeded Lord Auckland. He wound up the Afghan War, but was ultimately responsible (the direct responsibility rested with Sir Charles Napier, whom he sent there in military command) for the unprovoked attack upon Sindh and its conquest. In the big game of Imperial policy attention had already been drawn to Sindh, which was held by the Talpur family of Biloches, the Mirs or Amirs of Sindh, with their capitals at Haidarabad,* Mirpur, and Khairpur. Between 1830 and 1838 various attempts had been made to arrange for the navigation of the Indus through Sindh, but political considerations had doubtless been held in view as well as commercial. The Mirs were suspicious, but had allowed the passage of troops through their territory for the first Afghan War, and had refrained from hostility during the trying period of disasters to the British arms in Afghanistan. With a masterful and impetuous soldier like Napier their liberties were now doomed. They made their stand, but the brilliant battle of Miāni, near Haidarabad, in which General Napier fought like a common soldier, against odds of seven to one,

* In Sindh; not to be confounded with Hyderabad (Haidarabad), Deccan.

shattered their power. The Mir of Khairpur, who had been friendly, was allowed to retain his State, as a Protected State; the rest of Sindh was annexed (1843), and was attached to the Bombay Presidency.*

Sir Henry Hardinge (Lord Hardinge I.), 1844-1848: Went Out by the Overland Route.—The Court of Directors in London had never taken kindly to Lord Ellenborough, and he had done nothing to conciliate them. Patronage (including the powers of appointment and dismissal) was still in their hands, and they recalled Lord Ellenborough, although the Home Ministry was inclined to support him. The next Governor-General, Sir Henry Hardinge, came with a great military reputation, won in the Peninsula and Waterloo campaigns. He came by the overland route: across France, partly by railway; by sea to Alexandria; by river-boat to Cairo; by a four-in-hand, at a gallop across the desert, to Suez; and thence by steamer to Calcutta. The whole journey took him only forty-four days instead of the three or four (sometimes six) months that the Cape route took. The Suez overland route was inaugurated in 1841-1843.

Development of Steamer Communication.—The development of steamer communication in India had been rapid. The first steamship service in the United Kingdom had been between Liverpool and Glasgow in 1815; for Continental ports it was introduced in 1824. The steamer *Diana* was built at Kidderpur docks in Calcutta, and launched in 1823; she was very useful in the first Burmese War in 1824. Bombay built the s.s. *Hugh Lindsay* for Suez in 1829. In 1825 the s.s. *Enterprise*, of 500 tons, was sent from England to India by the Cape route. The conquest of Aden in 1839 and its incorporation in the Bombay Presidency gave a coaling station to the Company for the Egyptian route, for the development of which the P. and O. Company sent out a small fleet from England, beginning in 1842. The Ganges flotilla had been plying already under Lord William Bentinck.

Sikh Kingdom in Anarchy after Ranjit Singh.—The Sikh kingdom founded by Ranjit Singh in the Panjab broke up into anarchy after his death (1839). The civil power was paralyzed

* Napier is said to have announced his conquest of Sindh with a laconic pun: *Peccavi* (I have Sindh [sinned]).

by rivalries between various claimants to the throne and factions that claimed offices or provinces. A son and grandson of the Maharaja died in November 1840, and two ladies (Ranis) as well as others claimed the power in the State. Intrigues, insurrections, and assassinations became frequent. The only organized body that remained was the Sikh army, but instead of being the servant of the State, it became its master. It became itself the Sikh people, the Khalsa, and was run by committees or panchayets, without a controlling head or guide. The European generals gradually withdrew. In 1843 Dalip Singh (Dhuleep Singh) (born 1837) was proclaimed Maharaja; his mother, Rani Jindan, who was hostile to the British, became regent. Peace in the Panjab was a British interest; the anarchy had been dangerous to the British in their withdrawal from Afghanistan in 1842. The Sikh army was all-powerful. It was animated by an intensely patriotic and religious spirit, and military preparations were made on a large scale on the British side of the Satlaj to meet any eventualities. The Sikhs believed that the British were preparing for invasion, and anticipated the movement by crossing the Satlaj into British territory in December 1845. There is reason to believe that the Sikh leaders themselves, finding the power of their army awkward to themselves, hurled it to destruction against the British.

First Sikh War (1845-1846): Panjab comes under British Control.—The Governor-General (Sir Henry Hardinge) and the Commander-in-Chief were already at Ambala, and moved up to meet the Sikhs. Their preparations were not quite complete, and they were inferior to the Sikhs in heavy guns. The Sikhs were the first to attack, and they fought well. The casualties on both sides were heavy. Three pitched battles were fought between December 18, 1845, and January 28, 1846, at Mudki, Phiru-shahr (Ferozeshah), and Aliwal. The fourth, on the river bank opposite to Sobrāon, was decisive, and practically destroyed the Sikh army. Its rank and file and subordinate commanders fought well; "few escaped, and none surrendered." Among the British heroes may be mentioned Sir Harry Smith, who had an independent command at Aliwal, and whose name is commemorated in South Africa by the towns of Harrismith and Aliwal North, while his romantic Spanish wife is remembered in the town of Ladysmith. The British army now marched to Lahore, where the treaty of peace was signed (March 1846). The infant Dhuleep Singh was recognized as Maharaja, but the regency was to be under a British Resident; the Jalandhar Doab (tract between the Satlaj and Beas rivers) was annexed by the Company; a heavy indemnity was imposed, and as it could not all be paid, part of it was taken in territory—viz., the Hazara District and the province of Kashmir; Hazara was retained as British, and Kashmir was sold to the Dogra* chieftain Gulab Singh, who had risen from a humble position to be a favourite of Ranjit Singh; and the Sikh army was to be limited in future. A later agreement authorized the maintenance of a British force in the Panjab.

Lord Dalhousie (1848-1856); Railways and Telegraphs; Coal-Mining; Cheap Postage; Public Works.—In January 1848, Lord Hardinge (who got his peerage for the Panjab campaign) was succeeded by Lord Dalhousie (1848-1856). Dalhousie was the youngest Governor-General to come out to India; his age was only thirty-five. But his Cabinet experience in England at the Board of Trade enabled him to design large schemes of railway policy with a view to State ownership, which he had been unable to carry out in England. The first railway in India, from Bombay to Thana, was opened in 1853, and small lengths were laid down in the other two Presidencies. In Bengal the railway from Calcutta to Raniganj opened up the coal-fields, and laid the foundations of coal-mining on a large scale, and later of the iron industry. A telegraph line between Calcutta and Agra was laid down between 1853 and 1855, and Delhi and Lahore were already in telegraphic communication before May 1857. The first postage stamp was issued in 1854, simultaneously with cheap rates for inland postage (a half-anna† for letters, and a quarter-anna for post-cards), which were maintained till the revision of economic values in the Great War. A civil Public Works Department was organized (1855), and roads and canals received a great impetus.

* The Dogras are a hill tribe of Rajputs round Jammu. The style of the ruler of Kashmir is: Maharaja of Jammu and Kashmir.

† Half anna=¾d. according to the rate of exchange then current.

Second Sikh War (1848-1849): Panjab Annexed.—There were two big wars, and three large accessions of territory and various minor ones without war. In the Panjab the attempt made to govern indirectly was a failure. The Sikh notabilities, who had been deprived of real power, were never reconciled. The remnants of the Sikh army chafed at the restraints put upon them. The Sikhs formed an alliance with the Afghans. An insurrection at Multan in April 1848, caused dangerous excitement in the army of the Khalsa. Multan itself was handled in the earlier stages by the frontier British officers with Pathan and other levies. But a large army was assembled on the British side and sent out to meet the Sikh army near the Jhelam river. The first pitched battle at Chilianwala (January 13, 1849) was indecisive, and the British casualties were heavy. But when reinforcements arrived, including the troops from Multan, which had been captured on January 2, a second battle was fought, February 21, at Gujarat, which decided the campaign. The Panjab was annexed; Dhuleep Singh was deposed, and went to live in England, where he received much sympathy and kindness from Queen Victoria; and the famous Koh-i-nur diamond passed into the regalia of the Crown of England. Under the strong administration of Sir John Lawrence, order was restored to the Panjab, under the Non-Regulation system of government, which was simpler and more personal than the complicated machinery which had grown up in Bengal.

Second Burmese War: Conquest of Pegu.—The second Burmese War (April to December 1852) arose out of certain grievances of British merchants. It was carried through with swiftness and decision. As a result the port of Rangoon, and the whole delta of the Irawadi, comprising the province of Pegu, as far north as Thayetmyo and Toungoo districts, were annexed. The Burmese lost access to the sea, and their court at Ava led a secluded existence until 1885.

Doctrine of Lapse; Nagpur Annexed; Berar Assigned; Creation of the Central Provinces; Oudh Annexed.—The Nagpur territories were annexed (1854) on the failure of natural heirs to the Bhonslê ruler. Lord Dalhousie believed in the extinction of Indian States, and disapproved of adoption, by means of which Hindu law perpetuates families. In other cases, such as Satara (1848) and Jhansi (1853), the ruler had actually made a death-bed adoption, which was not recognized. The doctrine of lapse and annexation was applied to several minor States. In 1853 the fertile province of Berar was taken over ("assigned") from the Hyderabad State for payment of the Hyderabad Contingent and the settlement of other financial claims, it being stipulated that any surplus revenue would be paid to the Nizam. This stipulation was cancelled for a consideration in 1902, and the assignment was converted to a perpetual lease. The Nagpur territories, together with the Sagar and Narbada territories, were constituted into the "Central Provinces" in 1861, to which Berar was added in 1903. The kingdom of Oudh was annexed for maladministration in 1856.

Open Competition for Civil Service : Comprehensive Educational Policy.—Thus Lord Dalhousie had added four large kingdoms to the Indian Empire, with an immediate increase to the revenue of not less than 4 millions sterling; in Berar and Nagpur he had acquired the finest cotton tracts in India; and his administrative reforms had modernized India. The Charter Act of 1853 had enlarged the Governor-General's Council for legislative purposes as distinct from the Executive Council, and had abolished the Company's patronage, and substituted open competition for the Indian Civil Service in England instead of the limited competition of twenty years before. Sir Charles Wood (afterwards Lord Halifax) in his dispatch of 1854 laid down a comprehensive educational policy, for the foundation of Indian universities, for the development of Anglo-vernacular secondary education, and for the systematic organization of primary vernacular education. India's reaction to all these varied movements and activities was complex. We can only judge of it by the history of the next half century.

CHAPTER XXII

THE GREAT MUTINY AND THE EXTINCTION OF THE COMPANY. 1857-1858

GOVERNOR-GENERAL: LORD CANNING, 1856-1862 (TITLE OF GOVERNOR-GENERAL AND VICEROY FROM NOVEMBER 1858).

Lord Canning (1856-1862): Principles of His Government.—Lord Canning, who assumed the Government of India in February 1856, was the youngest son of George Canning, the Conservative statesman of Liberal views, who had controlled British foreign policy from 1822 to 1827. Lord Canning succeeded to the strenuous autocracy of Lord Dalhousie in India—as his father had succeeded to the autocracy of Castlereagh at the London Foreign Office. In dealing with the great military and political convulsion in India, he tried to conciliate the two complementary principles: firm, unflinching assertion of authority, and sympathy and consideration for the vanquished dupes of other men's ambitions.

Unrest in Northern India: Dispossessed Principalities.—There was a general feeling of unrest in Northern India. In spite of the wholesale annexations of Lord Dalhousie, about three-sevenths of the area in India still remained under Indian princes. They sympathized with the feeling in the minds of some of the expropriated princes or their heirs, which was very bitter. The Delhi territory was still under the nominal sovereignty of the Mughal emperor, Bahadur Shah II. Though his family had long ceased to exercise real authority, a show of sovereignty had been maintained, which was abandoned when the Company ceased to present nazars (or ceremonial offerings symbolical of fealty) in 1818, and ceased to issue coins in the Mughal's name in 1835. Lord Dalhousie proposed to terminate the dynasty of Timur altogether after the death of the "present King of Delhi," but agreed, as a compromise, to recognize an heir-apparent if he would quit Delhi. While Delhi was smarting under a sense of wrong and indignity, the Oudh dynasty, which had been loyal to the Company, was deposed for maladministration. The King of Oudh had been in complete accord with his nobles, and the feudal tie kept the ryots attached to the nobles. The Oudh people did not weigh standards of administration. To all classes the punishment by the Company of a friend of the Company seemed unjust. The dispossessed Peshwa's son, Nana Sahib, lived near Cawnpore; the Company had refused to continue to him the pension which his father had enjoyed, and he hated the Company. There was another Maratha dignitary, the young widowed Rani of Jhansi (she was only twenty in 1857), who felt that she had been wronged by the Company's annexation of her little State under the doctrine of lapse. The neighbouring big Maratha State of Nagpur had also been recently annexed, but it had thrown up no strong character to make a fight. To the Hindu rulers the non-recognition of their cherished principle of adoption seemed an invasion of their ancient institutions. There was a general feeling of insecurity, but the strongest centres of discontent were Delhi, Lucknow (the capital of Oudh), Cawnpore, and Jhansi (with other centres in Central India in touch with the Maratha feeling in Cawnpore or Jhansi). These were the active foci of the Mutiny.

The Sepoy Army.—The sepoy army of the Company had also suffered a deterioration, both in discipline and in its sentiment of loyalty to the Company. Its experienced and ambitious British officers had been taken up for civil duty, and there was no satisfactory understanding between the new British officers and their men. The Bengal army was the largest, and had been the most employed in recent warfare. It was drawn from Northern India, and was affected by the sentiment of the general population. In the Burmese wars, in Sindh, and again in the Panjab wars there had been disquieting symptoms of its insubordinate spirit. Many of the sepoys were drawn from Oudh, the Delhi territory, or the North-Western Provinces (now the United Provinces), which looked to Delhi. The proportion of British troops to Indian troops in the country was as one to five or one to six, and the disposition of the troops over the rapidly expanding territory of the Company was faulty. News of the Crimean War (1853-1856) had not been very complimentary to the British, and Russo-British hostility had also necessitated a demand upon India for the war with Persia (November 1856 to April 1857) and with China (1856-1860).

The Masses and the Thinking Classes.—The vast mass of the people were passive, but the innate conservatism of the thinking classes, who had lost their power and influence, and frequently their means of livelihood, with the Company's advance, looked upon its new intrusive policy with suspicion and even hatred. A link was established between the different discontented elements and the Company's Bengal army, and the result was the conflagration of the Mutiny (May 1857 to January 1859).

Outbreak of the Mutiny.—The immediate occasion was the issue of greased cartridges in connection with the new Enfield rifle. The Hindu sepoys thought (or were made to believe) that their caste was endangered, and the Muslims that their ideas of ceremonial purity were insulted. Isolated outbreaks occurred in Calcutta and elsewhere, from February 1857 onwards. On May 9, 1857, eighty-five sepoys were imprisoned in irons for insubordination in Meerut, a large cantonment only forty miles from Delhi. Next day the sepoy regiments at Meerut rose, released their comrades, committed wild excesses, and marched to Delhi, where the Delhi sepoys joined them, and the Mughal emperor was proclaimed as ruler of India. The British in Delhi were taken by surprise; most of them were massacred; but a young telegraph lad had the presence of mind to wire a message to Lahore, while a young British subaltern blew up the magazine in order to deprive the mutineers of ammunition. A fortified, walled town, full of troops, the capital of pre-British India, and the residence of the Mughal emperor—Delhi became the centre and headquarters of the mutiny. The movement spread rapidly over the North-West Provinces and Oudh—to Bareilly, Lucknow, Cawnpore, Jhansi, and surrounding districts. By the middle of June, when the Gwalior contingent mutinied, though the young Maharaja Sindhia and his minister, Dinkar Rao, remained loyal, the mutineers were in possession of the maximum area ever in their possession, though sporadic outbreaks occurred here and there later.

Fight for Delhi (June to September 1857).—The first care of the Government was naturally to recapture Delhi. Panjab was the province marked out for this task. It was nearest to Delhi, with no rebel forces to bar the way. Its ruler, Sir John Lawrence, quickly disarmed the province. The Afghans on the frontier were friendly, and were maintained in their good relations. Sikh rule had long estranged the Panjab from Delhi, and its annexation had been too recent to re-establish touch. The martial instincts of the Sikhs were provided with an outlet by the recruitment of irregular corps under daring British leaders like Nicholson and Hodson. The famous corps of Guides, horse and foot, raised in 1847, and originators of what was then the informal khaki, took up with alacrity their duties in the three months' attack on Delhi (June 8 to September 14, 1857). Gurkhas, Sikhs, Jammu troops, and some loyal regiments of the Company co-operated with the British troops. The British position was on the Ridge to the north-east of the town. Early in September the heavy siege guns arrived, drawn by elephants. On September 14 five columns stormed the city, and entered it by the northern gates and the breaches made between. It took a week more to clear the city. General Nicholson, the soul of the assault, died of his wounds. Bahadur Shah was captured, and was afterwards exiled, and his dynasty terminated.

Cawnpore and Lucknow (June to September, 1857).—The capture of Delhi very much eased the situation, but it was only the first (though the greatest) blow in killing the Mutiny. Further east and south the operations were not so successful in the early stages. At Cawnpore General Wheeler's garrison capitulated on June 26, 1857, but the Nana's fury led to two wholesale massacres and subsequent reprisals by an avenging force. At Lucknow Sir Henry Lawrence had made prudent provision to withstand a long siege, and the British and loyal Indian garrison were shut up in the Residency from July 1 to September 25, 1857. Sir Henry died of a shell wound on July 4, and lies buried in the Residency, where a simple inscription bears witness that he "tried to do his duty." It was not easy to arrange for the relief of Lucknow. The western troops were engaged before Delhi, the key position of India. The troops from Bengal had to march through many hundred miles of disturbed country, fighting their way. Sir Henry Havelock led a movable column, Havelock's "Ironsides," strengthened by civilian volunteers, but his communications were constantly threatened. Leaving Allahabad on July 7, he occupied Cawnpore on the 17th. He started for Lucknow on the 20th, but his flanks were exposed, and his force was very much reduced by casualties from fighting, from the heat, and from disease, and he had to fall back on Cawnpore. On September 15 he was superseded by Sir James Outram, who brought reinforcements. But that "Bayard of India" (as Outram has been called), though senior to Havelock, served under him in order to give him the glory of relieving Lucknow, which they did jointly on September 25. They were, however, shut up in the Residency in their turn, and were not strong enough to fight their way out with the women and children of the Residency.

Great Drive, North and South of the Jamna (September 1857 to January 1859).—Delhi and Cawnpore were captured, and Lucknow was heartened. Now began the final drive which re-established the Government. Reinforcements began to pour in from England. The troops from Delhi were available from the west. The naval brigade of 500 handy men, under Captain Sir William Peel,* were ready to go anywhere, and more could follow. The new Commander-in-Chief, Sir Colin Campbell (afterwards Lord Clyde), arrived in Cawnpore in November 1857, and arranged, in conjunction with his lieutenant, Sir Hugh Rose (Lord Strathnairn), the great drive which terminated the Mutiny. Campbell took the northern operations, while Rose worked up his Central India force south of the Jamna. Campbell lost no time in evacuating the Lucknow garrison and ineffectives from the Residency (November 14 to 18); Peel's bluejackets were conspicuous for their gallantry. Campbell hurried off to Cawnpore, defeated the Gwalior rebels and the Maratha leader, Tantia Topi, and cleared the district, finally capturing Lucknow on March 15, 1858. Meanwhile, Rose had cleared various points in Central India, and arrived before Jhansi on March 21, 1858, where Tantia was operating in support of the young Rani. The Rani made a daring raid on

* Third son of Sir Robert Peel, the Conservative Prime Minister.

Gwalior, when the Maharaja's troops joined her and ejected their own prince, Sindhia, who was loyal to the British. On June 16, 1858, Sir Hugh Rose captured Gwalior; the Rani died fighting with her troops in male attire. The main operations were now ended, although various rebel parties had yet to be rounded up. Order was declared to have been restored in Oudh in January 1859. The Hyderabad State, under its capable minister, Nawab Salar Jang I., kept peace in the Deccan, and sent troops to fight in Central India, while Nepal, under its minister, Jang Bahadur, sent troops to assist in the northern operations.

Lord Canning's Patient Work of Pacification: Extinction of the Company.—All this while, the Governor-General, Lord Canning, worked patiently, organizing the campaigns, reorganizing civil government, punishing foes, and rewarding friends. Racial feeling ran high, and he had to stem the tide of "rapid and indiscriminate vindictiveness" on the part of his own countrymen. He was reproached with showing too much clemency on the one hand; on the other, his Oudh proclamation (1859), declaring all land in Oudh to be forfeited on account of the rebellion (for so it was in Oudh), and conferring new titles to land as from the British Government (though actual disturbance of titles took place in only a few cases), was considered too drastic. The Company was extinguished, as from November 1, 1858, and he was created the first Viceroy of the Queen as from that date. He continued to govern India till March 1862. The reforms carried out after the Mutiny will be best considered in the next chapter.

CHAPTER XXIII

BRITISH SPIRIT SUPREME: MILITARY, ADMINISTRATIVE, AND ECONOMIC REFORMS; SAFEGUARDING THE FRONTIERS. 1860-1888

VICEROYS: (2) LORD ELGIN I., 1862-1863; (3) SIR JOHN LAWRENCE (LORD LAWRENCE), 1864-1869; (4) LORD MAYO, 1869-1872; (5) LORD NORTHBROOK, 1872-1876; (6) LORD LYTTON, 1876-1880; (7) LORD RIPON, 1880-1884; (8) LORD DUFFERIN, 1884-1888.

Modernization; British Spirit Predominant; Universities.—The first twenty years of the direct government of India by the Crown were, except for the second Afghan War and the conquest of Burma, years of peace and internal development. The modernization which had been begun under Lord Dalhousie and interrupted by the Mutiny was continued, but at a much-accelerated pace. The civil population of British India had (except in Oudh) shown no active sympathy with the mutineers, and in many instances had succoured the British. The old Conservative irreconcilables had died out or been exiled. The new intellectual classes were fed with good mid-Victorian British doctrines. The three Presidency Universities wer started in 1857, after the model of the London University; Lahore followed in 1882, and Allahabad in 1887. And there was an Education Commission in 1882-1883. The British spirit—of restlessness, reform, kindliness without intimacy, and an inordinate belief in institutions—was predominant. It had an unshaken belief in itself, and required—and obtained—an unquestioning belief from the new Indian Intellectuals. The latter used the same terms, but they understood them in a different sense. The conflict came in a succeeding generation.

Army; Indian Princes; Doctrine of Lapse Abandoned; Oudh Talukdars.—The army was remodelled (1860-1863) in two directions. The Company's British troops were amalgamated with the Queen's army, not without protest from the former. The proportion of British troops to Indian troops was increased, and artillery was made an almost exclusively British arm. As regards the Indian States, they had remained loyal during the Mutiny, and some of them had rendered valuable assistance to Government. Such assistance was rewarded with titles, extensions of territory, etc. The Queen's Proclamation (1858) confirmed the treaties and engagements with the Indian princes, and promised to respect their "rights, dignity, and honour . . . as Our own." The doctrine of lapse, which had caused so much feeling of insecurity among Hindu States before the Mutiny, was withdrawn (1859), and the principle of adoption was freely conceded. In Oudh the big landholders (talukdars) were given (1861) special privileges, including English primogeniture and other incidents not usually connected with land in India. Lord Canning wished to create and maintain a landed aristocracy on the English model. His hopes have not been completely fulfilled.

New Constitution; Legislative Councils; High Courts; Codification of Law.—Constitutionally, apart from the elimination of the East India Company, and the creation of the Secretary of State for India and his Council in London, important changes were made in the Viceroy's Council (1861). A fifth member was added to the Executive Council. For legislative purposes "Additional Members" were to be appointed to sit with the five "Ordinary Members." These Additional Members were nominated by the Viceroy, but they included non-officials and Indians, and the germs of the representation of classes and interests were introduced. Similar Legislative Councils were created for Madras and Bombay, and later on for other provinces. By a separate Act (1861) High Courts were created at the Presidency towns, which absorbed the jurisdiction of the earlier Supreme Courts of the Presidency towns, as well as the other superior courts which had dealt with appeals from the interior and other matters relating to purely Indian litigation. The Code of Civil Procedure (1859), the Indian Penal Code (1860), and the Code of Criminal Procedure (1861) were promulgated. The contents of *general* Indian law were gradually modernized, but various provisions of religious and personal law continued (and still continue) to be applied to matters of succession, inheritance, marriage, and family rites or usages.

Finance: First Budget.—In finance the first Budget was introduced in 1860. For this purpose the British Treasury had sent out its secretary, Mr. James Wilson, M.P., the founder of *The Economist*, of London, to the Government of India. From 1840 to 1860 there had been only four years with small surpluses; for the other years there had been deficits, mostly above a million sterling. The Mutiny had cost the Government £40,000,000, and the total debt of India in 1860 was nearly 100 millions sterling, and it was (unlike the modern debt of India) mainly unproductive. On the revenue side nearly three-fifths of the receipts were from land revenue and excise, which were not elastic sources. On the expenditure side the interest on the debt was higher than it need have been under skilled and prudent management of the finances, and the military item was much swollen by the recent events. The system of accounts and audit was also unsatisfactory. Mr. Wilson sought for a remedy for all these shortcomings, and he introduced the Income Tax. He lived for only a year after taking over office, and was able only partially to carry out his reforms; but his Budget marks an epoch in the financial history of India. He also introduced the Government paper currency.

Frontier; Orissa Famine; Famine Policy and Irrigation.—Sir John Lawrence (1864-1869) was sent out as Viceroy for his special knowledge of the North-West frontier, gained during his successful administration of the Panjab. Afghanistan was torn with internal dissensions, and the Russian menace was getting appreciably nearer. Sir John fulfilled expectations by keeping India out of the trouble. The chief points of interest in his period are the Orissa famine and the Bombay cotton crisis. The famine and floods in Orissa (1865-1866) caused a mortality of over a million lives, and a loss of crops estimated at 3 millions of pounds sterling. The first stone in the edifice of a systematic famine policy was then laid. The Irrigation Department was then organized, and 2 millions sterling were spent (Productive Debt) on the Mahanadi Canals. Since then irrigation has been much extended. Over 28 million acres, being 13 per cent. of the cropped area, is now irrigated in British India. The capital outlay on canals has been 84 crores of rupees, equal to 84 millions sterling, with the rupee at 2s. exchange.

Cotton and Jute Industries.—The cotton boom in India (1862-1864) has an interesting history, connecting it with both earlier and later history. Cotton has been grown and woven in India from before the Christian era. But it was a hand industry. With the mass production that grew out of the Industrial Revolution, India was left behind, and the United States of America supplied Manchester with raw cotton, of a longer staple. The East India Company had tried from 1788 onwards to improve the quality of Indian cotton, but had made little impression. The American Civil War (1861-1865) stopped the supplies from America, and the cotton trade of Bombay experienced an extraordinary boom, resulting in gambling and speculation, and a financial crash (1865). When the Civil War stopped, America resumed her supplies of cotton, but Bombay was able to utilize the unwanted Indian supplies in her own modern mills. The first mill had been started in Bombay in 1851, with the import of English coal; but from 1865 the progress became very rapid. There are now 264 cotton mills in India, run with Indian capital, and employing over 300,000 persons. A similar war necessity gave the fillip to the jute industry of Calcutta. The Crimean War cut off the supplies of Russian flax, and the first jute mill in Calcutta was started in 1854. There are now eighty-one jute mills in India, employing nearly 300,000 persons. But the capital is mostly held in Scotland.

Frontier and Finance Dominate Indian Policy.—Lord Mayo (1869-1872) and Lord Northbrook (1872-1876) carried the reforms and policy of their predecessors some stages further. They were both known as benevolent Viceroys in sympathy with the people of India. Lord Mayo (sixth Earl) took the first steps in the direction of a decentralized provincial finance as distinct from the finances of India. His fine work was prematurely brought to an end by an assassin's knife on his visit to the convict settlement of the Andamans. Lord Northbrook was a member of the famous financier family of Barings; he brought to India as his private secretary his cousin, Captain Evelyn Baring, who, as Finance Member of Council (1880-

1883), left his mark on Indian finance, and subsequently as Lord Cromer left his mark on the history of Egypt and the world. Under both these Viceroys frontier questions claimed much attention.

Lord Lytton's Imperial Policy: Its Relations with Disraeli's Eastern Policy.—Lord Lytton's viceroyalty (1876-1880) was full of picturesque ceremony, Imperial sentiment, military movements, and breadth of ideas in finance and policy. It also had to deal with widespread distress from famine (1876-1878), and to curb the vernacular press in India (1878). To understand it fully we must read its detailed history along with the detailed history of Mr. Disraeli's administration of 1874-1880 in England. For Lord Lytton was a devoted disciple and close associate in policy of the great statesman who purchased the Suez Canal shares for England (1875), who in the teeth of much opposition built up a well-defined Eastern policy (1876-1878), and who gave a new Imperial outlook to British statesmanship and a new progressive policy to the British Conservative Party. Lord Lytton wished to support the aristocracy in India. To him the Indian Intellectuals were "a deadly legacy from Metcalfe and Macaulay." He strongly supported the new Muslim movement for modern education, and personally opened (1877) Sir Saiyid Ahmad's new Anglo-Oriental College at Aligarh (now the Aligarh University). In his view "the interests of the British Empire were not exclusively material, or even exclusively English." In January 1877, he held a grand Imperial Assemblage at Delhi, at which Queen Victoria was proclaimed Empress of India. In dealing with the famine he looked to more than the immediate needs. He stimulated the policy of more irrigation and better communications, and the Budget of 1878 inaugurated the Famine Insurance Fund.

Russian Expansion; Afghanistan and Baluchistan; Second Afghan War (1878-1880).—His Afghan policy must be interpreted in the light of the Empire's Eastern policy of that day. Russia had expanded rapidly east and south, and that expansion, unless checked, constituted a danger to the Empire. She had by 1858 acquired, by treaty with China, the basin of the Amur, including the port of Vladivostok, which gave her an opening into the Pacific. Her ambitions towards the Mediterranean had been checked

GEORGE PHILIP & SON, LTD. THE LONDON GEOGRAPHICAL INSTITUTE

MAP OF AFGHANISTAN AND THE NORTH-WEST FRONTIER

To accompany "THE MAKING OF INDIA," BY A. YUSUF ALI (A. & C. BLACK, LTD., LONDON)

in the Crimean War (1853-1856) and the Russo-Turkish War of 1877-1878. She was now in contact with Persia, Afghanistan, and China; and Afghanistan was subject to internal revolutions. The Amir Sher Ali seemed to favour Russia as against Britain. Lord Lytton's plan was to partition Afghanistan, retain Kandahar under India, and support on the throne of Kabul Sher Ali's son, Yakub Khan, on terms more favourable to British prestige. On the first military advance from India (November 1878), Sher Ali fled to Russian territory (December), and Yakub Khan was recognized as Amir (May 1879). He ceded the Kurram valley and other approaches to Afghanistan, and agreed to receive a British envoy at Kabul. The envoy (Sir Louis Cavagnari) and his staff and escort were, however, massacred (September 1879); there was a rising of the Afghans, and Yakub Khan was a fugitive for British protection; and more than one claimant fought for the throne of Kabul, until Sher Ali's nephew, Abdur Rahman, won the prize (July 1880). Abdur Rahman was recognized as Amir, but it took him another fourteen months to become the ruler of united Afghanistan. In this second Afghan War (1878-1880) General Sir Frederick Roberts (afterwards Lord Roberts) won great distinction by his march to Kabul (October 1879), and from Kabul to Kandahar (1880). Lord Lytton's plans were not fulfilled; but the permanent results of the events of those years were: (1) the establishment of British influence in Baluchistan by treaty with the Khan of Kalat (1876), mainly through the influence of Sir Robert Sandeman; (2) the establishment of advanced posts in Quetta and Kurram (Agency), commanding the roads to Kandahar and Kabul respectively; and (3) the establishment of a strong kingdom of Afghanistan, subsidized with arms and money from India, and leaving its foreign policy in the hands of the British Indian Government. This arrangement about foreign policy was revised in 1919.

Lord Ripon and Local Self-Government; Lord Dufferin and Burma; Safeguarding the Eastern Land Frontier.—Lord Beaconsfield's defeat by Mr. Gladstone in England in 1880 led to Lord Lytton's resignation of the viceroyalty, to which Lord Ripon succeeded (1880-1884). The policies in India underwent a similar alteration. Lord Ripon was thoroughly in sympathy with the new Intellectuals of India. He repealed (1882) the Vernacular Press Act, and began (1883) to give effect to a scheme of local self-government through municipalities and district and local boards all over India, "as a measure of political and popular education." His successor, Lord Dufferin (1884-1888) was more a diplomatist than an administrator, and both he and Lady Dufferin filled their rôles with tact, dignity, and distinction. In 1885 a slight collision between the Afghans and Russians at Penj-deh led to a Russian scare, which was smoothed over. The Indian Princes offered military and other assistance, and the scheme of Imperial Service Troops was worked out. The Burmese king, Thibaw, adopted an aggressive attitude, and intrigued with France. The short military operations (November 14 to 27, 1885) are known as the Third Burmese War. Thibaw surrendered, and Upper Burma was annexed (January 1886). This removed the danger on the eastern frontier. Annam and Tongking had come under French protection in 1883-1884, and Russian policy under Alexander III. was, about 1885, receding from Bismarck, and gravitating towards France. Lord Dufferin's action in Burma thus strengthened both the land frontiers of India against Russia or Russian allies.

CHAPTER XXIV

GROWTH OF NATIONALISM, AND THE SPIRIT OF DISCONTENT. 1888-1910

VICEROYS: (9) LORD LANSDOWNE, 1888-1893; (10) LORD ELGIN II., 1894-1899; (11) LORD CURZON, 1899-1905 (Lord Ampthill acted for him during the interval April to December 1904); (12) LORD MINTO II., 1905-1910.

Gulf Between Rulers and Ruled.—The East India Company had, in their dignified protest to Parliament against their own extinction (1858), deprecated the anti-Indian feeling, "among our countrymen in India and at home," evoked by the Mutiny. They had claimed to be the guardians of the principle that the Government of India "acknowledged no such distinction as that of a dominant and subject race," and "that its first duty was to the people of India." This principle was also embodied in a guarded form in Queen Victoria's Proclamation of 1858. But the very efforts to improve the administration produced a wide gulf between the rulers and the ruled, between British and Indian, in the thirty years following the Mutiny. A belief grew up in the Indian mind that the "governing caste," which was supposed in 1833 to be ruled out of British India, had, in fact, grown and flourished. The fruit of this belief was reaped in the events that marked the close of the nineteenth and the beginning of the twentieth centuries.

The Crown's Indian Civil Service.—The servants of the East India Company, with all their faults, at least adapted themselves to the people and the country to which they gave their services. The Crown's Indian Civil Service, selected by an open competitive examination of a very high standard in London, gave a type of man (the "Competition-wala") of a much superior education, but a much less Indian outlook. The opening of the Suez Canal in 1869 and the Red Sea cable in 1870 made communication between England and India rapid and easy, and the special "European Service" Leave Rules, enabling Government officials to go "home" every few years in the course of their service, made their outlook even less distinctively Indian. As regards the external policy of British India, and the broad lines of her internal policy, British considerations had always prevailed, but now even details of her administration began to be affected by the breezes of British politics. There also began to be a free movement of British non-officials, without the training and responsibility which made for tact and smooth inter-racial relations. Some of these stood for Liberal or even Radical tendencies. But many ranged themselves under the banner of the "ruling caste" idea. Their claim gave the more offence, as, without being rulers, they claimed the status of a ruling race.

Indians Educated in English: Political, Economic, and Social Grievances.—On the other hand, the generation of university-educated Indians reached their maturity about the time of Lord Ripon, and received considerable encouragement from the general trend of British institutions towards political freedom. There was a certain inconsistency between the political institutions worked by the British in India (mainly adapted from earlier Indian institutions) and certain fundamental doctrines of British (or European) political creeds, such as the separation of executive from judicial functions, representative control of taxation, the discussion and criticism of Government measures by means of public meetings and writings, the idea of a unified and organized nation, and the organization and recognition of a constitutional Opposition to the Government. These ideas had taken hold of English-educated India, and were encouraged by Englishmen like Mr. A. O. Hume, who, after his retirement from the Indian Civil Service (1882), devoted himself to the work of the Indian National Congress. Another devoted friend of the Congress was Sir William Wedderburn, who retired from the Indian Civil Service (Bombay) in 1887, presided over the Congress in 1889, and zealously watched over its interests in England till his death in 1918. With political theory was joined a certain amount of economic discontent. The universities were turning out graduates in increasing numbers, who could use the English language for public controversies as well as Englishmen, and to whom the English language and

English ideas were a bond of union amid the great diversities of the vernaculars and of social and religious institutions. Indians in increasing numbers studied in England, and entered the learned professions, especially the Bar. In the commerce and industries of Bombay and the commerce of Calcutta Indians occupied leading positions, although they believed themselves to be at a disadvantage in the economic relations between India and England. In the higher ranks of the civil and military services, and in the practical shaping of administrative and political policy, they were hardly represented. And the social gulf between them and the English governing class grew wider every year.

Indian National Congress formed, 1885.—Such were the conditions that led to the formation of the Indian National Congress in 1885. It was the response of English-educated India to the political gospel as preached by Edmund Burke (*d.* 1797), Jeremy Bentham (*d.* 1832), John Stuart Mill (*d.* 1873), and John Bright (*d.* 1889). When Lord Dufferin described the supporters of the Congress as a "microscopic minority," he was statistically correct, but he failed to take account of certain factors of vital importance in political development. It was a growing minority; its slogans were such as must ultimately win the support of the British man in the street; and, through the legal and educational professions, it had access to channels of influence entirely closed to a Government machinery out of touch with the people. It represented at first a phase of the ascendancy of English ideas over the Indian mind. It was, after thirty-one years, swallowed up in a movement bitterly against the Government, and hostile to everything English.

Hindu and Muslim Religious and Social Movements: Transformations and Reactions.—There was a similar transformation of the progressive religious and social movements. The Brahmo Samaj, founded in Calcutta in 1830, became and remains a small eclectic cult (or cults) for the few, but remote from the tidal waves of Indian life. The galvanic force for the reform of Hinduism came from the Arya Samaj, whose first lodge was founded in Bombay by a Gujarati Brahman, Swami Dayanand Saraswati, in 1875. This movement became hostile both to the Government and to the Muslims. It found its inspiration, not in modern civilization, but in the Vedas. With a modern organization it had an archaic outlook. Its attitude started afresh the hostility between the Hindu and Muslim religions and the Hindu and Muslim communities. Sir Saiyid Ahmad's movement in Aligarh (1877) aimed at a Muslim "Oxford." In 1916-1917 it was saved with some difficulty from being engulfed in a fierce revolutionary wave. Both in Hinduism and Islam the latent reactionary resistance has shown more strength than the reform movements.

The Pamirs; the "Vanishing Rupee"; Elective Principle in Councils; Indian Home Rule.—Lord Lansdowne's viceroyalty (1888-1894) saw the completion of the chain of defence on the North-West frontier in the direction of the Pamirs, where the Russian advance had created a threat; British authority was established over Hunza and Nagar (1891). The fall in the price of silver relatively to gold had greatly depreciated the Indian rupee. The movement had gone on ever since 1874, and as India had (and has) large payments to make annually in England, the "vanishing rupee" had deranged Indian finance. In 1893 the mints were closed to the free coinage of silver, and India began to have a "managed" currency. The Indian Councils Act of 1892 broadened the basis of the Legislative Councils and introduced the principle of election. It also gave members the right of asking questions and of discussing, but not of voting on, the Budget. But the logic of events moved faster than the Act of Parliament. The dying Conservative Parliament which had passed the Indian Councils Act was replaced in the summer of 1892 by a Radical Parliament. The new Ministry was headed by Mr. Gladstone, whose remarkable oratory was enlisted in the cause of Irish Home Rule. And the election to that Parliament, for a London constituency, of an Indian member, Mr. D. Naoroji, established, in a very real and practical form, the contact of India with Irish politics, the link between the Indian National Congress and actual work-a-day British Radicalism, and the vague stirrings for an Indian Home Rule.

Frontier Risings, Famine, and Plague: Deccan Anarchical Movement, 1896-1897.—In the viceroyalty of Lord Elgin, ninth earl and second Viceroy of that name (1894-1899), there were serious frontier risings (1897-1898); a disastrous famine (1896-1897); and the first official notice of the outbreak of plague in Bombay (1896), an outbreak which has not yet been stamped out of the country. All these calamities helped to react on the sensitive mind of India, and produced an atmosphere of confusion, suspicion, and estrangement. The principles of famine relief were reviewed anew by Government, and the Famine Code overhauled. But the deeper causes of famines were much discussed, and connected by the popular school with the Government's economic policy. The plague regulations and the quarantine and other connected measures were so resented as to cause riots and murders, and to strengthen the hands of the anarchical movement in Poona and the Bombay Deccan.

Character of Lord Curzon's Viceroyalty (1899-1905).—In the next viceroyalty (1899-1905) Lord Curzon's personality became the dominating power, the passion for efficiency the ruling motive, and universal discontent the prevailing feature of the Indian atmosphere. With all Lord Curzon's splendid gifts, his untiring energy, and boundless knowledge, he never really understood the machinery of the Indian Government or the psychology of the Indian people. He came at a difficult time; and he left India a seething mass of discontent. There was hardly a department which he did not try systematically to overhaul—with what permanent results it is too early yet to judge.

Frontier Policy; Indian States; Darbar; Universities; Army; Partition of Bengal; Discontent.—He carefully worked out a new frontier policy, and created the new North-West Frontier Province (1901). He was an authority on Central Asian politics; the pressure of Russia from the north induced him to send an armed expedition to the Forbidden City of Lhasa (1904). There was a note of Imperial splendour in his relations with the Indian States; his bargain with the Nizam about the Berars (1902) has ever since been a sore point with the premier Prince in India. Queen Victoria having died in January 1901, Lord Curzon held a great Coronation Darbar at Delhi two years afterwards to announce the coronation of King Edward VII. as Emperor of India, and he initiated the Victoria Memorial at

Calcutta, the most beautiful building yet erected in the British period in India. His university reforms (1904) brought him into collision with educated India, which criticized them as officializing higher education. His views on army administration brought him into collision (1905) with Lord Kitchener, then Commander-in-Chief, and led to Lord Curzon's resignation. His partition of Bengal (1905) caused such a violent and persistent agitation that it had to be reversed in 1911.

Lord Minto as Viceroy and Lord Morley at the India Office (1905-1910); Sedition and "Justifiable Discontent."—Lord Minto (1905-1910), fourth earl and second Viceroy of that name, came to India to give (in his sporting simile) the galloping horse a rest. The administrative machine certainly had rest. But the anarchical and seditious movements required strong handling, and he was determined to understand and differentiate from such movements the "justifiable" political discontent which they were also exploiting. Events in other parts of Asia were a spur to India: Japan had triumphed over Russia (1904-1905) and become a world power; the Persian Constitution had been promulgated (1905); the Turkish Revolution was accomplished without bloodshed in 1908; and the Chinese movement which ended in the proclamation of the republic in 1912 had begun. The Liberal flood in England placed Mr. John Morley (Lord Morley of Blackburn) in power at the India Office (December 1905 to November 1910). He had dealt with political idealism in his *Life of Burke*, and faced actual racial antagonism and sedition as Irish Secretary (1886 and 1892-1895), and in consultation with the Viceroy he now introduced a scheme of Indian Reforms, known as the Minto-Morley Reforms (1909).

Minto-Morley Reforms; Suppression of Anarchy; China Opium Agreement.—Parliamentary institutions were not attempted, but the Legislative Councils were enlarged, and their powers expanded, so as to enable members to move resolutions on the Budget or other matters of public interest, and to divide the Councils on them. The principle of election was developed, and the Muslims, as a minority community, were given the power of separate (communal) representation. Indians were appointed to the India Council in London and to the Viceroy's and Provincial Executive Councils. The

Muslims formed a separate political organization, called the Muslim League (1908). Lord Morley's aim was to "rally the Moderates," and he succeeded. The Indian National Congress of 1907 split into two parties: the Moderates led by Mr. G. K. Gokhale, and the Extremists led by B. G. Tilak. At the same time vigorous measures were taken to stamp out anarchical crime in the shape of assassinations, terrorism, bombs, and secret revolutionary societies (1907-1908). Laws were enacted to control public meetings and the Press. A measure of Imperial idealism may also be mentioned: India agreed (1907) to abandon a revenue of about 5 to 6 millions sterling annually in order to help China to extirpate the opium habit.

CHAPTER XXV

THE GREAT WAR AND THE NEW CONSTITUTION. 1910-1925

VICEROYS: (13) BARON HARDINGE OF PENSHURST, 1910-1916; (14) LORD CHELMSFORD, 1916-1921; (15) LORD READING, 1921- .

Lord Hardinge (1910-1916); King George V.'s Darbar; Delhi made the Capital, and Provincial Autonomy Foreshadowed.—Lord Hardinge, both by training and temperament, was marked out to make the Reforms of 1909 a success, and he succeeded in winning the confidence of the people of India to a remarkable degree. King George V. succeeded King Edward VII. as sovereign of the British Empire in May 1910. His Majesty, with his consort, Queen Mary, announced their Coronation in solemn Darbar in Delhi in December 1911, and the occasion was taken to inaugurate some important changes. The capital of India was removed from Calcutta to Delhi; the partition of Bengal, which had created so much discontent, was cancelled; in the consequent rearrangements the new province of Bihar and Orissa was created; the claims of education were recognized on a generous scale; the Indian Army received certain boons, including the eligibility of Indians to the Victoria Cross; and certain concessions were made to the Indian Princes. In preparing for these measures Lord Hardinge's Government had adumbrated a scheme of autonomous provinces for India.

Revolutionary Crime; Indians in the Dominions; Sanitary Reforms.—There was a recrudescence of revolutionary crime in Bengal in 1912, and an attempt was made on Lord Hardinge's own life with a bomb at Delhi (December 1912). This movement was not connected with the nationalist movement, but pursued its own course, until it was temporarily suppressed under the Defence of India Act, a War measure, of March 1915. A universal feeling of bitterness was caused by what Lord Hardinge called "invidious and unjust laws" against Indians in South Africa. Indentured emigration of Indian labour to Natal was prohibited from India in 1911, and the whole system of indentured emigration was abolished five years later,* as inconsistent with India's self-respect. Sikhs from the Panjab had also had difficulties in Canada, and the unsatisfactory position of Indians in the British Dominions generally was forced to the front in Indian politics. Lord Hardinge's sympathetic personality prevented the question from being used against his Government. He held his course straight in the "resolute struggle against disease and death,"—in the sanitary reforms which the ravages of plague had made more urgent than ever.

Great War (August 1914 to November 1918); Help with Materials, Man Power, and Finance; Spirit of People and Princes.—When the War broke out in August 1914, Lord Hardinge's popularity and his smooth working of the administrative machinery enabled India to make a response which materially improved both her credit and her position in the Empire. A certain amount of panic was at first inevitable among the ignorant masses, and the revolutionary movement among Indians in foreign lands was adroitly used by the enemies of the Empire. But all classes in India joined the Government in a hearty effort to put all their resources in the common cause. A political truce was agreed to by both the Moderate and the Extreme parties. Raw materials (leather, jute, metals, etc.) and food for man (wheat) and beast (fodder) were supplied, with some sacrifice to the home population. Railway waggons, engines, railway materials, and tents were sent for the Eastern campaigns. The Munition Board and the Tata Steel Works at Jamshidpur (a romantic industrial town that has grown to a population of 100,000 in ten years) worked strenuously. The value of Indian supplies to the Empire and its Allies during the War has been estimated at 250 millions sterling. In man power India contributed 800,000 combatants and 400,000 non combatants. They went to most of the theatres of the war—France and Flanders, East Africa, Aden, Mesopotamia, Gallipoli, Salonika, Egypt, and Palestine, besides undertaking

* The abolition was decided on before Lord Hardinge left India, but it was carried out in 1917.

duties at the fringes of the war, as in Persia, the Persian Gulf, and the Afghan border. The Mesopotamian and Palestine campaigns were mainly won from India. Indian casualties amounted to over 100,000, including nearly 30,000 deaths. Eleven Victoria Crosses and hundreds of minor decorations were won. India's financial help may be judged from the addition of 250 crores to her rupee debt (more than 250 million sterling according to the rate of exchange in 1919-1920), in addition to the large sums she contributed to numerous war funds. All her Princes placed their resources unreservedly at the Empire's disposal, and many of them offered personal services in a splendid spirit of co-operation.

Lord Chelmsford (1916-1921); New Men and Battle-Cries; New Scheme of Constitutional Development.—It fell to Lord Hardinge's successor to see the end of the war. But Lord Hardinge left a great record in India—only marred by the military disaster at Kut in Mesopotamia (December 1915) and saddened by the death of Lady Hardinge (July 1914), whose work for women and children in India had won universal admiration. Lord Chelmsford (1916-1921) had to deal with the later phases of the war and the difficulties and disillusionments of the peace. The political situation was now altered for the worse. New men had come on the scene, and new battle-cries were in the air. A new approach was tried for the development of self-governing institutions, in the scheme known by the joint names of Mr. E. S. Montagu (Secretary of State for India, 1917-1922) and Lord Chelmsford.

Lead Passes to the Extreme Wing.—In 1916 the Indian National Congress came under the direction of its extreme left wing. The moderating influence of two of its stalwarts was lost by the death, in 1915, of Mr. G. K. Gokhale, who had founded in 1905 the Servants of India Society, to be a secretariat and a permanent organization of the constitutional Opposition, and of Mr. Phirozeshah Mehta, who had shown his capacity, power, and robust good sense in the national cause, as well as in civic work in Bombay. The lead now was with Mr. B. G. Tilak, the Poona leader already mentioned, and Mrs. Besant, the old colleague of Mr. Bradlaugh, and the founder of the Hindu College at Benares. She was now the most eloquent expositor of a scheme of Home Rule for India. Bengal was free from violent constitutional agitation. She had found a national voice in Dr. Rabindranath Tagore, whose world-wide fame was evidenced by Sweden's award of the Nobel Prize for Literature to him in 1913. Her national art had found expression in the new School of Oriental Art, and her drama was taking a national tinge. Sir J. C. Bose had advanced her fame by his scientific researches. "Swadeshi," the movement for the promotion of home industries by the boycott of Manchester cloth, had been prominent in the agitation against the partition of Bengal, but became quiescent after the partition was cancelled. It took a new form under Mr. Gandhi, as we shall see. The Panjab was suffering from Sikh discontent on account of the treatment of the Sikhs in Canada, and on account of a reform movement among the Sikhs themselves. Many schemes of Home Rule began to be propounded, and the word "swaraj" (self-government) became fashionable.

India's Partnership in the Empire Recognized.—In August 1917, Mr. E. S. Montagu, the new Secretary of State for India, announced in Parliament the policy of His Majesty's Government in the direction of "the progressive realization of responsible government in India as an integral part of the British Empire." Already in the spring of that year India had been represented in the Imperial Conference and the Imperial War Cabinet, as she was again in 1918, and in the Peace Conference (1918-1919). India, like the self-governing Dominions of the Empire, became a party to the Treaty of Versailles (June 1919) and an original signatory to the Covenant of the League of Nations. Her people's representative at all these gatherings was Sir S. P. Sinha, who was elevated to the British peerage as Lord Sinha (1919) on his appointment as Under-Secretary of State for India in the British Parliament. At the end of 1920 he was appointed Governor of Bihar, but he resigned within a year.

Montagu-Chelmsford Reforms.—While all these official marks of India's partnership in the Empire were being emphasized, the Montagu-Chelmsford scheme was worked out in 1918, and embodied in an Act of Parliament in 1919. It created, in place of the Viceroy's Legislative Council, a two-chambered

Legislature—the Legislative Assembly and the Council of State. In eight major provinces (since increased to nine) it established single-chamber Legislative Councils. In all these Legislatures there are non-official majorities composed of directly elected members. The electorate in 1919 numbered over 6 millions. A germ of responsible government was introduced into the provincial Legislatures, but not into the central Legislature, by making over a limited number of "transferred subjects" to Ministers appointed from among the elected members, the other subjects (the "reserved subjects") being still retained under the Executive Council appointed by the Governor. This dual system of government has been called the Dyarchy. The Governors and the Viceroy (in their respective spheres) retained the power of "certifying" Bills or supplies as necessary if refused by the Legislatures. On such "certification," which has in practice been exercised freely, the measures refused by the Legislatures are deemed to be passed, as if voted by them. A High Commissioner for India has been established in London, to take over the "agency business" of the Government of India, and to represent India in business and social life like the High Commissioners of the Dominions.

How the Moderates (Liberals) were Disheartened.—The framers of the scheme intended it to be a compromise, to be worked for ten years and then revised in the light of experience. But the majority party in the Congress refused to accept it. The minority party—the old "Moderates," now the "National Liberal Federation"—accepted office as ministers in the various provincial governments, but they lost touch with the country. The financial stringency also prevented the development of the "nation-building departments." The third Afghan War (May to August, 1919) and the subsequent military operations against the frontier tribes, the Mahsuds and the Waziris (October 1919 to May 1920), cost India 15 millions sterling, and created financial embarrassment. Afghanistan was now freed from the control of its foreign policy, but this did not make the problem of defence on the North-West frontier any easier, with the Bolshevik passion for revolutionary propaganda. The Rowlatt Bills against sedition (early in 1919) and the troubles in the Panjab (April 1919) caused racial estrangement between British and Indian, which was further strengthened by the anti-Indian policy in Kenya, which was much discussed from 1920 onwards. Thus, while the friends of Dyarchy were disheartened and powerless, the new forces in the Congress brought popular fury to bear on its destruction.

Mr. Gandhi: His Ideals and the Factors in His Influence.—Tilak died in the summer of 1920, but already before his death a new force had appeared in the Congress and in the country. Mr. M. K. Gandhi (born 1869) had distinguished himself in South Africa by leading the Indian Passive Resistance movement against the Anti-Asiatic Laws (1906-1914). During the War he returned to India, and his intervention in certain agrarian disputes on the "no rent" side gave him much prestige with the masses. He introduced two elements into Indian politics, which greatly added to their dynamic force—viz., the ethico-religious element and the ideal of Hindu-Muslim union. To Government he applied the word "satanic." He condemned Western civilization, and its manifestations in railways, Western trade, and Western teachers and doctors. To him the Manchester textile industry is "immoral," because it has killed India's manual textile industries. The primitive "charkha," or spinning wheel, is to him a symbol not only of economic, but of political and spiritual regeneration. He preached the boycott of the Councils, the schools, and the law courts established by Government, but deprecated violence. The phase "non-violent non-co-operation" meant nothing to the masses, whose resistance and repression led to much disorder and the dreadful Martial Law régime of the Panjab in April 1919. In the summer of 1920 the publication of the proposed Sèvres Treaty, imposing humiliating terms on the Turks, inflamed Muslim opinion, and threw it and the Khilafat* organization into the arms of Mr. Gandhi and the Congress. The post-war distress of 1921 caused agrarian and labour troubles, and these elements also swelled the tide of Gandhiism. The Mopla rebellion of

* The Khilafat movement was—or is—a Muslim movement for maintaining the unity of Islam under one head. That head was for some time recognized by a great part of the Muslim world as the Sultan of Turkey. The Turks have since abolished both the Sultanate and the Khilafat as far as their new national State is concerned.

August 1921 shattered the hopes of either a non-violent non-co-operation or of Hindu-Muslim unity.

Lord Reading's Skilful Handling: Change in the Political Situation.—When Lord Chelmsford was succeeded by Lord Reading in April 1921, Mr. Gandhi was in the plenitude of his influence. Lord Reading analyzed the factors in that influence, and his patience and skill gradually unravelled the knots. In November 1921, the brothers Muhammad Ali and Shaukat Ali were convicted of tampering with the loyalty of Muslim soldiers and sentenced to two years' imprisonment. The Prince of Wales's visit in the cold weather of 1921-1922 was marred by some ugly incidents which did not help to promote British and Indian unity. Apart from that, many crimes of violence had occurred. In March 1922, Mr. Gandhi was put on his trial, and convicted of sedition. He was sentenced to six years' imprisonment, but he was released for reasons of health in February 1924. Meanwhile, the political situation in the country had changed. The labour and agrarian upheavals had subsided. In place of Hindu-Muslim unity there raged fierce Hindu-Muslim antagonism, which had produced sanguinary riots in many places in 1923-1924. The ablest and most practical of Mr. Gandhi's lieutenants had broken away from the boycott of the Councils, and had won considerable successes in the second General Elections in the autumn of 1923. They form the present Swaraj Party, led until his death by Mr. C. R. Das, of Calcutta. The Swarajists have captured a great many municipalities and local bodies. They profess to have entered the Councils to destroy them. But events were shaping, under Mr. Das's lead, towards a possible compromise. His sudden death (June 16, 1925) adds enormously to the uncertainties of the political situation.

Present Position (June 1925).—The present position can be read in diverse ways according to the reader's point of view. The Legislatures have been flatteringly called, even semi-officially, Parliaments. But the repeated exercise of legislation by certification shows how far we are yet from having responsible Parliaments. The Swaraj party have majorities in Bengal and the Central Provinces, but they have not been able to undertake any constructive work. Mr. Gandhi himself seems to be shaken in his belief in the boycott of Councils; certainly the majority of his followers have left him on that point, and the orthodox Hindu community has shown no disposition to follow his teaching about the depressed classes. The Hindu-Muslim tension seems to be growing in politics and among the leaders. The denominational Universities established in Benares (Hindu), 1916, and Aligarh (Muslim), 1920, may accentuate intellectual differences. Anarchical crime still calls for exceptional measures in Bengal. India's tariff policy has turned in the direction of protection. Steel and iron are already heavily protected. The proposal (1923) to officer ten units of the Indian Army exclusively with Indian officers does not lead very far yet towards India's ability to undertake her own defence. The Indianization of the Civil Services is proceeding more rapidly, but at a snail's pace in the view of Indian publicists. In India there is an insistent demand for quicker and more substantial political progress. In England there is an idea that the pace is perhaps too rapid already, or a suspicion at least that it has been in the wrong direction. The Conservative Ministry which came into power in the autumn of 1924 has sent for Lord Reading (April 1925) for consultations as to future policy. The dissolution of the Tsarist Empire during the War has not eased the situation on the North-West frontier. Soviet propaganda is active in Central Asia, and the situation both in Eastern and Western Asia has been so completely transformed that there are no elements of stability in it. The Afghan nation is now free in its foreign policy. The Khaibar Pass Railway (twenty-seven miles, from Jamrud to Landi-khana), to be opened in November 1925, and the Razmak road on the Mahsud section of the frontier, are evidences of a vigilant policy as regards communications. But the salvation of India will depend on her own powers of internal consolidation, and co-operation with the forces making for harmony, law, order, and progress.

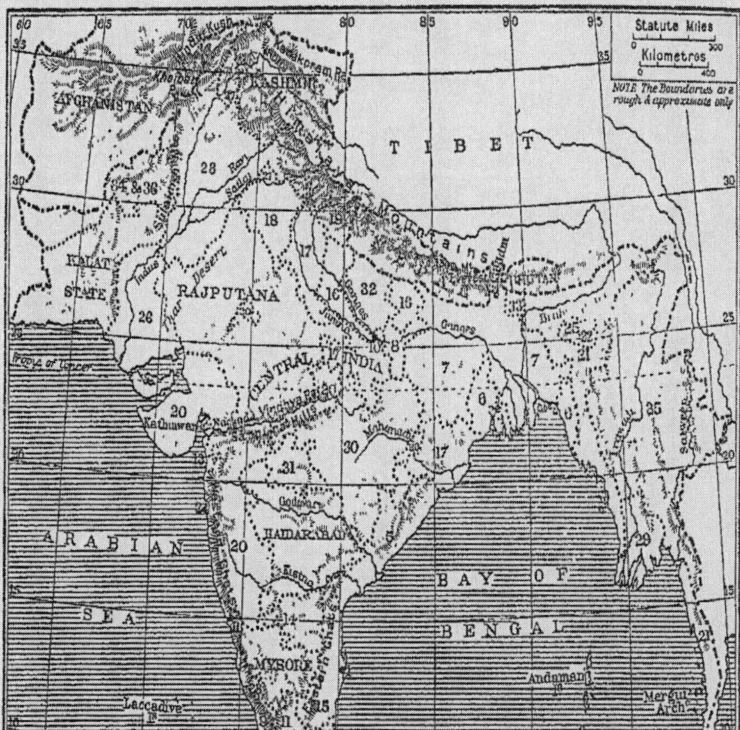

SKELETON MAP OF INDIA.

The figures shown on the map refer to the numbers in the first column of Appendix I.

APPENDIX I

TABLE SHOWING THE PRINCIPAL STAGES IN THE GROWTH OF THE BRITISH EMPIRE IN INDIA

Serial Number. (See Map.)	*Date.*	*Name of Tract.*	*From whom acquired.*	*Modern Name of approximately corresponding Tract.*
1	1639-40.	Madraspatam.	Raja of old Vijayanagar dynasty after it was overthrown by the Muhammadan kingdoms of the Deccan.	Madras (Presidency Town) — Fort St. George.
2	1661.	Bombay.	Portuguese, who got it from the Muhammadan dynasty of Gujarat, 1534.	Bombay (island; Presidency Town).
3	1690.	Villages of Kali Kotta, Chatanati, and Gobindpur.	From the Nawāb of Bengal, confirmed by Mughal Emperor, 1698.	Calcutta (Presidency Town) — Fort William.
4	1757.	Clive's Jagir of the twenty-four Parganas.	Zamindari, from the Nawāb of Bengal; confirmed by Mughal Emperor, 1759.	District of Twenty-four Parganas (Bengal).
5	1758.	Northern Sarkārs.	Conquered from the French, to whom they were ceded by the Nizam in 1753, confirmed to the Company by the Mughal Emperor, 1765.	Districts of Guntur, Kistna, Godāvari, Vizagapatam, and Ganjām (Madras).
6	1760.	Districts of Burdwan, Midnapur and Chittagong.	Zamindari from Nawāb of Bengal.	Bardwan Division and Chittagong District (with presumably Chittagong Hill Tract).
7	1765.	Provinces of Bengal, Bihar, and Orissa.	Diwani, from the Mughal Emperor. The greater part of Orissa was, however, occupied by the Marathas.	Bengal. Bihar (including Orissa).
8	1775.	Benares Province.	Nawāb Wazir of Oudh.	Benares Division.
9	1792.	Malabar (Coorg restored to a local Raja, but annexed to British India in 1834).	From Tippu Sultan, after Third Mysore War.	District of Malabar (except Wynaad sub-division, which accrued in 1799).

Serial Number. (See Map.)	Date.	Name of Tract.	From whom acquired.	Modern Name of approximately corresponding Tract.
		Dindigul.		Portion of Madura District.
		Baramahal and the Lower Ghats.		Major portion of district of Salem.
10	1798.	Fort of Allahabad.	From Nawāb Wazir of Oudh.	Allahabad.
11	1799.	All maritime territory belonging to Mysore.	From Mysore, after the Fourth Mysore War.	Districts of South and North Kanara.
		Coimbatore and Dhārāpuram.		District of Coimbatore.
		Wynaad.		Wynaad sub-division, in Malabar District.
12	Oct. 1799.	Tanjore.	Raja of Tanjore, pensioned off.	District of Tanjore.
13	May 1800.	Surat.	From the Nawāb of Surat, descended from a Governor appointed by the Mughal.	District of Surat (portion).
14	Oct. 1800.	Ceded districts. Territory assigned to Nizam after the Third and Fourth Mysore Wars, 1792 and 1799.	Ceded by the Nizam.	Districts of Bellary, Anantapur, and Cuddapah (portions). Karnul was a distinct Nawabi, annexed in 1842.
15	July 1801.	Karnatik.	Deposition of the Nawāb of Arcot (capital of Karnatik).	The Madras Districts between the Eastern Ghats and the Bay of Bengal, from District Nellore to Cape Comorin.
16	Nov. 1801.	Ceded districts from Oudh.	Nawāb Wazir of Oudh.	Gorakhpur Division, Allahabad Division (north of the Jamna), eastern portions of Rohilkhand and Agra Divisions.
17	1803.	Bundelkhand.	From the Marathas (Second Maratha War).	Bundelkhand Division, U.P., except Jhansi, which was annexed in 1853.
		Katak (Cuttack).		Orissa.
		Broach.		Broach District.
		Sindhia's possessions north and east of the Jamna.		Western Districts of the United Provinces, and Portions of Delhi and Hissar Districts.

Serial Number. (See Map.)	Date.	Name of Tract.	From whom acquired.	Modern Name of approximately corresponding Tract.
18	1809.	Territory between the Jamna and the Satlaj.	By negotiation with Ranjit Singh and the minor Sikh chiefs.	Delhi Division, with influence in the cis-Satlaj States, which then included Ludhiana and Ferozepur Districts.
19	1816.	Province of Kumaun and adjoining hill territory.	From Nepal.	Kumaun Division, U.P. Dehra Dun District. Part of Simla District.
20	1817-19.	(a) Sambalpur.	Bhonslê Raja.	(a) District Sambalpur, then given to a Raja, but annexed in 1853.
		(b) Sāgar (Saugor) and Narbada Territories.	Bhonslê Raja.	(b) Sāgar, Jabalpur, and Damoh Districts, and portions of Districts Narsinghpur and Hoshangabad.
		(c) Peshwa's Territories.	Deposition of Peshwa.	(c) Central, Northern and Southern Divisions, Bombay Presidency.
		(d) Ajmir Province.	Ceded by Sindhia in exchange for other territory.	(d) Ajmir Province.
		(e) Ahmadabad.	Gaikwar, as Peshwa's Deputy.	(e) City and District of Ahmadabad. (Some portions of the District had been previously acquired in 1802-3.)
		(f) Khandesh.	Holkar.	(f) Khandesh District.
21	1826.	Assam. Arakan. Tenasserim (including Martaban but not Rangoon).	Annexed after First Burmese War.	Assam. The Coast Districts of British Burma, except Rangoon and the delta of the Irawadi from the Salween to Bassein.
22	1830.	Kāchār.	Lapse on local Raja's death.	Kāchār District.
23	1834.	Coorg.	Raja of Coorg	Province of Coorg.
24	1835.	Darjiling.	Purchased from Raja of Sikkim in return for an annuity, stopped for misconduct in 1888.	Nucleus of Darjiling District, to which further hill territory, acquired from Bhutan in 1865, was afterwards added.
25	1835.	Jaintia Parganas.	From local Raja.	Jaintia Parganas.
26	1843.	Sindh.	Conquest from the Amirs of Sindh.	Sindh Province (attached to the Bombay Presidency).

Serial Number. (See Map.)	*Date.*	*Name of Tract.*	*From whom acquired.*	*Modern Name of approximately corresponding Tract.*
27	1846.	Jalandhar Doāb Hazāra.	From the Sikhs after the First Sikh War.	Jalandhar Division, Hazāra District.
28	1849.	The Panjab	From the Sikhs after the Second Sikh War.	The rest of the Panjab, including the present North-West Frontier Province.
29	1852.	Pegu.	Conquest and annexation from Burma, Second Burmese War.	The whole of the coastal tract of the Irawadi Delta, as far north as the districts of Thayetmyo and Toungoo.
30	1853.	Nagpur Territories.	Extinction of the Bhonslê family (Marathas), and lapse to British Government.	Central Provinces, to which 20 (*b*) was transferred from the North-West Provinces (now the United Provinces).
31	1853.	Assigned Districts.	Assigned by the Nizam for payment of the Hyderabad Contingent.	Berar (administered with the Central Provinces). Leased in perpetuity to Government of India in 1902 The Raichur Doāb and the Dhārāsiv District were restored to the Nizam in 1860.
32	1856.	Oudh.	Deposition of the King of Oudh.	Oudh
33	1865.	The Duārs (Dooars)	From Bhutan by conquest.	Eastern Duārs in Goalpara District. Western Duārs in Jalpaiguri District.
34	1876.	Quetta Territory.	By negotiation with the Khan of Kalāt.	Assigned territory which became British Baluchistan in 1887 (see No. 36, below).
35	1886.	Upper Burma.	Annexation after deposition of King Theebaw; Third Burmese War.	Upper Burma.
36	1887.	British Baluchistan.	Tracts formerly assigned for British administration (see No. 34, above) were declared British territory.	British Baluchistan

APPENDIX II

BOOKS FOR FURTHER STUDY

GENERAL

1. Smith, Vincent A.: *The Oxford History of India*, to 1921, 2nd ed. by S. M. Edwardes. Oxford, 1923.

2. Elphinstone, Mountstuart: *History of India: the Hindu and Mahometan Periods*, 9th ed., by E. B. Cowell. London, 1905.

   Earlier chapters require modification in the light of recent research.

3. Roberts, P. E.: *Historical Geography of India.* 2 vols., Oxford, 1920.

   For the British period this gives a useful modern sketch: vol. i., under the Company; and vol. ii., under the Crown. This author's chapter on "British Empire in India," in vol. xii., pp. 457-499, of the *Cambridge Modern History*, deals with the events after the Mutiny.

4. Mill, James: *History of British India*, 4th ed., with notes and continuation by H. H. Wilson. 9 vols., London, 1848.

   Mill (vols. i. to vi.) covers the period from 1599 to 1805; Wilson (vols. vii to ix.) the period from 1805 to 1833.

5. Ilbert, Sir Courtenay: *The Government of India: A Brief Historical Survey of Parliamentary Legislation relating to India.* Oxford, 1922.

   Authoritative introduction to the study of Indian Constitutional History in the British Period.

6. Muir, J. Ramsay: *Making of British India*, 1756 *to* 1858. Manchester, 1904.

   Documents illustrating constitutional growth.

7. Keith, A. B.: *Speeches and Documents on Indian Policy*, 1750 *to* 1921. 2 vols., Oxford, 1922.

   Includes, besides constitutional documents, letters, speeches, and notable non-official papers.

8. Ronaldshay, Earl of: *India, a Bird's-Eye View.* London, 1924.

   A picture of modern India by an ex-Governor.

Chapter I

9. The geography of India may be studied in Colonel Sir Thomas H. Holdich: *India.* London, 1904.

Chapter II

10. Risley, Sir H. H.: *The People of India*, 2nd ed., by W. Crooke; with illustrations and ethnographical map. London, 1915.

11. The vernacular languages of India were comprehensively studied by Sir George Grierson in his monumental *Linguistic Survey of India* (Oxford, 1907), and the results are summarized in the *Imperial Gazetteer of India* (Oxford, 1907), vol. i., pp. 349-401.

See also his article on "India and its Languages," in the *Nineteenth Century* for May, 1925.

CHAPTER III

12. RAPSON, E. J.: *Cambridge History of India*, vol. i., "Ancient India." Cambridge, 1922.

Period: from the earliest times to the middle of the first century A.D.

13. BARNETT, L. D.: *Hinduism*. London, 1906.

14. BARNETT, L. D.: *Antiquities of India*. London, 1923.

Chapter ii. contains a valuable chronological summary from 600 B.C. to A.D. 1200.

15. SLATER, DR. GILBERT: *Dravidian Element in Indian Culture*. London, 1924.

CHAPTER IV

16. RHYS DAVIDS, T. W.: *Buddhism*. London, 1910.

17. The Jatakas can be consulted in the English translation, edited by Professor E. B. Cowell, and published at Cambridge, 6 vols., 1895–1907. A selection in one volume has been edited by H. T. Francis and E. J. Thomas (Cambridge, 1916).

18. BERRIEDALE KEITH, DR. A.: *Buddhist Philosophy in India and Ceylon*. Oxford, 1923.

19. RONALDSHAY, THE EARL OF: *Lands of the Thunderbolt*. London, 1923.

Buddhism in Sikkim, Bhutan, and the Chambi Valley of Tibet. Rites of the Greater Vehicle and its metaphysics sympathetically described in a travel narrative.

20. *Encyclopædia Britannica*, 11th ed., 1910–1911; article on Lamaism.

Sacerdotal Buddhism as it appears in Tibet; terms used in the philosophy and mythology of the Mahayana (Greater Vehicle), which are reflected in Buddhist art.

CHAPTER V

21. For Alexander the Great: B. I. WHEELER: *Alexander the Great*. New York and London, 1900.

Pp. 382-465 are concerned with India, but the earlier pp. 122-148 deal with the political ideas which made it possible for the Macedonian to subdue Greece and "merge East and West in universal history."

For the Mauryas, Indo-Greeks, Scythians, Parthians, etc., see No. 12 (above), *Cambridge History of India*, vol. i., chapters xvii.-xx., and xxii.-xxiii.

CHAPTER VI

22. For Asoka: SMITH, V. A.: *Asoka*, Oxford, 1900.

23. For the Guptas: SMITH, V. A.: *Early History of India*, Oxford, 1908.

Pp. 264-295.

24. For Harsha: ETTINGHAUSEN, M. L.: *Harśa Vardhana, Empereur et poète de l'Inde Septetrionale* (A.D. 606–648). *Étude sur sa vie et son temps.* London (Louvain), 1906.

25. For the Kingdoms of the South: AIYANGAR, S. KRISHNASWAMI: *Ancient India.* London, 1911.

Chapters i., ii., iii., iv., and vi. should be read, especially the last, which describes the Chola system of administration.

CHAPTER VII

26. The life of the Prophet may be studied in a brief compass in SYED AMEER ALI: *The Spirit of Islam, with a Life of the Prophet,* revised ed., London, 1922.

For the early Muslims in India there is no satisfactory brief account in English. We have to go to the original authorities, among which the following may be consulted in translations:

27. FERISHTA: *History of the Mahomedan Power in India, till the Year 1612.* Translated from the Persian by J. Briggs. 4 vols., London, 1829.

The Arab invasions of Sindh are dealt with in vol. iv., p. 401 *et seq.*

28. ELLIOT, SIR H. M.: *History of India as told by its own Historians,* 8 vols., London, 1867–1877.

Vol. i. is concerned with this chapter.

CHAPTER VIII

No. 27 above—Ferishta.

Vol. i. gives the pre-Mughal dynasties of Delhi; vols. ii. (latter part) and iii., the Deccan kingdoms; and vol. iv., Gujarat, Malwa, Khandesh, Bengal etc.

No. 28 above—Elliot.

See vols. ii., iii., and portions of vols. iv. and v.

CHAPTER IX

29. LANE-POOLE, STANLEY: *Babar.* Oxford, 1909.

30. BEVERIDGE, MRS. A.: *History of Humayun : Life and Memoirs of Gulbadan Begam.* London, 1902.

Picture of the family life of the early Mughals.

31. SMITH, V. A.: *Akbar, the Great Mogul.* 2nd ed., revised. Oxford, 1919.

Views on Akbar's religion the least satisfactory part of the book.

CHAPTER X

32. ROE, SIR THOMAS: *Embassy to the Court of the Great Mogul,* edited by W. Foster. London, 1899.

33. PRASAD, BENI: *History of Jahangir.* London, 1922.

Spirit of Mughal administration sympathetically studied.

34. BERNIER, FRANÇOIS: *Travels in the Mogul Empire,* 1656 *to* 1668. Ed. by A. Constable. London, 1891.

35. LANE-POOLE, STANLEY: *Aurangzib.* Oxford, 1893.

CHAPTER XI

36. DANVERS, F. C.: *The Portuguese in India, being a History of the Rise and Decline of their Eastern Empire.* 2 vols., London, 1894.

There is no English work on the Dutch in India on the same scale as the preceding, but the following may be consulted:

37. EDMUNDSON, G.: *History of Holland.* Cambridge, 1922.
See pp. 82 109, 159-185.

38. ROGERS, J. E. T.: *Holland* ("Story of the Nations"). London, 1888.
See pp. 134-137, 144-150, 168-184.

CHAPTER XII

39. CUNNINGHAM, W.: *Growth of English Industry and Commerce in Modern Times.* 2 parts, constituting vol. ii. of *The Growth of English Industry and Commerce,* Cambridge, 1903.
There are later editions, but I have used the third edition, in which the first part of vol. ii. will be found helpful in studying the part which the East India Company played in the development of English national life.

40. RYLEY, J. HORTON: *Ralph Fitch, England's Pioneer to India and Burma: His Companions and Contemporaries.* London, 1899.

41. ROGERS, J. E. T.: *Industrial and Commercial History of England.* London, 1892.
Pp. 113-137; a rapid sketch of Chartered Trade Companies, from which the true significance of the East India Company in the economic life of the nation will be understood, as well as its position in the national controversies of the seventeenth century.

CHAPTER XIII

42. WHEELER, J. TALBOYS: *Early Records of British India.* Calcutta, 1878.

43. CAPPER, J.: *The Three Presidencies of India.* London, 1853.
Social, moral, and economic factors described.

CHAPTER XIV

No. 2 above: Elphinstone.
Successors of Aurangzib, in the last section, book xii.

44. KEENE, H. G.: *Fall of the Mughal Empire.* London, 1887.
Requires correction in places.

45. GRANT DUFF, J. C.: *History of the Mahrattas.* Edited by S. M. Edwardes. London, 1921.

CHAPTER XV

46. MALLESON, COLONEL G. B.: *Dupleix.* Oxford, 1890.

CHAPTER XVI

47. MALLESON, COLONEL G. B.: *Clive.* Oxford, 1893.

48. FORREST, SIR GEORGE W.: *Life of Lord Clive.* 2 vols., London, 1891.

Chapter XVII

49. Lecky, W. E. H.: *History of England in the Eighteenth Century.* vol. iv., pp. 262-285. London, 1892.

Relates Indian facts to English politics.

No. 4 above: Mill and Wilson, book iv., chapters vii. and ix.

Chapter XVIII

50. Trotter, L. J.: *Warren Hastings.* Oxford, 1890.

Captain Trotter's defence of Hastings in the affairs of the Begams of Oudh and of Chait Singh may be compared with Mr. Roberts's more judicious remarks in No. 3 above. Macaulay's Essay on Warren Hastings contains a brilliant account of the impeachment, but its historical judgments should be read with caution.

51. Seton-Karr, W. S.: *The Marquess Cornwallis.* Oxford, 1890.

Pp. 25-73 explain clearly the points of Indian revenue administration and the Permanent Settlement of Bengal, and pp. 74-100 the reforms in the Civil Service and the judicial system.

52. Ascoli, F. D.: *Early Revenue History of Bengal, and the Fifth Report,* 1812. Oxford, 1917.

A detailed consideration of the questions that confronted the early British Administrators.

Chapter XIX

53. Owen, S. J.: *Selection from the Despatches, Treaties, and other Papers of the Marquess Wellesley during his Government of India.* Oxford, 1877.

The Editor's valuable "Survey of Lord Wellesley's Administration," pp. xiii-xlvii, gives a reasoned summary of the policy of that masterful Viceroy.

54. Malcolm, Sir John: *Memoir of Central India.* Abridged and edited for colleges and schools by C. H. Payne, London, 1922. (The original Memoir was first published in 2 vols. in 1823.)

Malcolm's pacification of Central India (in which term Malwa is included) was the keystone of the arch on which the modern system of Indian States rests.

55. Tod, Colonel James: *Annals and Antiquities of Rajasthan.* Calcutta, 1894. (First edition, London, 1829-1832, in 2 vols.)

Somewhat imaginative, and requires correction. Mr. C. H. Payne's abridgment (London, no date) gives the Annals of the most important State, Mewar (Udaipur); its last three chapters (xv.-xvii.) cover the period of Maratha invasion and the final rescue.

Chapter XX

56. Sleeman, Sir W. H.: *Rambles and Recollections of an Indian Official,* edited by V. A. Smith. Oxford, 1915.

A miscellany of Indian matters, written by Sleeman for his sister in 1835-1836. Chapter xvi. describes a *sati* on the Narbada: chapter xiii. is on Thags and poisoners; and chapter xlix. describes the Pindari system.

57. Oswell, G. D.: *Sketches of the Rulers of India,* vol. ii. (Company's Governors). Oxford, 1908.

Read specially the sketches of Munro, Malcolm, Elphinstone, Metcalfe, and Thomason, with reference to the development of provincial and personal administration.

Chapter XXI

58. Griffin, Sir Lepel: *Ranjit Singh.* Oxford, 1882.

A good account not only of the Maharaja, but of the Sikh nation and theocracy in the nineteenth century.

59. Cunningham, J. D.: *History of the Sikhs.* Edited by H. L. O. Garrett. Oxford, 1918.

Ethnology, religion, and history of the Sikhs, to 1846.

Chapter XXII

60. Holmes, T. Rice: *History of the Indian Mutiny, and of the Disturbances which accompanied it among the Civil Population.* Reprint of 5th ed. 5 maps and 6 plans. London, 1913.

61. Roberts of Kandahar, Field-Marshal Lord: *Forty-One Years in India: from Subaltern to Commander-in-Chief.* London, 1901.

The best one-volume edition. The siege of Delhi and the relief of Lucknow are illustrated with plans, as is also the Russian frontier, which figures in the next Chapter.

Chapter XXIII

62. Balfour, Lady Betty: *History of Lord Lytton's Indian Administration.* London, 1890.

No. 61 above: Lord Roberts's *Forty-One Years.*

For the part which that great soldier played in the second Afghan War.

63. Buckle, C. E.: *Life of Benjamin Disraeli.* Vols. v. and vi., London, 1920.

A continuation of earlier vols. by W. F. Monypenny. Chapters xi. (an Imperial Foreign Policy) and xii. (Suez Canal and Royal Title) in vol. v., and chapter x. (Afghan War) in vol. vi. explain much in Lord Lytton's Viceroyalty.

Chapter XXIV

64. Dutt, Romesh: *Economic History of India in the Victorian Age, 1837 to 1900.* London, 1906 (2nd ed.).

Voices the statement of the Intellectuals on India's economic discontent.

65. Morley, John, Viscount: *Recollections.* 2 vols., London, 1917.

Vol. ii., pp. 149-346.

66. Buchan, John: *Lord Minto, a Memoir.* London, 1924.

Pp. 209-335 deal with Lord Minto's Indian Viceroyalty.

Chapter XXV

67. The Montagu-Chelmsford Reforms can best be studied in the Official Report—East India Constitutional Reforms: Report, with appendices and supplementary papers. Published by His Majesty's Stationery Office, London, July, 1819, price 1s. 3d.

68. There is also an official summary—Indian Constitutional Reforms; the Montagu-Chelmsford Proposals: a brief version of the Official Report by the Secretary of State and the Viceroy. London, 1918.

69. ARCHER, WM.: *India and the Future*; 36 illustrations. London, 1917.

A critical review of India's claim to nationalism, by a vigorous writer, who faced the problem from other than a purely political standpoint.

70. CURTIS, LIONEL: *Dyarchy*. Oxford, 1920.

71. RONALDSHAY, LORD: *The Heart of Arya-varta: A Study of the Psychology of Unrest.* London, 1925.

72. TAGORE, DR. RABINDRANATH: *Nationalism*. London, 1917.

STATISTICS

73. *Statistical Abstract of British India.* Blue-book published annually by His Majesty's Stationery Office in London.

Ten years' statistics are included. But the statistics are published a long time after the last year included—for example, in No. 57, just published (1925), the last year treated is 1921–1922.

74. *The Indian Year-Book.* Published by the *Times of India*, Bombay, giving facts and statistics in a handy form.

APPENDIX III

CHRONOLOGICAL TABLE

B.C.	
c. 2000–1000.	Aryan invasions of India.
c. 1200–1000.	Composition of Rig-Veda.
c. 560–480.	Life of Buddha.
326–325.	Alexander invades India.
323.	Death of Alexander.
c. 305.	Chandragupta defeats Seleucus.
c. 300.	Megasthenes in India.
c. 300.	Treatise of Kautilya.
c. 273–236.	Reign of Asoka.
206.	Antiochus III. of Syria attacks N.W. India.
c. 135.	Bactrian kingdom overwhelmed by Sakas (Scythians).
c. 75.	Sakas established in the Panjab.
58.	Sambat (or Vikram) era commences.
A.D.	
78.	Kushāna supremacy in N.W. India: Saka era commences in Western (and Southern) India.
226.	Rise of Sāsānian dynasty in Persia.
320–445.	Gupta Empire in its vigour.
375–413.	Reign of Chandra Gupta II.
c. 402–411.	Fa-Hien visits India.
c. 406–453.	Attila in Central Europe.
c. 500.	Toramana in Malwa.
c. 570.	Birth of the Prophet Muhammad.
606–647.	Reign of Harsha.
622.	The Hijra (Hegira) era commences.
630–645.	Hiuen Tsang visits India.
632.	Death of the Prophet Muhammad.
636.	Muslims invade Broach and (643) Sindh.
712–715.	Expedition of Muhammad Kāsim.
788.	Birth of Shankar Acharya.
c. 944.	History of Mas'ūdi.
973–1048.	Life of Al-Biruni.
c. 1000.	Supremacy of Chola Kingdom.
1000–1026.	Mahmud of Ghazni's invasions of India.
1142–1236.	Life of Chishti of Ajmir.
1162–1227.	Life of Jenghiz Khan.
A.D.	
1164–1197.	Reign of Parākrama Bāhu in Ceylon.
1173–1265.	Life of Baba Farīd of Pak Pattan.
1186–1206.	Ghori period in India.
1294.	Ala-ud-din Khilji invades Deccan.
1321–1422.	Life of Gesu-daraz of Gulbarga.
1325–1351.	Reign of Muhammad Tughlak.
1334–1337.	Ibn Batuta in India.
1351–1388.	Reign of Firoz Tughlak.
1378–1396.	Reign of Bahmani Sultan Mahmud of Gulbarga.
1398.	Invasion of Timur (Tamerlane).
1453.	Turks take Constantinople.
c. 15th century.	Death of Ramanand the Theist.
c. end of 15th century.	Poet Kabir flourished.
1469–1539.	Life of Guru Nanak.
1492.	Columbus discovers America.
1493.	Pope Alexander's award of West and East to Spain and Portugal.
1498.	Vasco da Gama reaches Calicut.
1500.	Portuguese discover Brazil in sailing for India.
1509–1515.	Albuquerque Governor in the East.
1510.	Portuguese occupy Goa.
1511.	Portuguese capture Malacca.
1515.	Portuguese capture Ormuz.
1517.	Ottoman Turks conquer Egypt.
1519.	Batavia founded.
1520–1521.	Magellan's voyage round South America to Philippines.
1526.	First battle of Panipat.
1526–1530.	Reign of Babar.
1532–1623.	Life of Tulsi Das.
1540–1545.	Sher Shah Sur *de facto* ruler.
1542.	Birth of Akbar.
1554.	Russia or Muscovy Company founded.
1555.	Restoration of Humayun.

A.D.
1556. Death of Humayun.
Second battle of Panipat.
1556–1605. Reign of Akbar.
1560. Inquisition established at Goa.
1571. Turks defeated at Lepanto.
1572–1573. Akbar's conquest of Gujarat.
1581. Proclamation of Dutch Republic.
Turkey and Levant Company founded.
1585. Ralph Fitch at Fatehpur Sikri.
1588. Defeat of Spanish Armada.
1600. East India Company founded.
1602. Dutch East Indies companies amalgamated.
1603. John Mildenhall at Agra.
1605–1627. Reign of Jahangir.
1609. Dutch get footing in Southern India.
1609–1611. William Hawkins at Agra.
1611. English factory at Masulipatam.
1612. English factory at Surat.
1615–1618. Sir Thomas Roe in India.
1622. Ormuz captured from the Portuguese.
1623. Amboyna massacre.
1627. Birth of Shivaji.
1627–1658. Reign of Shah Jahan.
1639. British settlement at Madras.
1647. Balkh lost to India.
1652. Dutch build Cape Town.
1653. Kandahar lost to India.
1653. Pearl Mosque and Taj Mahal completed.
1658–1707. Reign of Aurangzib.
1664. Surat plundered by Shivaji.
French E.I.C. (Colbert's) founded.
1668. Bombay handed over to E.I.C.
1672. Aungier's Convention (Bombay).
1674. French settlement at Pondicherry.
1680. Death of Shivaji.
1688. French settle at Chandernagore.
1690. British settle at Calcutta.
Elihu Yale establishes a factory at Cuddalore.
1693. New Charter granted to E.I.C.
Death of Job Charnock.
1695. Gemelli Careri's audience with Aurangzib.
1696. Original Fort William (Calcutta) begun.
1698. "*English* Company trading to the East Indies."
1702. Amalgamation of English and London Companies.

A.D.
1707. Danish Protestant Mission established at Tranquebar.
1713. Treaty of Utrecht: England's position strengthened.
1719–1748. Reign of Muhammad Shah.
1722. French settle at Mahé.
1739. Invasion of Nadir Shah.
French occupy Karikal.
1742–1754. Dupleix governor of Pondicherry.
1742–1750. Maratha invasions of Bengal.
1746. French capture Madras.
1747. Afghanistan united under Ahmad Shah Abdali.
1749. Madras restored by Peace of Aix-la-Chapelle.
1751. Clive captures Arcot.
1754–1775. Rule of Shuja-ud-daula (Oudh).
1756. Siraj-ud-daula captures Calcutta.
1756–1763. Seven Years' War.
1757. Clive retakes Calcutta, and turns the French out of Chandernagore.
Battle of Plassey.
1759–1806. Reign of Shah Alam II.
1760. Battle of Wandiwash.
1761. Invasion of Ahmad Shah Abdali.
Siege and destruction of Pondicherry.
Third Battle of Panipat.
1763. Peace of Paris.
1764. Battle of Baksar.
1765. Acquisition of the Diwani.
1766. Mutiny of European officers in India.
1767–1769. First Mysore War.
1770. Bengal famine.
1773. Regulating Act.
1773–1774. Rohilkhand annexed by Oudh.
1774–1785. Warren Hastings Governor-General.
1775–1782. First Maratha War.
1775–1797. Rule of Asaf-ud-daula (Oudh).
1780–1784. Second Mysore War.
1782. Treaty of Salbai.
Death of Haidar Ali.
1782–1783. Admiral Suffren in Indian Seas.
1783. Peace of Versailles.
1784. Treaty of Mangalore.
Pitt's India Act.
1786–1793. Lord Cornwallis Governor-General.
1788–1795. Trial of Warren Hastings.
1789. French Revolution.
1790–1792. Third Mysore War.
1793. Permanent Revenue Settlement.
1793–1798. Sir John Shore Governor-General.

A.D.	
1794.	Death of Mahadaji Sindhia.
1795.	Battle of Kharda.
1796–1798.	Conquest of Ceylon.
1798–1805.	Lord Wellesley Governor-General.
1799.	Fourth Mysore War.
	Tanjore annexed.
1801.	Karnatik annexed.
1802.	Treaty of Bassein.
1802–1805.	Second Maratha War.
1803.	Battle of Asāi (Assaye).
	Treaty of Surji Arjungāon.
1806.	British occupy the Cape.
1807–1813.	Lord Minto I, Governor-General.
1813.	E.I.C.'s Charter renewed: Indian Trade monopoly abolished.
1813–1823.	Lord Hastings Governor-General.
1814–1816.	Nepal War.
1816.	Hindu College (Calcutta) founded.
1817–1819.	Third Maratha War.
1818.	Peshwa's dominions annexed.
1819.	Capture of Singapore.
	Kashmir annexed by Ranjit Singh.
1823–1828.	Lord Amherst, Governor-General.
1823.	First steamer launched in Calcutta.
1824–1826.	First Burmese War.
1825.	Storming of Bharatpur.
1829.	*Sati* forbidden by law.
1831–1881.	Mysore under British administration.
1833.	Charter renewed: company ceases to be commercial.
1834.	Annexation of Coorg.
1835.	Calcutta Medical College founded.
	Restrictions on Indian Press removed.
1836–1842.	Lord Auckland Governor-General.
1839.	Conquest of Aden.
1839–1842.	First Afghan War.
1840.	"Opium War" with China.
1842.	Relief of Jalalabad.
1842–1844.	Lord Ellenborough Governor-General.
1843.	Battle of Miāni; annexation of Sindh.
1844–1848.	Lord Hardinge I. Governor-General.
1845–1846.	First Sikh War.
1848.	Engineering College at Rurki founded.
1848–1849.	Second Sikh War: Panjab annexed.
1848–1856.	Lord Dalhousie Governor-General.
1851.	First cotton mill started in Bombay.
1852.	Second Burmese War.
1853.	First Indian railway opened (Bombay to Thana).
1853–1856.	Crimean War.
1854.	Nagpur annexed.
	First Indian postage-stamp issued.
	First jute mill started in Calcutta.
1855.	Public Works Department organized.
1856.	Oudh annexed.
1856–1862.	Lord Canning Governor-General (Viceroy from 1858).
1857.	Universities of Calcutta, Bombay, and Madras founded.
1857–1859.	Indian Mutiny.
1858.	E.I.C. extinguished; Lord Canning becomes Viceroy.
1860.	First Indian Budget.
1861.	Central Provinces constituted.
1861–1865.	American Civil War.
1862–1863.	Lord Elgin I. Viceroy.
1864–1869.	Sir John Lawrence Viceroy.
1865–1866.	Orissa famine.
1869.	Opening of Suez Canal.
1869–1872.	Lord Mayo Viceroy.
1870.	Red Sea submarine cable.
1872–1876.	Lord Northbrook Viceroy.
1875.	Arya Samaj founded.
1877.	Aligarh College founded (now University).
1877.	Imperial Assemblage at Delhi.
1878–1880.	Second Afghan War.
1880.	Lord Roberts' march from Kabul to Kandahar.
1880–1884.	Lord Ripon Viceroy.
1882.	Lahore University founded.
	Vernacular Press Act repealed.
1883.	Scheme of Local Self-government.
1884–1888.	Lord Dufferin Viceroy.
1885.	Third Burmese War.
	Indian National Congress formed.
1887.	Allahabad University founded.
1888–1894.	Lord Lansdowne Viceroy.
1892.	Indian Councils Act.
1894–1899.	Lord Elgin II. Viceroy.
1896.	Plague in Bombay.
1896–1897.	Famine; Deccan Anarchical movement.
1899–1905.	Lord Curzon Viceroy.
1901.	North-West Frontier Province created.
1903.	Coronation Darbar at Delhi.
1904–1905.	Russo-Japanese War.
1905.	Partition of Bengal.
	Servants of India Society founded.

A.D.	
1905–1910.	Lord Minto II. Viceroy.
1907–1908.	Anarchical movement and its repression.
1908.	Muslim League formed.
1909.	Minto-Morley Reforms.
1910–1916.	Lord Hardinge II. Viceroy
1911.	King and Queen in Darbar at Delhi.
	Capital moved from Calcutta to Delhi.
1912.	Attempts on Lord Hardinge's life.
1914–1918.	Great War; India's effort.
1915.	Defence of India Act.
	Death of Mr. G. K. Gokhale.
1916–1921.	Lord Chelmsford Viceroy.
1917.	Indentured emigration of Indian labour abolished.

A.D.	
1919.	Treaty of Versailles.
	Khilafat movement.
	Montagu-Chelmsford Reforms.
	Rowlatt Bills against sedition.
	Troubles in the Panjab.
1921–	Lord Reading Viceroy.
1921.	Mopla Rebellion.
1921–1922.	Prince of Wales visits India.
1922–1924.	Imprisonment of Mr. Gandhi; emergence of Swaraj Party under Mr. C. R. Das.
1925 (June).	Death of Mr. C. R. Das.
1925 (Nov.).	Khaibar Pass Railway opened.

INDEX

Map accompanying "The Making of India," by A. Yusuf Ali (A. & C. Black, Ltd., London)